At Eighty-Two

Kinds of Love
As We Are Now
Crucial Conversations
A Reckoning
Anger
The Magnificent Spinster
The Education of Harriet Hatfield

NONFICTION

I Knew a Phoenix
Plant Dreaming Deep
Journal of a Solitude
A World of Light
The House by the Sea
Recovering: A Journal
At Seventy: A Journal
After the Stroke: A Journal
Writings on Writing
May Sarton—a Self-Portrait
Honey in the Hive
Endgame: A Journal of the Seventy-ninth Year
Among the Usual Days: A Portrait
(*edited by Susan Sherman*)
Encore: A Journal of the Eightieth Year

FOR CHILDREN

Punch's Secret
A Walk through the Woods

At Eighty-Two

A Journal

By *May Sarton*

W · W · Norton & Company · New York · London

First Edition

The text of this book is composed in Caledonia with the display set in Garamond Composition and manufacturing by Haddon Craftsmen, Inc.

Library of Congress Cataloging-in-Publication Data

Sarton, May, 1912–
    At eighty-two : a journal / May Sarton.
       p.   cm.
    1. Sarton, May, 1912–1995—Diaries.   2. Women authors,
American—20th century—Diaries.   3. Aged women—United States—Diaries.
I. Title.
PS3537.A832Z4626   1995
818'.5203—dc20   95-7744
    [B]

ISBN 0-393-03889-0

W. W. Norton & Company, Inc., 500 Fifth Avenue, New York, N.Y. 10110
W. W. Norton & Company Ltd., 10 Coptic Street, London WC1A 1PU

1 2 3 4 5 6 7 8 9 0

For Maggie and Susan,
who helped me through this hard year
with unfailing verve and understanding

August 26, 1994

Author's Note

In FORMER journals I have abided by my rule to add nothing to the day's notation. But when I read the typed manuscript of the journal of the eighty-second year, which I had dictated, I felt a strong wish to enrich it here and there with afterthoughts, to make a kind of dialogue out of what had been a soliloquy. I've enjoyed doing this, enlarging on a brief description that seemed to demand a little more in background or discussion. I hope it will give my readers pleasure now for the extra indulgence in explaining experience first on the pulse and then reflectively.

KAIROS

*A unique time in a person's life;
an opportunity for change.*

At Eighty-Two

Sunday, July 25, 1993

I AM MORE and more aware of how important the framework is, what holds life together in a workable whole as one enters real old age, as I am doing. A body without bones would be a limp impossible mess, so a day without a steady routine would be disruptive and chaotic.

I tell myself, this marvelous blue ocean morning, that it is not ridiculous that I feel put upon if the framework gets tampered with, if I am kept waiting a half hour by a visitor, for instance, because I am ready for a visit but then use up the necessary energy by trying to be patient. These days I am rather impatient.

Yesterday the framework was done away with temporarily by Pierrot, who decided to stay out instead of sleeping on my bed with me as he usually does while I rest after lunch. He often lies on his back, a long sumptuous scarf of pale fur for me to stroke, and his purrs make me as relaxed as he is. Yesterday, for the first time in a year perhaps, he did not come, and I felt outraged, especially as he was outside meowing for his breakfast at 4:00 A.M. and, having devoured it, went right out to the field, burnished gold these days of drought, to hunt. But I had been awakened from sound sleep and never got it back.

I am reading Barbara Kingsolver's new book, *Pigs in Heaven*, a Book-of-the-Month Club selection. I am happy for her sake, but this novel is not as good as the one before, *Animal Dreams*. What seemed like a marvelously human broadness of vision about all sorts of people in the earlier book becomes a bit like a cartoon. Irony replaces tenderness. America seen as a cartoon country may make you laugh, but it is not really a pleasure. The laugh hurts and maybe that is what she means.

Monday, July 26, 1993

PIERROT CAME yesterday afternoon and rested with me, so that lonely time is over. Absurd, but he is a key figure in my joy these summer days. The birds bathing ecstatically in the large pottery bowl on the terrace wall are another joy I could not easily do without, and the constant stir of wings in the air another.

Susan makes everything to do such fun, cooking delicious meals and looking appreciatively at a video with me. Yesterday and the day before it has been *Jane Eyre*, which Sue Hilsinger and Lois gave me for my birthday.

It is not quite as overwhelmingly wonderful as Dickens's *Little Dorrit*, which we saw for hours last week, but it is a far more limiting scene. What I enjoy most is being inside a great English country house. I have never actually experienced this except perhaps that weekend at Dorothy Wellesley's in the thirties. That was the real thing one longs for as a tourist being "shown around" dead-feeling rooms, and oneself unrecognized.

Ruth Pitter introduced me and arranged that I join her at Penns-in-the-Rocks for a weekend. One of the things that impressed me were the extraordinary bibelots, a small table in the drawing room covered with lapis lazuli small boxes, also the decoration over the fireplace in the dining room painted by Vanessa Bell and Duncan Grant. I watched Cornish, the butler, with admiration. Lovely to hear Dorothy addressed as "Your Grace." She looked at that time rather like the White Queen in *Alice in Wonderland*. I slept in the bedroom that Yeats had always slept in, enough to keep me awake hoping for a ghost. The next day Dorothy Wellesley did read from some of her poems, of which I have learned a few by heart.

Thought

I seem to hold thee like a dream
With pargeter's hands, now light now dense,
My exquisite compound of sense,
My lifted water glittered on,
My form, my matter Plato knew.

Thou art a dream within a dream;
So I am quiet till my last day,
Capable now of air or clay,
Contesting neither holding either,
Content thou in my vision too;
Take thou the hard Platonic way.

For love one way is greatly told,
But greatlier far than men have seen,
Unless within a block of ice
Within a block of veriest green
Thought makes eternal sacrifice.

It is tragic to see a genius as she was deteriorating in old age. We had no wine at dinner because Dorothy was an alcoholic, drinking claret in her bedroom all day, but Cornish was persuaded to bring me a gin and tonic, thank goodness.

How often I thought of her and Wordsworth's poem for the poet Chatterton: "We Poets in our youth begin in gladness;/But thereof come in the end despondency and madness."

Friday, July 30, 1993

Two DAYS ago we had a tremendous time of joy and communion with three dear friends, Nancy and George Mairs and Susan Kenney. George is so expert at getting Nancy out of the car and into her special wheelchair it seems like an easy thing, but of course, it is difficult, and then the wheelchair has to go over the flat stones of the path and terrace and up two steps into the house. Nancy has MS and George has cancer, in remission now, but last year it was very bad, so they are a little like magicians making the impossible happen every day. What flows out to others is simply love, such warm, understanding love, one feels nourished and blissful.

Susan Kenney lost her beloved husband, Ed, eight months ago. For two years her life was given over to taking him back and forth from hospitals and the doctors hoping to find a cure or even at one time a diagnosis. It was a long hell.

We were all walking wounded except Susan, the youngest of us, and all writers except George. It is so rare for me to be with writers, writers I greatly admire and feel at home with. That was bliss also.

Champagne is the best drink to foster good conversation, and we created it together for almost two hours. I felt quite exhausted then, but fulfilled in some area of my being which is often rather bereft.

I don't suppose anything can happen as life-giving as this for a year—I'll be thinking of it often.

Saturday, July 31, 1993

TODAY A remarkable letter from Cathy Sander, the Wellesley student who was hired by Eleanor Blair to do odd jobs and became deeply involved and caring in the last two years. There is something so touching about that relationship between an eighteen-year-old and a ninety-six-year-old woman, blind and quite deaf, living alone, coming to the end of her strength. Cathy says in her letter:

"You know, May, the most giving relationship I've had my entire life was with Eleanor. I always felt so loved when I was with her. Eleanor really taught me how to love, to give of myself without asking in return, to love because love is beautiful not because I want love in return. Our love for each other just seemed to flow, giving and taking in turn. The hours I spent with her were among the best times in my life. Nothing was expected. Nothing was taken that was not offered."

Otherwise a rather dim day here, humid and foggy. I'm packing up copies of *Encore* for friends, and it is fun but tires me. However, I did manage to write Cathy right away, an imperative.

Sunday, August 1, 1993

How GOOD it is to see old friends after a long interval and pick up as though one had seen them a day before. Serena Sue Hilsinger and Lois Byrnes made the percipient selections for my *Selected Poems*, which remains the best introduction to my poetry and goes on selling year after year.

Sue and Lois are such invigorating people, and we had so much to talk about that I was hardly tired at all after two hours, even though they only arrived near 1:00 P.M. instead of noon because of the traffic.

Of course, they were interested in the books about me, the new event this year, books published by the university presses. There are two remarkably interesting books: *That Great Sanity, Critical Essays on May Sarton*, edited by Susan Swartzlander and Marilyn R. Mumford, University of Michigan Press; and *A House of Gathering, Poets on May Sarton's Poetry*, edited by Marilyn Kallet, University of Tennessee Press, for me a dream come true, serious critical consideration of the poetry.

Sue teaches *Mrs. Stevens* every year at Clark University and says her students are "crazy about your work."

They commented that bookstores everywhere, even Belfast, Maine, had shelves of my books. It is heartening.

As we talked about the horrendous state of the world, Lois said she had stopped reading newspapers this year, but she added, "You have never ceased to face the worst in your poems, 'At Kent State,' the Holocaust poems."

I felt restored by their love and their true admiration for

my work, and also restored by their warm, beautiful presences. They look so well, flourishing, and now have five cats they tell me. It was all a summer holiday for me who cannot travel these days, a visit resembling a dazzling trip.

Tuesday, August 3, 1993

MY MOTHER's birthday. Pat Carroll is bringing my lunch. What a lucky woman I am! And Susan is taking me out to dinner. I think about how wonderful it would be if my parents had seen this place. I imagine my mother in the chaise on the terrace, my father smoking a cigar. But I learned from Margot Peters, who knows everything I forget because she is my biographer, that both my parents died in their seventies, my father five years after my mother. Seventy seems so young! And I feel lonely because they never knew what real old age asks of one, what an effort it becomes even to get dressed. I can't take courage from their old age and so feel somehow put upon.

The night before last I hardly slept. I have been too shaky to get down to the picking garden for months, but day before yesterday, after Lois and Sue had gone, I suddenly wanted to see what was what, got my cane, and set out with Susan to support me the hundred yards or so. What met my astonished eyes was simply a very large garden of weeds, dotted by a few struggling nasturtiums. I had spent about forty dollars on seeds, most from Thompson and Morgan—where were the cosmos, the zinnias, the calendulas, the poppies, love-in-a-mist, bachelor's buttons? Not anything to be seen but rich, flourishing grass!

I imagine my mother in the chaise on the terrace. . . .

I could not sleep, I felt too dismal. Pat Robinson, who gardens for me, gets four hundred dollars a month, but that only provides five hours a week and it is a big garden, before the terrace and behind the house and along the fence, so the picking garden is a small part of what has to be done, and five hours a week is not enough. I cannot afford more, and all night I worried about this and felt despair. I have created a visually lovely garden for twenty years, and now do I have to watch it disintegrate? A bad night—

—followed by a long nerve-racking wait for the Salvation Army to pick up a lot of bags and boxes of clothes because I lost fifty pounds last year and so cannot wear a lot of beautiful things. The wretched driver never did find us though I had given him directions. Susan had to go down and meet him in York.

Yesterday was a frustrating day altogether. We did not even look at a video although the afternoon before we had laughed very much at Whoopi Goldberg in *Sister Act* and eaten a huge bowl of popcorn. I have been rereading Nancy Mairs's book *Ordinary Time*. It is right to reread it now when I have been so miserable at how little we Americans seem to care about Sarajevo or whether Clinton gets some support at long last after all the meanness of spirit.

What Nancy says is that we must simply do something *ourselves*, whatever we can, instead of being so overwhelmed by the bad news everywhere that we become passive. Act now to wrest some positive thing out of the chaos.

Wednesday, August 4, 1993

ERIC SWENSON is coming at eleven. I have spent one hour trying to find a paper I need to photocopy, a business letter. It came yesterday or the day before, and as so many other things have in these forgetful years, it has disappeared. Susan tells me when I have lost something, "Don't say 'lost,' just 'misplaced.'" Sometimes she can find things for me that I have called "lost."

Thursday, August 5, 1993

AND SHE did find the letter!

Pat Carroll came like an angelic godmother on August 3, bearing sandwiches and brownies for our lunch, and such wonderful talk ensued. Unlike most stars, she is very human and never apparently "acting" herself offstage. Of course, there is always the hearty, infectious laughter. I read her the poem "For My Mother," which I wrote last year, the only one I have managed to do that seems almost worthy. She was a Leo, and Pat was interesting about Leos she knows, who are apt, she said, to be very aggressive. My mother was not at all. Unless the lion was roused by an injustice. For instance, when the Germans invaded Belgium in 1914 and soldiers marching through our village at Wondelgem climbed the fence to steal plums, Mother was so furious she forgot the danger and ran out and berated them. They climbed out of the tree very meekly and went on their way. She might have been shot.

I ask myself, captivated by Pat, this bundle of energy, How can anyone as childlike in her abundance also be so wise? She is looking indomitable and will soon, she told me, be directing a production of *Alice in Wonderland*. As a child Pat loved *Alice* whereas I found her terribly irritating and only enjoyed her when I was grown up and Le Gallienne did her production at the Civic.

Pat, like me, was an only child, which is a great bond. She has grown-up children, but she told me how lonely it is for an only child when the mother dies. She was speaking of herself. True, you simply have to go it alone in a new strange way.

Sylvia Frieze was here one day when I was feeling very ill and I said, "Even at eighty-one, when you are ill, you want your mother." Dear Sylvia had tears in her eyes. Her mother died when she was ten, the youngest of nine children.

After our communion here on Tuesday it was lovely to know we would be at the matinee of *Nunsense*, which Pat is playing in Ogunquit, so I would see her onstage as well. The musical comedy creates a great deal of innocent merriment. Hard to take ones eyes off Pat's marvelously expressive face even when others are singing.

Eric Swenson came yesterday morning, and we too had a good talk about everything. He promised Norton would do some advertising on *Encore*, which has sold 11,500 although it only comes out August 15. It was cheering to hear how committed they still are, though Eric is now officially retired.

He is a few years younger than I and still sails his boat in the Bermuda race and just now the Halifax race with a crew of thirteen.

He wants a few more poems for the book of new poems which they will publish next year, so I must try to invent, easier said than done. Poetry is a a balky donkey.

Saturday, August 7, 1993

On Reading the Greek Anthology

This people with unchanging vision sees
The silent-footed hours,
That love as simply as the almond trees
In his season flowers,

That certain as the winter to the wood
Is sorrow for the beautiful and good.
                    Frances Cornford

Frances Cornford, the granddaughter of Charles Darwin and
Emma Wedgwood, and daughter of Francis Darwin and
Emma Crofts, was born in 1886. She married Francis Cornford, a professor of classics at Cambridge University, and
lived in Cambridge until her death. She had a daughter and
three sons, one of whom, John, fought in Spain and died in
that war at twenty-one. She published seven or eight books of
poems, of which the last two were *Collected Poems*, 1954, and
On a Calm Shore, 1960. In 1959 she was awarded the Queen's
Medal for Poetry.

Louise Bogan used to say that it might be fun to compile a
silver treasury of lyric poems. By "silver," I believe she envi-
sioned a collection of minor perfect lyrics, many of them by
women. The pure lyric is never in fashion and never out of
fashion. It stands outside time and comes to any poet as a
Providential gift. We cannot call such poems great, but they
are rare and precious. A very few poets have written nothing
else, Housman, for example, and Frances Cornford is among
them. Pure lyrics embed themselves in the memory and have
the power to haunt. They may be elegiac or explosive, ironic
or passionate, but they always strike the ear as the closest
thing in poetry to song itself and have the same power to
move the reader beyond reason.

I have kept Frances Cornford's *On a Calm Shore* on the
turning bookcase by my desk for years and must have pulled it
out a thousand times as though for a drink of water from a
spring.

When I think about lyric poetry and wonder how I can
give Eric a few more real poems, I always come back to
Frances Cornford and her poems like music for a clavichord.

How unforgettable they are! But I slept badly, worrying about new poems, stupid of me. For poems never come out of worry, only perhaps out of joy or pain. Life taking the poet by surprise.

I have begun this journal at a time of difficult transition because I am now entering real old age. At seventy-five I felt much more able than I do now. Forgetting where things are, forgetting names even of friends, names of flowers (I could not remember calendula the other day), what I had thought of writing here in the middle of the night—forgetting so much makes me feel disoriented sometimes and also slows me up. How to deal with continual frustration about small things like trying to button my shirt, and big things like how to try for a few more poems. That is my problem.

It does help to keep this journal; it forces me to be alive to challenge and to possibility. I want to learn to walk again with Pierrot, who precedes me, tail in air and meowing for fear that we are getting lost, but "the walk" makes a circle and when he realizes we are home, he runs very fast and leaps up the stone steps to the terrace, a magnificent sight for me, who plod slowly on a single path toward the lawn.

Because of the drought the lawn is pale brown these days, a parched world, and no rain today although it was expected.

Later, while I lay down after lunch, I thought that one difficulty is the balance of accepting dependence and at the same time not giving in, doing everything possible for oneself.

Kairos, a Greek word referring to a unique time in a person's life and an opportunity for change, is what I shall call this journal.

Sunday, August 8, 1993

I AM behind on everything because of signing, packing, and sending off books (*Encore*) to friends. It is hard work, but I love doing it and remembering each of the faces, often of friends I see rarely. We are all getting older, travel less, and in some ways these journals are like long letters, telling much of what I have done and thought in a whole year.

Last night Susan and I had invited Margaret Whalen and Barbara Martin to dinner out, such happy extravagance! This was a very late celebration of Margaret's birthday and had been supposed to take place in February, but then I was too ill. We decided on the Cape Neddick Inn as the most festive with an imaginative menu. We talked a little about the poems which I gave them some time ago. Barbara has collected the books for years, but I was rather surprised to hear her say that she felt the "younger poems were more innocent." I cannot see a loss of innocence in any of the last poems in the book, so perhaps she did not really mean "innocence." Youth is not really innocent because it is too full of curiosity about the mysteries of life with the sexual door usually only half open. Old age is the truly innocent time, I think, and in my case a poem like "The Cosset Lamb," "Christmas Light," or "Who Knows Where the Joy Goes" surely shows that this is true. One has grown beyond something, the eternal puzzle, and come into something, the peace of acceptance of reality however painful.

Thus innocence is so often cruel, like the cat's torture of a mouse. The cat is not evil but was created with a mouse- and bird-hunting instinct that makes it do wicked things. This innocence is not responsible for the harm it does, and innocence is lost when guilt enters the scene. I suggest some of this in my poem "Giant in the Garden," where a mature person without guilt is a monster of innocence.

I get rather upset thinking of all this, how few people really know anything about lyric poetry, so unfashionable today. Of the few people who invest in my poems, how many will read them aloud? Not to is like reading a score and not hearing it played. But I feel certain that there are poems in this book that will haunt readers as so many have already been used by lovers to explain their love, at weddings, at funerals, and by the bedside of the sick. Why am I so on the defensive?

Monday, August 9, 1993

I HAD such a welcome letter from Janette Turner Hospital in answer to a rather depressed one from me. She is the Australian writer who wrote a superb long review for the *Times Literary Supplement* of the three books of mine The Women's Press in London has brought out this year. In answer to my depressed letter she says, "It often seems to me that the biggest single issue for a writer is how to stay buoyant enough to go on writing. How not to drown." How right she is. It is the more moving because she is such a productive writer herself, though she teaches at least one semester in Australia.

Lying in bed after breakfast as I always do, sometimes watching the "Today" show, I thought how good it is to find myself in such a beautiful space, early in the morning, after

The red and blue stained-glass phoenix.

lunch when I have a nap, and at night before I go to sleep and read for an hour or two. My bed faces a white wall divided between a beautiful fireplace over which hangs Ann Woodson's painting of the Nelson hills with three of the ancient gravestones at their feet, a semiabstract painting of great simplicity and force. It reminds me that my ashes will be buried in Nelson, my home there the only home I have ever owned.

On the right side of that wall is a big many-paned door onto the porch roof, and at its top hangs a blue and red stained glass phoenix Karen Saum had made for me years ago and which the sun illuminates early in the morning.

The east side of the room is all windows, four casement windows that open out. I do not see the ocean from my bed, but I hear it all night, the most soothing murmur accelerating as the tide rises, and I have only to get up and look out to see it

CREDIT: SUSAN SHERMAN

The long field . . . like some huge magic animal.

lying there below the long field like some huge magic animal which at any moment high wind may rouse.

As everywhere in this house, everything has a meaning and, as I look around, evokes memories of all my lives—a small blue vase on the mantel was given me in memory of Ernesta Green, for instance. She was one of the most beautiful young women I have ever seen, with her sapphire eyes and dark eyebrows, and she shot herself before she was thirty, having burned in the stove letters she had written perhaps to explain why.

Tuesday, August 10, 1993

IN DESCRIBING the charm of my bedroom as I lie in it and enjoy, I forgot yesterday several important things. By the fireplace there are two stuffed toy sheep, one quite big I bought in Lewiston, Pennsylvania, when I was staying with Marilyn Mumford; the other someone gave me. In front of them is a low table covered a foot high with books I am reading or looking forward to reading. Then a small television set in the middle of the room, and to its right a fantasy goose with her gosling sitting high up on a suitcase which rests on an armchair. By the window a lovely big donkey, lying down, its ears pricked in two directions. He was brought by an admirer of *Joanna and Ulysses* who gives me some kind of donkey every Christmas, a card, a small dear fellow, a yearly surprise. She brought the big one in a shopping bag to a book signing in Cambridge.

To left and right of my big bed are revolving bookcases, one tall one containing autobiographies and Henry Adams's

Mont-Saint-Michel and Chartres, which I must reread one of these days. The other table close to my bed is low and round and nearly always has a small bunch of flowers on it, a box of my medicines, an electric clock, and a few poetry anthologies, the most precious being the *London Book of Verse*, which contains long poems that are too long for inclusion in the *Oxford Book of English Verse*. There I reread Thompson or Tennyson, Francis Thompson's "The Hound of Heaven," which Letty Field and I used to recite on our walks in Cambridge. Above this useful little round table I hang two English calendars, this month a scene of rolling hills and pasture and a great tree in a field in Yorkshire.

So the room is filled with my life and gives my life back to me as I lie in my bed and look around me. The changing light on the white walls makes it always luminous in daytime.

Wednesday, August 11, 1993

Two DAYS ago Marilyn Kallet, her husband, Lou, and daughter, Heather, now eight years old, came for an hour at four. Lou took Heather down to York Beach, where she braved the icy water up to her knees. Marilyn is a poet and critic who teaches at the University of Tennessee and has given me this year an immense joy, a book she has edited, *A House of Gathering: Poets on May Sarton's Poetry*. It is something like a very unlikely dream come true, for there has been so little serious criticism of the poetry in the fifty years since it has been published. I felt like a happy bear with a pot of excellent honey as I absorbed it. There is such a variety of comment by both men and women, and much to my delight, many are young.

This is not the place for me to comment at length on this book, for what I want to do here is celebrate Marilyn Kallet herself. She looks beautiful and, in spite of all the stresses of family life for a fundamentally dedicated poet to handle, happy. It was a joy to drink a glass of champagne and sit and talk for an hour about all that concerns us.

Thursday, August 12, 1993

WE MISSED the magic rain of meteors last night because of a cloudy sky, and today is gray and cold. I have on a wool sweater. Yesterday afternoon Susan helped me clear away a mountain of papers and objects on the two cocktail tables in front of the couch up here in my study. Much of this went back to 1992. So many people send me privately printed books, little presents. It is all so kind, but I have to confess, unwelcome. I spend an enormous amount of energy and time thanking people for things they want to give me far more than I want to receive them. It sounds meanspirited, but so much now has to be counted as far as energy goes. I say to myself a hundred times a day, "Yes, I want to answer this or that friend," but there are fifty letters I should answer first, and all at once I am buried alive in the chaos, and my mind balks at the effort.

Saturday, August 14, 1993

Two DAYS ago Marge Piercy and Ira Wood came by. They live on the Cape. I hope this can be a yearly tradition. Marge is such a life giver in spite of awful problems with her eyes, and worse to come, she fears. Ira is a warm and loving man. I will not forget his being really moved by my reading in Cambridge for the Poetry Society in late April, how warmly he embraced me. As for Marge, she took over in the most admirable way like an experienced general before a battle. I had had a small stroke in London three weeks before this and was shaky and extremely nervous. It seemed like hubris to imagine I could still read my poems—and those all new poems—at eighty-one and ill. Then I saw the auditorium, in a science building at Harvard University, a deep trough with a table and microphone miles below where we stood as we came in. I knew at once that I could not go down very flat stairs with no banister to hang on to. What to do?

Meanwhile, the audience was piling in, and I had to greet old friends. Marge took over, determined to find an elevator and some way for me to reach the stage safely, and she did succeed though it involved walking quite a distance. She also introduced me when the time came, better than I have ever been introduced, and this followed dear Diane de Hovanessian's introduction. I felt truly blessed and sent forward into the reading armed. It went well. Molly Howe came, such a present to see her in the front row. She must be ninety. And Bob and Eleanor O'Leary, and so many other old friends. It felt like a festival.

Bosnia! Bosnia! It haunts my nights, and the agony of Sarajevo is never not in my heart. This is something quite new. Evil is done before our eyes morning and evening on the TV and every day in the newspaper. We are witnessing genocide while it takes place. It is as though we had seen the Holocaust, watched the naked Jews being herded into the gas ovens, and the emaciated few still alive being beaten and forced to work themselves to death. Seen it every day. But then, at that time, we did not know what was happening. Would anything have been done to stop it if we had? We finally made war. But now in Bosnia we see and do nothing.

I do not know how to deal with it. I am haunted. It is like a constant dark foreboding in the air.

And the temptation in these circumstances is to forget it, to push it down out of our consciousness, and deal with other things. What more dangerous to the soul than this forced passivity? "The ground is littered with corpses; the intensity of the Serb bombardment makes it all but impossible to bury the dead." (*New Statesman*, August 6, 1993) Fourteen thousand children, terribly wounded, need to be flown to hospitals in the West. Today only four will be flown out.

Sunday, August 15, 1993

THE NEW mattress is a dream. Karen Kozlowski drove me to Jordan Marsh two weeks ago, and I lay on the hard ones first, but I have so little flesh on my bones my back hurt. Then I tried a slightly less hard one—heaven! I had had the old one for forty years. I got it for the guest room at Nelson when I moved there. It had become very lumpy, so I feel like a princess, especially as the mattress is higher than the old one.

Yesterday Andrea Lockett came to interview me for the *New York Quarterly.* She is a charming African-American woman, elegantly dressed, and I realized at once that she truly knows and cares about my work. The questions were cogent and challenging, and I enjoyed answering as best I could. This was a "craft interview," so I had a chance to talk a little about the new poems, the rather austere style I came to use when I was seventy-nine. Andrea said it is quite true that the young know my work and persuade their professors who do not to let them write a paper or thesis on Sarton. What could be better at eighty-one, not to be old-fashioned but discovered by the young? New-fashioned, as I never was when I was first published.

She brought me a delightful present, a glass pen. I could hardly wait to try it and did yesterday afternoon with a bottle of ink I found up here.

Before Andrea left at around twelve-fifteen—she had come at eleven—I realized that I was frightfully exhausted. I felt like a balloon suddenly emptied, a limp mass.

So I minded that Bruce Conklin and Deborah Straw were picking me up at five for dinner. I rested on my delicious new mattress until four after my lunch, but still felt overtired. I try not to schedule two important things in one day, but August is the crowded month, so overdoing is inevitable.

Wonderful to see Deborah and Bruce again after all these months. They are among my friends who read the most and with the greatest taste, so they always bring something to lend me, this time also flowers. We had a great talk about everything at Stage Neck Inn.

Today no one comes, so Susan and I are alone with peace, quiet, and ourselves. No rain in sight, alas, but bright sun and a pale hot-looking ocean.

Tuesday, August 17, 1993

YESTERDAY WAS old home day, for Sears brought and installed
the new rug I had ordered for the cozy room where we eat
and where I watch TV. The old rug was eighteen years old
and terribly dirty; the new one is less orange and more purple, very distinguished. I am doing things about the house as
everything felt neglected because I have been ill most of the
summer so I celebrate now with renewal here and there.

Wednesday, August 18, 1993

A LOW day, overcast, and we waited for rain that did not
come. I had a frustrating morning looking for a letter I could
not find, and then for the small book of photographs of me in
Wondelgem at eleven months old. These things happen every
day and make me feel crazy, but considering how much falls
in here every day, how much I have to keep sorted out, I
suppose some misplacing is to be accepted as part of the complex life I still live.

In the late afternoon Susan and I had the very moving
experience of seeing a video called *A Woman's Tale* (Illumi-
nation Films, Australian Film Finance Corporation). It is a
masterpiece as we follow a seventy-eight-year-old woman
who is dying of cancer through her spirited, life-giving days.

She is helped by her married son's lover, who is a nurse. The whole atmosphere is of love, a person surrounded by love because she is so loving and alive herself. The film does not deny the physical decadence, we even see her taking a bath, the sagging breasts, the disfigured hands, but it is always inspiring. I feel so grateful for it.

Yesterday just after the film Fred Rogers called me from Nantucket to tell me that Ruth Carter had died. She was a great fan of his and of mine, looked at Fred's show every morning. He called her now and then, answered her longing for attention, and made an immense difference in the last ten years and more of her life that ended in a nursing home, happy but not quite all there. I too tried to keep in touch over the years. She was a great egotist with a firm sense of humor and a real gift for light verse. She lived in Oregon.

A much heavier loss for me was to read in the *Times* the obit of Irene Sharaff, two columns making it clear what a distinguished stage and costume designer she was, dying at eighty-three after a very successful life in New York and Hollywood. She wrote a warm paragraph for my *Festschrift* which touched me especially because we had not corresponded for years. But when I spent a year in Paris when I was nineteen, I saw Irene almost every day and often spent the night with her at the Foyot Hotel because I lived in Montrouge and the metro closed down at midnight so I could always knock at her door under the eaves. Then when I went to Florence in April, very unhappy, she and I stayed in the same apartment as P.G.s and Irene was a tender and loving friend. I wish I could imagine what she was like in her years of fame. Aware of her own genius, defensive and arrogant, I think.

Sunday, August 22, 1993

I FORGOT to say that Deborah Straw and Bruce Conklin brought me an entrancing book by Terry Kay, *To Dance with the White Dog* (Washington Square Press). It is so real and so imaginative about children overanxious about an aging parent who is taking refuge in an elusive white dog. I was in tears as I finished it, for I could not bear it to be over. I have ordered two copies to lend or give.

Ann and Charles McLaughlin came a little after four. What a celebration of our long friendship and really of our lives, three survivors. They got polio just before the Salk vaccine. Ann was in an iron lung for a long time. Charlie will always be in a wheelchair. Their children are grown up, Ellen an actress now in that play about AIDS, *Angels in America*.

How beautiful they are, especially Charlie, who has white hair now and shining brown eyes, an extremely gentle but humorous and giving presence, a great talker. Their marriage is a true wonder of mutual understanding and mutual help. They reminded me that I had written a poem for their wedding and Susan will find it for me.

Epithalamium

for Charlie and Ann
Now from all mountains you come down
Radiant after those reaches of despair
Which you climbed once on courage alone,
A footstep's span from the dreadful air.
Now from interminable empty seas

Where the unwavering compass was your hope,
You land at last as radiant as those
Saints who discover a mysterious home,
Where out of conflict the most difficult joys
Like poetry, like love, search and find poise.
You give us a new world. Tenderness flows
Out from your hands like some amazing news.
And in this marriage rooted deep in trust
We bless a legend we had almost lost,
The miracle of balance and of gentleness
That steadfast love may slowly bring to pass.
                              With love from
                              May Sarton
                              July 14, 1952

I found blackberry brandy, and we sat on the terrace in a lovely glow of happiness to be together, survivors, after so many years.

Wednesday, August 25, 1993

I HAVE now to accept that what I do every day is all right— that is, to answer the day's mail or as much as has to be answered, and accept that what is not answered the day it arrives will probably never be. This morning I have worked for an hour, mostly to put together Medicare material for AARP, hoping they will pay a fairly large hospital bill. Then I wrote Rosemary Mattson. Howard Mattson died after a long illness at their home in Carmel, holding Rosemary's hand. He was eighty-five, a Unitarian minister, a poet, and a tremen- dously giving presence among migrant workers in the civil rights movement. I met Rosemary when I was a summer professor at the Starr King Unitarian School of the Ministry in Berkeley, California, and stayed with the Mattsons for a while at that time.

It is going to be a terribly hot, humid day, but when I went down to give Pierrot his breakfast at a little after five, the whole sky was a brilliant orange over a very blue ocean, all so calm and beautiful early in the morning.

Thursday, August 26, 1993

YESTERDAY DOROTHY Jones came for our yearly lunch together and exchange of news. Dorothy said we have known each other for ten years. Such friendships are precious stable joys for me. New people tire me, but I enjoy Dorothy's lively appreciation of life.

Today was a little more demanding, an hour of intense talking with Erika Pfander, who is producing my play *The Music Box Bird* in October. I have never met anyone as intense as I was at her age, but I think she is even more so, a very perceptive reader who sees the connections in my work as few ever have. I find I trust her to get everything out of the play that is there between the lines. I wrote it perhaps thirty years ago! It is thrilling that a work of art has no age, for it might have been written yesterday.

Susan is in Connecticut seeing her parents, so I have a taste of what it will be like when she goes back to Riverdale September 5. I am playing records, now Janet Baker singing Fauré songs and Chausson's haunting "Poème d'Amour et de la Mer. Awhile ago I got completely wet setting the hose as the garden is bone dry. On Sunday two days ago I was rocked by a phone call from Canada from Lewis Pyensen, who wants to do a biography of my father. I felt struck by lightning, another biography to help get done besides my own! My heart sank as I arranged for him to come here and see what I have in the files on Sunday and Monday of the Labor Day weekend. Susan leaves on the Saturday. Well, I am in for it. But I have always hoped a biography would be written, so it is good news. Only I am a rather burdened donkey already.

Monday, August 30, 1993

I HAVE not said anything for four days because it was a humid horrible heat wave which broke yesterday after mid-nineties on Saturday, to give us a beautiful day, extremely clear air, everything sharply defined, dry and cool like a blessing. Every atom in my body felt relieved and playing Fauré's wonderful passionate songs, *l'Invitation au Voyage*, to Baudelaire's poem. What a *frisson* these songs and Baker's moving voice give me! I wrote two small poems, one semihumorous one about my difficulties with getting dressed every morning. It is a problem to be overcome only by patience with my clumsy fingers.

In the afternoon I finished the stunning novel by Ruth Moore, *The Walk down Main Street,* Connie Hunting sent me because I had asked her about Moore, unknown to me, but I now realize a very good writer indeed, her novels rooted in Maine. This one, first published in 1960, is about the wreck-age in a small town when the basketball team in the local high school wins a local championship and goes on to a bigger test, how the boys become arrogant and obsessed, and the men take to betting on the game and become more and more involved, a corrupting process. The plot is fast-moving, but what held me was the language, the vivid slang so different from the endlessly repeated four-letter words novelists these days often use. I have not been so taken by a novel in ages.

The marvelous cool bright day ended with Susan and me going out to dinner at Dockside, a perfect evening for that scene of the harbor full of elegant boats, with a shining sky, the apotheosis of summer luxury and fun, and as we drove home, the sun was setting in a soft orange sky, the river reflecting it—such beauty! There are times—and this was one—when it would be hard to find a more beautiful scene anywhere in the world.

Wednesday, September 1, 1993

I HAVE to keep fighting back a fog of misery knowing that Susan leaves on Saturday. Once she has gone I shall remake a solitary routine and be all right, but the parting tears tender roots up that we have grown all summer, and before and immediately after she leaves are hard times. How huge and silent the house will become!

Perhaps it is a good thing that Lewis Pyensen, who wants to do a biography of my father, comes on Sunday to go over what is in my files here. We lunch on Saturday.

Yesterday Polly Tompkins and Molly took me out to lunch as they have done for maybe ten years. Polly was in the State Department and after she retired became very interested in South Africa. Always the conversation is thrilling for me, who do not have many friends as *au courant*. They summer in northern Maine and winter in Tucson. Polly had had a day with Winnie Mandela when she was still "banished" and was taken with her warmth and vivid personality.

Today at eleven Ellie Dwight, who is doing an essay on me with special emphasis on gardening, came. A good hour, but I felt tired at the end. After my nap Susan came in and was astonished at what an hour's sleep had done. "You look quite different," she said.

Friday, September 3, 1993

WE HAD a shower this morning. What bliss to feel gentle rain on one's face, but it has not turned into a real rain after all, terribly humid, hot, and altogether depressing. Susan and I are both depressed because of our imminent parting. It all feels heavy and sad, the life around here at the moment.

But I have found some snaps of Pierrot playing with Grizzle, a miniature dachshund. I had forgotten that they played quite fiercely, Pierrot sometimes on his back. I really should get him a kitten, but I am afraid he might be jealous.

After Tamas died, I felt so bereft that I decided to try again and obtain, if I could, a long-haired dachshund puppy. I had seen one years ago playing on the floor and fallen in love. Karen Saum knew a woman who bred them and would have one in a few months. I was seventy-five, and it never occurred to me that an untrained puppy might be too much for me. Tamas had been an exemplary dog with beautiful manners. When the time came to drive the four hours to meet Grizzle, as I named the dachshund, I was sitting in a chair across from the doorway where she was set down, and she flew across the room and jumped into my lap. What a sweetheart! It was a good beginning to our relationship.

A month later Karen brought her to me.

What brought her vividly to mind now were the snaps I discovered of Grizzle and Pierrot playing together. This was quite charming to see, and it was interesting because Pierrot had dominated poor Tamas, even driving him out of his bed. And now he was dominated by Grizzle, who also pushed him out of his bed and then romped with him.

Grizzle was just as charming as I had imagined and made me laugh a lot, especially when she raced down the drive to catch a ball, her long ears waving perpendicularly and her tail waving horizontally like mad. Her desire to chase a ball was constant. She was an hilarious, loving presence, but an untrainable dog. I learned the hard way that dachshunds are nearly untrainable. After a year she was still untrained and blithely did her business all over the house, unfazed by my shouts and even slaps. She had no sense of guilt. I loved her, but after two years of cleaning up I decided I was too old to keep an untrainable little dog.

When she first came, my friend Janice Oberacker took her and snuggled her into her parka and said, "If you ever want to get rid of her, I'll take her anytime," and she had not changed her mind. I had given a dachsie to Janice some years before, and Fonzi needed a companion. They became fast friends. What a lucky chance to find such a good home for darling little untrainable Grizzle.

For me it was a lesson on what I can no longer do. A puppy is too much for an old lady.

Susan and I have been out to dinner together for two nights. The first on Wednesday to celebrate my father's birthday. Susan invited me, and we had a fine dinner at Stage Neck in the grill. But the big event was stopping on the way at the Inn at Harmon Park on York Street where Susan had seen a small black pig. She bravely parked in front of the house and went to ask if we could view the pig. The owner, Sue Antal, was gracious, knew me luckily, and walked us round to the side of the house, and there on a long rope like a dog a delightful pig—quite large actually—came running toward us, wagging his tail. I scratched his head a little. Sue said she had had the pig for a year and a half, that he slept by the wood stove on winter days, was very clean and well behaved. I hear these Thai pigs are the most fashionable pets.

Today Karen, who drove me to the Golden Harvest to get vegetables, told me she had known a pig who was not killed because it had become such a pet became enormous. At the sound of the school bell at the end of the morning he broke out of the pen and ran to the school to let the children ride him! After a while the teacher called his owner to come and fetch him in the truck. Pigs can be very endearing creatures.

Saturday, September 4, 1993

"My life has not been my own for such a long while now," writes Char Radintz. Char and her husband have a dairy farm in Wisconsin with two children growing up fast, but what a hard life they lead, with less and less rest in it or time to enjoy, not push on to the next chore. Char is a good writer and wrote a stunning column about her life for a local paper. I felt some of these essays should be collected and made into a book. But now there is no time, I fear, for that creative side to be fulfilled. She is a great woman who stretches out to the whole world. Some years ago she joined a group of farm women and went to Nicaragua. Her letters always take me back to the essentials.

It is a momentous day because Lewis Pyensen has been here all day, going over the files concerning George Sarton. We had lunch together, and I was happy to get to know him as he seems to be the ideal biographer and I had always hoped this would happen. Expect a miracle! This indeed is one close to my heart.

Lewis Pyensen is well aware of the humiliations George Sarton suffered both from Harvard and especially Vannevar Bush at the Carnegie Institution. I feel this biography will at last do the great scholar, the universal man, justice. And I am learning things I did not know, for instance, that after World War II many Japanese scholars were penniless. Daddy apparently raised funds for at least one, and organized help from others in the academic groves. I sense that Lewis is quite humorous and ironic about academic life in general, the awful power struggles and sometimes meanness of spirit involved. People accept that about the business world, but perhaps still idealize the academic world. When I was teaching at Harvard, I saw how bitter the fight for promotion could be. I never suffered from that because as a Briggs-Copeland instructor of creative writing there could not be any question of promotion after the three-year stint.

Wednesday, September 8, 1993

IT IS the end of summer, a fraying end, without the autumn yet to lead us into its wide spaces and brilliant color. It feels like limbo.

When I was getting my supper, the phone rang five times just as the swordfish was in the broiler. Two interviews put off. One was to be today at eleven, a talk show in Wisconsin which would interview me by telephone and take questions for an hour. When I got back to the swordfish, it was ruined and uneatable though I swallowed it, some of it, somehow.

Writing all this frustration, I see why I am at sixes and sevens this morning, a dull dog. Interesting that we have the phrase "a dull dog," but a dull cat does not exist.

Margot Peters flies off to Belgium today. How I envy her! I am filled with nostalgia.

Sunday, September 12, 1993

I DO not know why I feel absolutely tired these days, but I think it is probably because the pressure is unrelenting—too many letters that must be answered. Maggie came yesterday before lunch, our first visit for a long time because Susan was here and Maggie was on North Haven. I expected Maggie at eleven-thirty, decided not to keep my weekly hair appoint-

ment because I needed time at my desk more than anything. I
wanted to get flowers for the house, get the mail, the *Times*
before I could feel free to work up here, and I did all that,
feeling extremely frail and off-balance. Luckily I keep a cane
in the car now. I drove home and on the way up the drive
could see there were nasturtiums ready to be picked in the
otherwise disaster area of the picking garden, so I got out of
the car and walked the few yards, but then I realized that
apples were all over the ground, and unsteady as I was, I
knew I would fall, so could not pick. It was the final frustration after quite a few yesterday—a glass slipped out of my
hand and broke. When I got to my desk, I could not find my
checkbook, and spent almost an hour trying to unearth a letter
from an editor at Norton wanting a blurb on a book I have
been reading bound proof of, *Life Notes: Personal Writings
by Contemporary Black Women,* a wonderful project marred
by the way it was organized with too little from the journals
and too much explanation. I tried on Friday to write something but was not pleased with it.

So when Maggie was here as I came home from shopping
not having picked nasturtiums for her, I simply burst into
tears. I felt totally unable to cope even with her, whom I had
so looked forward to seeing here again at last. Of course, we
hugged each other and laughed about the checkbook—she too
loses hers. Everyone over seventy does, I think. So I went up
to my desk and found it put by mistake in a drawer with my
English checkbook.

I then worked for an hour on a blurb for *Life Notes.* In
spite of my doubts about the editing, it is full of moving and
significant comment, a rewarding book *quand même.* It
makes one eager for more. How articulate those women are!
And how honest. Would an anthology of white women's journals have the same impact? I doubt it.

Judy Harrison, my part-time secretary, came on Friday

for the first time in months because I was not keeping a journal and was too ill to work with her. It was exhilarating to know the computer was being used again. She typed the new poems for the book to come out next year.

Wednesday, September 15, 1993

I AM back again dictating a journal which until now I have been writing in a notebook, but my hand is so illegible that even I cannot read it, so it is time that with Judy's help this got put on the computer. It is a terrifically hot, muggy day.

I have had quite a day because "All Things Considered" radio program sent three people to interview me this morning at nine, which seemed a hard time for me to pull myself together for, but they proved to be very sensitive. Katy Davis was the interviewer, and she had really studied my work and asked some questions, as everybody else does, about why solitude is so important and how it is different from loneliness. As I have said many times, one is lonely when one is in some way impoverished inside oneself. I do still love solitude and need it to discover where I really am, and one of the problems with these cluttered days where I have appointments either for interviews or with friends (because everybody comes to Maine in the summer) is that I almost never have a whole day to myself now, and that is what I crave. Perhaps come October it will happen, but then in October there is my play opening on the eighth, and I go to Maggie Vaugahn's for that weekend. So there is no clear time ahead.

Because I was upset by a letter that came today, I went out to do shopping instead of resting after my lunch. When I came back, there were flowers from the three sweet people from "All Things Considered." I was touched. They teased me because during the interview I had said, "Words do not obey me anymore," and that made them laugh. But the fact is that since the stroke I very often do not say the right word, the word I mean to say. I say another word. Sometimes it is all right. Sometimes it is slightly embarrassing. This was true several times during the interview. What I did discover was that reading a poem now, and I read three for them, is hard work. I felt exhausted at the end of the hour. Really exhausted.

On the card which came with beautiful lilies, the red and white ones so brilliant in this gray weather, the people from "All Things Considered" said, "Words don't obey us either." It was so good to laugh with them.

I am enamored of Muriel Spark's memoir. It is really a distinguished book, an unpretentious book in which one is totally convinced that she is being honest all the way through. She does not try to put her childhood memories together in any kind of sequence. She simply tells us what meals were like when she was a little girl, or what frightened her, or what delighted her, but not in a sequence. Reading it, one wishes to go to Scotland, so I am anxious to lend it to my friend Edythe Haddaway, whose grandmother was Scottish and who has a great feeling about Scotland, as all Scots do.

And now I must write a letter.

Friday, September 17, 1993

I AM sitting here looking out on a gray ominous ocean and sky. I think it is going to rain. It is very cold out. The only good thing about that is that Pierrot stays in a lot. He is now up on my bed and I hope will be there all day.

Last night I called Polly Starr, Polly Thayer, the painter, who painted a great portrait of me when I was twenty-five and my first book came out. It is on the jacket of *Encore*. I hope she will be pleased to see it although she is nearly blind and I think has to use strong magnifying glasses to see anything at all and probably will not be able to read the book. I felt, though, that I must send it to her after our talk. She laughs in such a wonderful way though she is ninety and has this problem with her eyes, which for a painter is particularly difficult. But she had a tremendous event to tell which amused me no end, and that is that a peacock has adopted her and lives apparently in the chimney. This I really do not understand and must get more news about. She had sent me two exquisite feathers, small ones, not the big feather with the eye in it but little ones with soft blue edges. I wanted to tell her how I loved them and also to learn about the peacock who is such a welcome visitor. I asked whether he screamed a lot, because when I stayed near the London Zoo when I was writing my first novel and the Huxleys lent me their apartment there, at night the peacocks screamed and woke me up. "Yes," said Polly, "at first he was marking his territory and he went all over the place, which is quite large, and screamed everywhere to say, 'Here I am, I am the peacock, I am the king.' " And then when that was done, which took some days, I gather, he became totally silent—unless he is frightened by the cat or something like that—which is amazing. I asked about his name and she gave me several. I am forgetting what her name for him is. One of her servants calls him Mr. Peacock. Unfortunately Polly has a cat of whom she did a magnificent drawing but who is not comforting and wanting to be petted or purr like Pierrot. I realize what a deprivation this is, especially as Polly cannot read and cannot see. I do not know what I would do if Pierrot did not purr.

Now I am looking forward to several interviews next week and to seeing Roger Finch, that remarkable poet who lives in Japan, on Sunday. So there is never a dull moment here, but sometimes I wish for a few empty days.

Saturday, September 18, 1993

IT HAS been gloomy weather, but today there is a silvery sky and a marvelous silver ocean with a dark blue band at the horizon.

The Muriel Spark memoir was a tremendous joy. Now I have been sent by Polly Starr an absolutely nourishing book, an extraordinary book for a Frenchman to have written, Jacques Lusseyran. It is called *And There Was Light*. Jacques Lusseyran became blind when he was eight years old and was run into from the back by mistake by a fellow student. One of his eyes was simply destroyed in that fall, and the other one soon went. So he had seen. The extraordinary thing about this man is that for him blindness is seeing. It is all the things that the blind person does and can do that the seeing person does not do that make the book so remarkable. For instance, the furniture comes toward him instead of his going toward it. Everything is animate. He can tell where the trees are on a French road, one by one where each is. The trees speak to him, if you will. That is extraordinary enough, but the thing that is most extraordinary is that there is this great light in him that he feels flowing from him and which affects everybody with whom he comes into contact. He is aware of the danger of a too-inward life and becomes active in every way. He runs, for instance, by having a student put a hand on his shoulder and run alongside him, being his guide. More than that, he is involved in all the life around him, and when he is sixteen, he becomes the head of one of the operative resistance groups against the Germans when they take France. When he was head of this group, it started with fifty and ended with six hundred. They were finally betrayed by one of them, and he was in a terrible French prison and then in one of the worst of the concentration camps. I have not got to this part of the book yet, but I could not wait to say how really illuminating in the deepest sense this book is for me right now.

It is wonderful to have Cybèle here, and Susan and we are going to see a video this afternoon of *My Life as a Dog*, which apparently we saw before but I do not remember. Now that is the extraordinary thing, that I forget things totally. I was sure that I had not seen Elizabeth Bowen's *The Death of the Heart*, so Susan brought it. We saw it again and I realized that some of it I did remember, but I had forgotten so much.

Phyllis Chiemingo is coming to take me to lunch, she who so often has sent flowers when I needed them most. Susan left after lunch, and at first when she leaves, it is a terrible empty cave I live in and I feel desolate. It reminds me of when I used to leave my parents, as I did so often to go to Europe or to go on a tour. Always I would see my mother waving at the door and then know that there was a bad time, maybe about a half hour, after the person is gone and one has to remake oneself. Today as I was lying there with Pierrot purring beside me— thank goodness he was there—I began to think of solitude in a new way. In solitude we are with ourself, and that is what is so frightening because what if there is no self there? Some people do not have a real self. And being with oneself is always a confrontation because there is always some human problem that one is involved with, even a small one that takes some thinking about. I have said so often that solitude is the richness of self and loneliness the poverty of self that I was glad to think just a little bit differently about it today.

Now the sun is out. It is a real autumn day, very cold, and I called Carol Heilbrun, whom I have not talked with in a while. We always laugh and have a wonderful time. I called Rene Morgan, who will soon be back in Albuquerque. It is a time always, the end of September and beginning of October, of transforming change. Already one is terribly aware of the lack of light. It is pitch-dark by seven or half past seven at most. Soon it will be much earlier than that. That is the hard time. It is why November is, I think, the worst month in Maine. November and March are the two bad months—November because of the darkness and March because the spring does not come in Maine until almost May.

Tuesday, September 21, 1993

"I WASTED time, and now doth time waste me," said Shakespeare's Richard II. It is certainly what I do a great deal. For instance, I have been trying to write a short note to Dean Frieze, who lost one of his brothers. Dean is such a brotherly man that it makes my heart ache to think of his losing an older brother. He is the youngest in his family, I believe.

While I tried to think of something to say, I as usual went back to Frances Cornford, hoping there would be a short poem there, and realizing once more how rare perfect short lyrics are and how marvelous when one comes upon one. Well, I did not find anything and so I had wasted quite a lot of time, but I did enjoy reading the poems nevertheless.

This has been quite a day because Edgar Allen Bean came from the *Maine Times* to interview me, an extremely gentle, sensitive man, and we had a good talk although I was not at my best because I had had such an exhausting day yesterday.

Yesterday I was in a small accident which was really quite a shock and, I think, was my fault although I wonder whether I could have blacked out for just a second. I turned in against traffic and ran into someone who was coming straight ahead. The strange thing is that there was almost no damage. One of his fenders was slightly dented. Nobody was hurt, thank goodness, so I guess I am well out of it. But it took so long for the policeman to make out all the papers. Then in the afternoon I had to fill out a lot of things for the secretary of state in Augusta. I found it hard to rest after that and then was up here in my office at about four trying to catch up with the mail

when Pat called me in much distress from the first floor to say
that she thought the septic tank, of all things, was overflow-
ing. At least she said there was a terrible smell. Later Susan
reminded me that it had been emptied two years ago so there
should not have been any trouble. But I felt that housekeep-
ing, coping with things, was an ordeal for me yesterday. So
when Bean asked me about the first phoenix poem ("The
Phoenix," in *In Time like Air*) I was really at a loss because I
had totally forgotten it. This is what happens. I mean there
are three or four hundred poems. I remembered it vaguely,
but I did not remember what the circumstances were, and
now I remember that the circumstances were Matthiessen's
death and in a way this poem has to do with my novel *Faithful
Are the Wounds*. I suppose it has to do also with me and the
fact that a temperament like mine can sometimes seem to do a
lot of harm, but in the end something has happened to whoever was involved with me, which is *not* negative.

I had a wonderful letter from Lewis Pyensen. I had given
him *Faithful Are the Wounds*, and he wrote so feelingly about
it I was really touched. He said, "There are no bad characters
and no shallow ones," which I found wonderful praise. "Pro-
fundity is everywhere if one looks for it," he says. But he also
said above all that, "Emotional electricity seems to suffuse the
story and it lights up each character in a special way. They
glow almost as if under the protection of halos like golden
illuminated byzantine saints." Well, I was in a state of high
emotion when I wrote that book. There is no doubt about it.
When I reread it recently, I felt that emotional tension again
and thought that perhaps I have never experienced it to the
same extent since. Lewis also spoke warmly of *A World of
Light*. He has written to Robert Merton, the great scientist
and friend of my father's, I am glad to say, and I am sure Bob
will see him. So altogether this was not as bad a day as yesterday.

Thursday, September 23, 1993

A DISMAL day, the sky closed in very low, but no rain, only a nerve-racking wind, and I am depressed. Tomorrow we are promised sun and everything will look different. How stupidly sensitive I am to the weather! Today was redeemed by Vicki Runnion, who came in her truck to have lunch with me. I have not seen Vicki since the champagne brunch here in 1992, when I invited some of the contributors to the three-day conference Westbrook College organized as a celebration of my eightieth birthday; it had been a perfect day, cool and bright, and so many people wandering around the place. Vicki I see very clearly in my mind's eye sitting on the terrace wall with Cybèle on her lap and looking blissfully happy.

She drove from Louisville, where she works in Hospice, twenty-two hours on the road with one stop overnight. But since then she has been with friends in Saco, walking the beach for hours, and she looked relaxed, brought me exquisite flowers, and we had a reviving talk about everything from politics to mutual friends and, of course, her little dogs. Vicki wrote a good essay about what I have written on death and dying, which she gave at Westbrook. It will be published with others next year by the Puckerbrush Press.

Vicki radiates what I call goodness. I know no one else who does so as simply and unself-consciously as she does. Being with her is restorative.

Friday, September 24, 1993

I CONTINUE to feel befuddled by how much goes on. Today, for instance, Nadine came as usual a little after seven, and that meant getting a tray ready and making a list of things for her to do. Then Judy Harrison, my secretary, came at nine when I was still reading the mail. At ten Karen came to take me to get in food as Susan arrives tonight close to eleven. But at least the sun is out. That is the great news. However depleted I felt this morning, the sun made all the difference. I saw the sun on three nasturtiums in a bunch that I had placed on the television set. It was so dramatic that it amazed me. This is what one misses when there is no sun.

Edythe, who came to get me for lunch, said that she is beginning to like having flowers in her apartment and had had some when people were expected the other night—some asters and white chrysanthemums and I cannot remember what else—but it is lovely to have her enjoying flowers at home. So many people feel that that is an extravagance, and I suppose it is to some extent, but to me when I am alone here, flowers are as important as food, perhaps more so. They are one of the joys of solitude. I look at their faces as if they were people.

Pierrot has become ravenous. He eats three or four cans of cat food a day, and I wonder if it is good for him. I must ask Dr. Beekman. I caught two fleas on him today. I have been aware that he was scratching in a way that suggests he might have fleas. It has been such a rare summer because he did not have any and did not have to go through the hell of being washed at the vet's, but of course, very soon there will be far

Flowers are as important as food.

more than two. They reproduce like rabbits; I must be prepared for that. I think I will wait until I can get his claws
clipped at the same time.

I have been thinking again about short lyrics and how rare

they are and, while seeking out a few I remembered, found this wonderful one of De la Mare that I had forgotten.

A Still Life

> Bottle, coarse tumbler, loaf of bread,
> Cheap paper, a lean long kitchen knife:
> No moral, no problem, sermon or text,
> No hint of a why, whence, whither, or if;
> Mere workaday objects put into paint—
> Bottle and tumbler, loaf and knife—
> And engrossed round spectacled,
> Chardin's passion for life.

I used to read that fairly often when I was doing poetry readings and always felt what a good poem it is. When one thinks of lyric poetry, how few short lyrics there are; it makes one want to write two or three, but they cannot be commanded.

Saturday, September 25, 1993

A PERFECT autumn day. Brilliant. Blue sea and the autumn crocuses in their glory down below the terrace. Such a hosanna of cups opening themselves to the sun. There is something about a flower that comes in autumn and only in autumn. So I rejoice especially in these today. Susan is here, so the house feels inhabited in a comforting way. Apparently Pierrot was asleep on the step by the side door when Cybèle was out on a run. When Susan came back to get her, she was stooping over Pierrot's head and he did not even move. I think they might even play together.

Today's mail brought a moving word from Janette Hospital to thank me for the poems. In a short card she said wonderful things about them. Because I am unspoiled about the poems, when a word like this comes, it makes the whole day— more than the day. But I am feeling particularly listless. Susan reminds me that this is always true at the beginning of the fall, the seasonal transition. I think it is really the instinct of the hibernating animal that cannot hibernate. What I want is to go to sleep for the winter and wake up in the spring. As I cannot do that, I do spend a great deal of time lying awake. I was awake from two o'clock this morning, anxious about something. I thought I had learned to manage depression. But because I am tired, I cannot do what I want. The little piece that I wrote for *Yankee* has come back with suggestions; they want revision, and I am not going to do it. A good thing about being eighty-one is that I can say that I do not want to do something and simply not do it instead of feeling I must show I can do it. It no longer matters.

Also in the mail was an announcement of Martha Wheelock and Kay Weaver's video of Berenice Abbott, the photographer. It is called *A View of the Twentieth Century.* They sent me an advance copy, not entirely edited, a year ago. Both Susan and I were tremendously moved by it. One of the things about it is that Berenice was ninety and such a vivid, warm personality. I fell in love with her the one time we met for lunch in Portland, and it was mutual; she often called to urge me to come up and see them in Monson, but it is a five-hour drive from here and I could not do it. And then she died.

Yesterday I started going over my translation of Péguy's "Présentation of the Region of the Beauce to Our Lady of Chartres." Such a great poem with a tremendous wind, if you will, behind it. It is a poem describing the yearly walk from Paris to Chartres as a form of celebrating the cathedral and the Virgin herself. I find translating like a fascinating game. I can hardly keep away from it. I had to stop yesterday because

I was getting nothing else done, and it is time that something was cleared away on this desk. Translation makes one aware of words and the value of each word. There are so many nuances. It is fascinating to try to find an exact equivalent, and of course, there is none, particularly perhaps with French. But I do not know if I can give the time. So much else needs to be done. I would put it in with the book of new poems with "Palme" by Valéry, which I have already decided to include because I have lived with both of these poems for over forty years, so the translation is more than intellectual exercise. It is a kind of homage that I am paying to those two great poets.

Sunday, September 26, 1993

I WOKE to the welcome sound of a steady rain that does not seem to be a deluge by any means but what we need—a fairly measured small rain. But of course it makes a melancholy surrounding just the same. And Pierrot wants an extra breakfast just because it is raining, he tells me.

Things are crowded these next weeks until my play is given on October 8; I have many interviews, and then there are people unexpectedly turning up, such as Martha Wheelock, who will be coming on Friday with Kay Weaver. They are coming for a first showing of their videotape on Berenice Abbott. Because they are coming from Los Angeles, it is not possible to say that I have a luncheon or an interview and I will be too tired. One cannot be too tired when it comes to old devoted friends like these.

I have been talking about the rarity of short poems, and it happened the other day that somebody sent me a wonderful one. This was part of an extremely moving memorial service for Judy Burrowes's aunt Adelaide Kennedy, who must have been a remarkable person. I have rarely read a service as moving as this. In the course of it a short poem of Langston Hughes's was quoted which I had never seen:

> Hold fast to dreams
> for if dreams die,
> life is a broken-winged bird
> that cannot fly.
>
> Hold fast to dreams
> for when dreams go,
> life is a barren field
> frozen with snow.

I like it because both the images are so simple and yet how much they say, especially the "barren field." There was another sentence in the service which I found good and that was "Adelaide's was a quiet, hopelessly optimistic greatness like the confidence of the tide, gentle and powerful, but absolutely confident that even though it goes out, in some new form it will most assuredly come back again." I thought the words "hopelessly optimistic" were marvelous. I guess that to be optimistic at all, one has to be so "hopelessly" because there are always so many bad things that have to be confronted or in some way understood.

It is awful when Susan comes for a weekend because it is so short. She has to leave after lunch today.

I am still reading Marge Piercy's very readable new novel, but I think she is a much better poet than novelist. She is a great poet. This makes me happy because I think it is much easier and less rare to be the good novelist that she is than a great poet as she is.

Monday, September 27, 1993

A DIM, foggy morning, rather beautiful. I can barely see the edge of the field and the whitish gray ocean that seems quite calm. Now that I have been thinking about short poems I keep finding them everywhere I look. Here is one that I have admired for years by Charles Causley.

Au Revoir

> I am the prince
> I am the lowly
> I am the damned
> I am the holy.
> My hands are ten knives.
> I am the dove whose wings are murder.
> My name is love.

I think I have used that somewhere. There are short poems, even shorter than five or six lines, that remain indelible. One of the poets who achieves this is J. V. Cunningham. Here is one of his, a two-line poem. It begins with a Latin title which is *"Nescit Vox Missa Reverti."* The poem reads:

> The once hooked ever after lives in lack,
> And the once said never finds its way back.

That has haunted me for years. It is, I am afraid, horribly true.

I am annoyed with the cat, who seems to have lost, for the moment at least, his charm though not his beauty. He used to follow me around, like a dog, and would often come up here to the study when I was working and lie on the rug or even climb up on the desk. Now he rarely even comes up to my bed on the second floor, and he meows as soon as he comes in for food, which means that he gets about five meals a day. I fed him at half past five this morning when I went down to fix my tray as I always do. When Joan came in at seven-thirty, he meowed at her so loudly that she called up and said, "Can I give him some food?" I said, "Of course, go ahead." He ate his food and then meowed some more because he wanted cream. He certainly makes it clear what he wants. After Joan left, he came in and asked me for more food and I was not about to give it to him so he was angry. When he is very angry, he sometimes sprays, which is what male cats do when they have not been altered, but he has been altered, so what he needs now I do not know. A psychiatrist. A vet friend of Maggie Vaughan's gave me a pill that I gave him for two weeks, but it has not done any good. I simply do not know what to do. It is a nuisance cleaning up all the time and stooping down. I would not mind that so much if he related more to me. He just, for the moment, does not seem to. We are both in our autumn mood no doubt, and once winter comes I hope he will come back to me like the dear friend he has always been.

There is nothing more exciting in the day's mail than when a poet friend sends me remarkable poems. This happened today when Marilyn Kallet sent me five poems as good as anything she has written. Very powerful. I am a little envious because the intensity of feeling in these poems is something I no longer have.

I am stuck on the translation of Péguy, which I had hoped to do quickly.

Tuesday, September 28, 1993

AT LAST we have sunlight after all the gloomy weather, but we did get rain; everything under the earth must be rejoicing. The trees had begun to look withered at the tops last week before these three days of rain.

This morning my stint was an interview with Ed Morin from Maine Public Radio, a sympathetic man who wanted to talk mostly about the play and will go and attend part of a rehearsal in Thomaston and review it on the radio before the play opens. It was interesting to talk with him. I was not sure that he cottoned to the play much as we talked about it. It is a sophisticated play. It is by no means everyone's dish. What work of mine is? He asked some good questions. He felt it was interesting that the four siblings were friendly when they remembered their childhood games and childhood names, such as Tigger. I said that I thought perhaps I was romantic about family life, being an only child. It is certainly true that I have great nostalgia for family life and always tried to adopt families when I was a child. It is certainly nothing to do with Maine, this play. It is a romantic . . . not really even a romantic comedy . . . a poetic comedy which Erika Pfander is kind enough to compare to Chekhov, and that is because she is an idealist and loves Chekhov, just as I do.

Meanwhile, Diane, the helper of my gardener, Pat, was digging out the wild roses which have planted themselves along the fence and really endanger it because it must not take too much weight; those wild roses are everywhere in the garden and have to be kept constantly at bay or they would take over completely.

I am in a quandary because a man who lives in York sent me a large manuscript to read; this is quite an imposition. I do not want to read it. At the same time, I do not know how to say no. This quandary is a description of my life at present, which is certainly ambivalent when it comes to what I am asked to do, because I need time. As I was lying down this afternoon, a short poem came to mind which I have now written, and that is wonderful. I believe the reason that I did it is that Deborah Pease's new book *Long before This* arrived this morning, and I read it at once. It is tremendously moving because one keeps thinking, "This is what I would say. This is what I feel." For the first time, I think, one gets the sense of somebody extremely loving who has been by life deprived of having a house, a real home of her own. A loving woman, very sensitive, very much a part of the world and yet isolated. This is perhaps what gives her book the flavor that it has.

Monday, October 4, 1993

I HAVE spent a half hour trying to get a tape into the machine that I talk the journal into—without success, only exasperation. I put in new batteries and did all I could think of. So now I shall write by hand, though slow and tedious writing by hand is.

It has been a roller coaster of a time all last week with interviews or visiting firemen every day. On Saturday a Belgian woman, a remarkable person, and her friend whom she is visiting came for an hour in the afternoon. Because of their emotion at being here with me, it was rather exhausting.

Meeting two new people who know me from my journals but whom I do not know is tiring, and two are always more tiring than one.

Claire, the Belgian, is the wife of a Protestant minister. They spent years in a kibbutz in Israel and now have a child living in New Zealand. She is very cosmopolitan, and it amazes me that she loves my work so much.

She brought me wonderful Belgian chocolates and *pain d'épice*, a kind of honey bread I loved as a child and still do.

Tuesday, October 5, 1993

EVERYTHING IS revving up for my play, which opens on Friday. Doris Grumbach and Sybil Pike are coming, and lots of people apparently will show for the reception at six. That is what makes me nervous. Of course I am always afraid of having another TIA or stroke.

I am hoping that Nancy Hartley, with whom I am having lunch, can fix the cassette so I can take it with me over the weekend. I have not seen Nancy for months so this is a fine prospect, and the sun is out, a glittering dark blue ocean.

This morning I began to pack. I have not packed for a trip since late March, the trip to London where I had a stroke. Packing is like going into a maze of decisions and physical efforts I am in no state to perform. What blouses? What slacks? I did try on what I am wearing for the reception. Taking things on and off is difficult, but at least I did it with a sense of triumph at the end. I did finally receive a tape of "All

Things Considered," the interview with me which was aired on Sunday afternoon. The best thing was when I talked my Pierrot language to Pierrot. They caught that without my knowing, and it is amusing.

But Pierrot is detached, detached and demanding these days. Is it autumn fever? He rarely comes up to my bed in the afternoon as he always has, and I miss that total relaxation he induces as he rolls over on his back and purrs.

Wednesday, October 6, 1993

THE DAY before I am to leave for Maggie's and for the viewing of the play. I am extremely nervous. But thanks to Nancy, at least the cassette is working, so I can take it with me and shall not have to write by hand all about the play, which is to be quite an event because of all the people who are coming.

It is a marvelous autumn day, and the leaves are beginning to turn. I think by next week, when I come back from Maggie's at Hallowell near Augusta, north of here, it will be at its prime in York, and now, when I go to Maggie's, it will be in its prime there. So it is an exciting autumn at last. It is exhilarating these days; one cannot help feeling a kind of wild joy.

Packing has been such a chore. I cannot tell you. Trying to decide what to wear. When I am looking, I find all these things that I had forgotten I even had, like a purple shirt that I had lost, did not know where it was; it turned up in a drawer yesterday, much to my delight.

I had a kind word from Helen Sheehy about the "All Things Considered" broadcast. She is writing the biography of Eva Le Gallienne, and I was thrilled to hear that she had listened to it and thought that I read well. My voice has come back. A year ago I had almost no voice and, in fact, had some lessons to try to improve it before the conference at Westbrook College.

Betty Friedan goes on being of great interest to me and a shot in the arm, to put it mildly. I feel better than I have in months reading her new book, *The Fountain of Age*. What she is after, which I am beginning to see, being less than halfway through this enormous tome, is to point out that all the tests of old people have been based on the tests of young people and that what old people have as they grow old is something that cannot be measured by usual tests. The questions are not right, because in old age we have a well of experience and wisdom to draw on, and in some good way we have changed from the person at twenty-five who might have gotten high marks on a test just about information or doing a puzzle or something like that. We still turn to the old because they have something to give us, and what is so terrible about the present state of affairs in America is that the old are relegated to a place where they are simply a burden. We hear every day that the young have to pay for the old. Well, the old paid for the young years ago. If we were willing to admit that old people have a lot to offer, then they would not be such a burden because they would be used. This is what we must hope and dream about.

Yesterday I managed to answer a wonderful letter from Nancy Mairs where she talks both about the Friedan book and about *Encore*. She says that I make old age happen in a new way. That is where art is different from an extended essay like Friedan's, because in an extended essay we do not actually experience what is happening, and in the best of my journals I think I do convey what is happening and make it seem real. I hope so. That is why I am not worried about this journal, which is written by a very old lady, an old lady who every day has so many things she has to contend with that it is not funny, although I have to laugh a great deal of the time because I do such stupid things.

The worst thing about my life right now is Pierrot, who is at a stage of distancing himself, I do not know why. He never comes up to my bed, almost never, and he is too heavy for me to carry. He eats like a pig. Whenever he comes in, he demands to be fed and meows at me and then wants to go out again. He never comes at night, but that was always true, except to be let in and fed at one in the morning. And that I do not have to worry about because of the cat door that Maggie Vaughan has made for him. He is something of a burden without being a pleasure at the moment, except it is lovely to see him always because he is so beautiful.

Friday, October 8, 1993

THE DAY that my play is being given, and here I am in Hallowell at Maggie Vaughan's, a most beautiful house, built in, I think, 1797, a grand farmhouse. I say grand because the ceilings downstairs are high and the rooms are very big and then upstairs there are a whole lot of bedrooms. But downstairs it is magnificent and everywhere one looks is beauty. Maggie has the most wonderful kitchen, a kitchen–living room with a great many paintings on the walls and a delightful tile mosaic over the stove of people bathing on a beach. Here is Maggie with her two dogs, who are very well behaved now, a gray poodle whose name is Hyacinth and a hunting dog called Cricket. I realize how shaky I am because I am terrified of the dogs. They are not dogs who jump much, but I am like a small vase that might tip over at any minute, and getting here, packing and all that, was almost beyond my strength. I feel tired and bewildered. I am in bed still; it is ten o'clock. Maggie brought my breakfast with an egg from the farm with homemade bread, homemade marmalade, what a treat! The only thing missing is the cat, Sheba, a wonderful Siamese, who has become an outdoor cat so she is rarely at home; she has enormous blue eyes. I miss my cat very much, and he was quite affectionate on the last day and stayed with the luggage, sleeping by the luggage downstairs until I actually left, so I think he had some idea that I was on my way somewhere. This time it is only five days, it is not like going to Europe, but five days is a considerable visit.

Quite a few people have written about the "All Things Considered" interview and spoken about my reading poetry so well.

I have now begun reading, I brought it with me, a book I know I am going to like enormously by James Salter: *A Sport and a Pastime*. It has an interesting epigraph from which the title comes: "Remember that the life of this world is but a sport and a pastime." That, strangely enough, is from the Koran. Gloria Vanderbilt kindly sent it to me because she read in one of the journals how much I admired another novel of his. He is one of the few writers today who has a style, a recognizable style, complex and beautiful.

And we now are trying to discover how to leave Somalia and yet not leave it in ruins or with a civil war to fight. I do not know how Clinton looks as young as he does considering the weight he is carrying on so many levels and on so many sides.

This afternoon we will be off to drive to Thomaston and see the first night of my first play, *The Music Box Bird*. The frightening thing for me is being on show for that long. There is first a reception of an hour, but I shall not have to stand, I hear. And then of course, the play, which takes over two hours. Finally we will get home, and then we are going to have fun . . . go to the movies and even do some shopping perhaps, a great event for me. The only thing I forgot to bring that I really need is my cane, but luckily Maggie has one.

Saturday, October 9, 1993

WHAT AN extraordinary day it was, or rather afternoon yesterday because at about quarter to five we started driving towards Thomaston for the premiere. It was not dark although it was overcast. The drive to Thomaston was a brilliant show of autumn leaves. Even in the lowering sky—it was not raining but a dark gray sky very low with fog in some places—we saw tiers and tiers of brilliant yellows and crimsons. That was the beginning, this spectacular drive through the autumn.

And then we arrived. The play is performed in the auditorium of a school, but there was first a reception for me, which I had dreaded because I knew people would come because I was there and I felt a little bit like an animal at a zoo. But the people were so kind, and there were many dear friends, Doris Grumbach and Sybil, one of my former students from Radcliffe, Jane Leonard. I had invited Ellen La Conte and her friend Dolly, and they sat beside us. Edythe Haddaway drove all the way from Boxford and arrived very excited, her eyes shining, to sit beside us.

That was in the theater itself, but first there was for me that exhausting hour of responding to people's coming to tell me what my work has meant to them. They were interesting people. It was a wonderful audience for that play because there were so many obviously intelligent people there and many people who had read me and wanted to talk about that. After signing one book, I said I would not sign books. If I did, I would be signing all the time instead of responding to people's longing to tell me what the work had meant to them. So it was a good idea that after signing that one book, I did not do more.

There I was with Maggie on one side of me and Edythe Haddaway on the other and Ellen La Conte and her friend just beyond them—very exciting. Then there we were finally, sitting in our seats, and I was much impressed by the set, which was exactly right. They decided to make it Victorian. That worked very well because in the middle of the stage on a small table was my music box bird, which Erika had had mended because it had ceased to function.

It was a tremendous experience for me to see the play and to hear the play. One of the things that worked very well was having Claude go off and play the piano offstage several times. I have always thought that music offstage is effective. It happens, you remember, in Chekhov in *The Cherry Orchard*.

Erika has done a superb job of directing. The way people are moved on the stage was so good, so well planned. She herself was very good playing Sybille. I would not have cast her for the role, but she did it in an interesting and convincing way. She did one thing that delighted me because Le Gallienne did it very beautifully in *The Three Sisters*. Erika was sitting on a chaise longue and she took the pillow and hugged it while she was talking. This I found extremely effective, but she did many things that were absolutely right in the direction and in the acting. Amazing that everybody was right in each part and did so well. One of the characters who represents the less neurotic or the nonneurotic of the children I had always thought of as a minor character of no great importance, but partly because she was so well acted, she turned into an important part of the play. That was thrilling to me. I certainly did write some good parts; there is not a single dull one. They each present a challenge, and the actors met it magnificently.

I am only sorry I was not able to talk a little more graciously at the end because I was by then exhausted and the audience also anxious to get away. It started at seven-thirty and was a little after half past ten when it was over. I knew that a long speech from me was not the thing, but I would have liked to have said something about art, which in the play is defined by Sybille as "magic without power," the point being that money is power and dangerous whereas art does no harm, is magic, but hasn't the power to destroy that money does. I was very pleased to see this come alive. I wrote the play forty years ago, when I was in my forties. I am now old and was afraid I couldn't stand when I had to stand at the end, but the play itself is exactly the age it was when it was written, and it did stand; the interesting thing is that it seems quite modern, a little bit ahead of its time, perhaps.

It was a thrilling night, and then dear Maggie had the long drive home in the dark, and when we got home, she did exactly the right thing, which was to make us a cup of cocoa. I went to bed feeling relieved because since I had two TIAs in London and a small stroke when I was under the kind of stress that this evening represented, I had been terrified that I would have another stroke. But there I was, safely in bed and very happy last night.

Now today it is a gloomy day, it is raining, but the colors are simply magnificent just the same.

Tuesday, October 12, 1993

HOME AGAIN! The play was really an enormous success. I still cannot get over it. It did not do what I feared, which was that it might seem too verbal; rather, the direction was so good, the actors on the whole excellent, and the audience like a gift, attentive and appreciative.

It is a gloomy day though there was a bit of crimson sun to the north as the sun rose, but now it is gray, cold, and going to rain. The time at Maggie's, which I had so looked forward to, was not entirely happy. Her house is a kind of treasure of beauty and luxury and a great sense of life, everywhere; there are beautiful things to look at, and the architectural proportions are such that it is possible it was designed by Bulfinch, who, of course, did the State Capitol at Augusta. We had two memorable drives. The leaves, which everybody thought would not be good this year, were unusually brilliant, and I was drunk on all that by the time we got to the theater. But I had not expected to feel at loose ends and depressed as I was away from everything which supports me here, the framework by which I keep at bay my pitiable state of weakness and inability to do anything much. It seemed tragic not to be able to walk around Maggie's garden, for instance, but I was afraid of falling. Most of the time I spent lying on her comfortable bed—she gives me her bedroom when I come—and looking out at the trees and a little glimpse of the Kennebec River and feeling depressed. There was in a way nothing for me to do. I had made a big mistake in the two books I took with me, neither of which was exactly what I needed, and I had left the

Friedan because it was too heavy to carry. I am constantly frustrated because I cannot carry things. Anyway, it taught me something, and that something is, I think, that I must not travel, even a little distance. Maggie is infinitely understanding, and I could even tell her I was depressed and she understood. We had a renewing drive back because the sun was out, the leaves were glorious, and we had a delicious lunch in Yarmouth. She went back and today is giving a speech at two o'clock to, of all things, the DAR about Mount Vernon, where she was one of the Mt. Vernon Ladies Associates for years. People may not realize that Mount Vernon is run by women from each state, and it is a great honor to be chosen to do that. They manage the whole business, which is a big business now, millions of dollars. One can rent Mount Vernon for a wedding, for instance.

I came back a day early partly because today was announced to be gray and bad and I did not want Maggie to drive all that way twice and then have to give a speech and because also it was time I got back. I needed to find the huge amount of mail, only two days of mail because of the weekend, but I had not expected to find what I did, which was almost too much for me. I did not open it till just before dinner, the first copy of Susan's book *Among the Usual Days*, which is a portrait of me through a mosaic of my letters and unpublished material, even some early poems or first drafts of poems. It is a stunning-looking book, and the editing that Susan has done is amazing, many letters in French but always translated and everything footnoted so well. It was a tremendous thrill for me to have it in my hands, but I was too tired to take it all in. That is the trouble with life. And then, just as I was feeling the exhaustion of getting home to all the mail, UPS came with a heavy parcel, an effort even to open, from Duffy Schade, with the manuscript of her book *From May Sarton's Well*, which includes her fine photographs with quotations from the journals, quite a few poems, I am glad to say. The photographs create the mood of the poem rather than illustrating it. She has done a sensitive job, and I am pleased it is going to be published. But to have two books, two major works to think about, immediately after the play, overwhelms me.

Wednesday, October 13, 1993

AND TODAY Duffy came to talk about *From May Sarton's Well*. I had gone over it yesterday and then again somewhat today. It can be extremely good, and we had a productive talk and then lunch. Hers are subtle, beautiful photographs which do not give themselves away immediately, ones you have to look at as if they were poems, which indeed they are. The first poem she uses is "A Glass of Water," about the water from my well in Nelson, and that is what the title refers to.

Things do get done here little by little. David Leavitt came to put on the storm windows. He has to get a man to help him because of the ladders and he found he could get one today, so suddenly—he was to have come over the weekend—there he was.

Including our time for lunch, Duffy was here three hours, but then I slept with Pierrot, who came up and purred beside me, stretched out full length; we had a rest. I decided not even to try to do letters up here. Instead I ordered the English calendars for friends whom I always send one to, paid a few bills, and that is satisfying. Tomorrow Judy comes and I must be ready for her, which means getting a cassette going.

I continue to be pleased and even surprised that the play

held the audience so completely; there was absolute silence except for the occasional ripple of laughter; my fear that it was too verbal was unfounded. Apparently some friends of Judy, my secretary, who saw it and who are professional reviewers said it was very much of its time, that it is an intellectual play, if you will, a play of ideas, which indeed it is, and that this is not fashionable today, which is also true. It is a play of a different era.

The weather, after terrific rain yesterday, has cleared up, and it is crystalline right now with the dark blue autumn sea. Unfortunately after heavy rain last night, many of the leaves have gone. I think the peak has passed here, but it has been a much better autumn than I thought was possible.

Friday, October 15, 1993

TODAY BEGAN with a wonderful sunrise, and there has been one marvelously clear day after another although we have had some rain, which we sorely need; the leaves are going, going, almost gone. I am slowly recovering from the play and the rather depressed weekend after it and now confronting the immense amount there is to do. It is not surprising considering that there are five books out which people write me about, and now, Susan's wonderful book. It is a triumph of organization and marvelously designed; the photographs are magnificent. I have to keep looking at it because it fascinates me and I think it will fascinate a lot of other people, the kind of book which one will go back to a little bit like a commonplace book. Very different from the journals, because it is essences, and very different from a novel.

Today I had lunch with Edythe. We had not seen each other since the play, nor had we seen each other since she got Susan's book, so we had a great deal to talk about and had a wonderful reunion. It was a treat for me after having worked three hours with Judy reading aloud to her as she put on the computer parts of the journal I had handwritten while she was away. Now, of course, I am speaking onto a tape, and she will be able to transcribe this so I won't have to do anything more except eventually revise.

It is amazing the numbers of people who continue to write about the poems I read on "All Things Considered."

Yesterday I spoke to Margot for the first time since she came back from Belgium. I wanted so much to hear about it, but she has had a hard homecoming because her mother had to be moved. She said there was a letter in the mail, although it did not come today. She did have a great time, I gather. What amused me was that she can't get over how much has happened to me: I was on "All Things Considered"; the play opened; Susan's book is there. Then there were various interviews to do with the play in local papers, so I have had my hands full since she left. But it is good to have one's hands full as long as one can handle it, as long as one does not feel utterly desperate as I did when I first came back from the weekend at Maggie's. Now I know that this business of being May Sarton will never be sorted out. I have piles of letters around me. I have written a postcard to someone who asked where they could find *A Light Left On*. Of course, all they need to do is go to the public library, but they don't. There were four or five permission requests for poems, and that I am glad about. If I can get people to read the poems, that is what matters most to me.

I still have not written a blurb for Margaret Robison. For some reason I am finding this difficult though I admire the

poems. I think it is simply congestion, too much going on in my
poor old head.

However, Betty Friedan is keeping me occupied at night.
I enjoy *The Fountain of Age* enormously, but it is too long. It
ought to have been edited, and yet every one of the stories she
tells about how one or another old person has solved the problem of retirement or what to do—whether to go into one of
these homes or not—is fascinating. Every one of the stories is
like a novel in itself. So I find that reading it for half an hour
before I go to sleep is a great adventure, and I want her to be
sent *Encore*. I must write Norton about this.

Friday, October 15, 1993

SUSAN'S BOOK is a constant delight. I get lost in it because it
brings back so many memories, and the photographs are evoc-
ative of so many people and places. Susan comes tonight, and
I have not yet written a word to welcome or to thank her, and
that I must do before anything else.

My mood is extremely low. I am in the perennial panic of
not knowing how to handle my life. Everybody laughs at me
and says that is the price of fame, but they are not eighty-one
and ill. I feel weak and unable to cope. I look at the pile, the
disastrous pile of letters before me. At night I think of what I
want to say to people, but then, when I confront my desk,
there is too much.

I have finally remembered the name of Vicki Runnion, my
friend who works in Hospice and who can connect me with
the person who took wonderful photographs of the play but

whose name I could not remember. That is my life now. Everything is a maze I am always trying to find my way out of. I would like to find a poem to read that would take me out of this conundrum and put me squarely down in some marvelous reality.

There is no doubt that I am in a serious depression, but it is hard to talk about. I expect that has always been so, for there are things I have never put into the journals. Only two or three things are depressing me now that I can speak of; one is something I have often written about already, and that is that when the new *Collected Poems 1930–1993* came and I saw the marvelous book it is, I mean Norton's beautiful production of it, Susan was surprised because I was not elated. The reason I could not respond is that I realized at once that it would not be reviewed, and that realization has bitten into me ever since the book came in March. Poetry, as everybody tells me, does not get reviewed right away, but the fact is there is no one who wants to review it, nobody back of me, and this has gone on for, well, at least thirty years. The *New York Times* used to review my poetry very well; the last one that got a good review I think was *The Lion and the Rose*. After Karl Shapiro's devastating attack, they never reviewed me again, and that is a matter of three decades and seven or eight volumes of poems that have simply never been registered. The people who could have helped me never have, beginning with Louise Bogan, so over and over again I have to try to make myself believe that eventually something will happen to these poems, that they are not going to be forever homeless people. It is costly, this making oneself come back over and over again. Yesterday we sent off the manuscript of new poems, *Coming into Eighty*. It represents a staggering change in my style, and it would be fitting if somebody cared, somebody out there with a critical sense saw that this was something new, but they will not. A few people will read them and may find their newness strange; a few people will read them and say, "Ah! Sarton's voice but in an altogether new form and timbre."

What I cannot speak of is a fight with a good friend. These things happen in every intense relationship, of course, and one must try to take them with as little vulnerability as one can. Easier said than done.

The third cause of my depression I have already described: the chaos of my life and all that is asked of me beyond my strength. Day after day I wait it out, wait for the time when I can lie down and have my nap. Luckily now Pierrot does come almost every day.

Saturday, October 16, 1993

It is wonderful having Susan here because we have had time to talk about her book at last. I have been so absorbed in the play and staying at Maggie's and the clutter to confront on my desk that I have not had time to concentrate on this extraordinary book, and it is extraordinary. I can hear Susan coming in from her walk on this gray day; the colors are beautiful now. She is probably reading aloud to her mother over the phone as she does every day that wonderful book about the blind boy by Jacques Lusseyran.

A dear thing happened today. I could not get the cat to come in and had wanted so much to have him for my rest; after a while I heard Susan's voice on the stairs saying, "Special delivery"; she was carrying this enormously heavy cat up to me, and here he is and has been for the last two hours, lying on his back, purring and bringing me peace.

It does seem always that when I feel I have reached the

end and think I cannot go on, that my life is out of control, that I do not have the energy for it, suddenly there is a new challenge which revives me. Yesterday was such a time. While I was resting, the phone rang and it was Susan Swartzlander to make a date, which we did, for her department at Grand Valley State University in Illinois to come and do a video interview with me as part of their program of teaching *As We Are Now*. It is an experiment. The department of English is taking four or five books and teaching them in depth. I am thrilled they have chosen *As We Are Now*. So there I was, absolutely exhausted, unable even to write a letter yesterday, and suddenly a voice long distance from the Middle West saying that on the thirteenth of November I must be ready for a whole day's photographing. It was an awakening; it summoned me back to life.

This morning I was able to write three letters that have been on my mind these last few days, and in fact, yesterday afternoon I was able to do the blurb for Margaret Robison. Today it was a letter to Martha Wheelock to say how excited I am about her proposal to do a new video about Sarton and old age which would also be a part of educating the American public that old age is not necessarily a total decline. This project was inspired by Friedan's new book. So I did write to Martha, and that was something off my mind. And I wrote to Bill Brown, who had written me a short but as always a wonderfully expressed letter. The photograph of him in Susan's book is superb. He is standing in front of a series of his self-portraits; the contrast is stunning. There are parts of a great many letters to him in *Among the Usual Days*, as there are to Juliette Huxley, Jean Dominique, Louise Bogan, and many others.

At four we are going to look at a video, and until then I am going to make a list of the people I want to give Susan's book to. Meanwhile, Pierrot lies on his back, a sumptuous sight.

Sunday, October 17, 1993

IT CERTAINLY is the season of mists. I cannot see the ocean; it is lost in dense fog today. Susan has to drive to New York, and apparently it is foggy all the way down. We have had a wonderful time because we were able to talk about her book, which is also my book as I wrote it all, and the wonderful selections she has made. We had so many things to talk about and exchange about this, so it was important that she come this weekend though hard for her because she has so much on her mind these days because of school and her parents leaving for Florida, and everything to do with sending out the book. I know so well the excitement it is and how one cannot wait to get the books out and see what people say. The most important thing is giving it to one's friends.

Yesterday she even managed to bring an absolutely extraordinary video, a Chinese film, made in China, called *Raise the Red Lantern*. It was very much like being inside Chinese paintings, the equivalent of a Vermeer, only Chinese with extraordinary light. It is a brutal and at the same time elegant film, a great work of art. There is no doubt about that. Strangely enough, its theme is more or less the same as that of Elizabeth Bowen's novel *The Death of the Heart*, which is also about innocence which creates devastation around it. In this case a very young woman arrives as a poor concubine in a rich man's house, and the film is all about the intrigue and the extremely formal life which this involves. The red lantern is lit at the door of whomever of his concubines he is going to sleep with that night, so there is a great deal of rivalry among these women. The young girl who comes at nineteen could not be more innocent, but in the end she is responsible for the death of two people, once because she got drunk and told about the unfaithfulness of one of the concubines, who then is hanged, and once because she betrayed a servant who had betrayed her and who dies of the cold out in the courtyard. This morning I was going over the whole thing in my mind and I could not stop, so I finally turned on the news just to get other, less tragic images into my head. It was painful but certainly worth seeing.

Now I am confronted by the mess and the horror of my desk and have managed only to write a few checks and to make a list, which is already enormous, of those to whom I want to send Susan's book. Luckily Norton will send out some copies to people who might review, like Doris Grumbach.

It was an extraordinary weekend, during which quite unexpectedly Susan found a video that had been sent me giving my performance at the Smithsonian in 1985, a few months before my stroke. This was a particularly fine audience, large, very silent and responsive, and, I think, perhaps one of the best readings I have ever given although at the beginning it was a little loud. When there is a microphone, one does not have to speak as loudly as one thinks. Otherwise, it was one of the best, and I was moved by the fact that I dared to read those long difficult poems like the poems for Perley Cole and for my father, long poems that take a lot of breath. That is the thing. I could not do it now, not possibly. I could not read for an hour, as I did then, such "demanding" poems, the autumn ones from the Nelson poems, for instance, which are not easy to read. Susan was visibly moved, and I was surprised at how moved I was because it gave me back a person I no longer am and can never be again because I no longer have that vitality, that actual physical strength, the breath that I had then. So I was often in tears, but of joy, because here it is. I am old and incapacitated, but here is this record which will be there forever and people can hear it after I am dead.

So it was an extraordinary day though gloomy in other ways. It is foggy, and I am worried about Susan driving to New York now and, of all things, Pierrot has a tick in his cheek which he will not let me touch and which I cannot get out; I have tried several times when he was asleep. He immediately brushes my hand off with his paw without using his claws; his soft big paw says, "Don't do it, don't do it." I do not know now what to do, or whether I should try to get him into the cat box tomorrow and take him to the vet as an emergency; surely they can do something. If necessary, I can leave him there, but it seems to me the last straw in what has been an exhausting few weeks beginning back with the play, which right now must be about to begin its final Sunday matinee. Sylvia and Dean are there, and I can hardly wait to hear what they say.

Tomorrow I shall get mailing envelopes and hope Susan's book will come so I can start sending it out.

Monday, October 18, 1993

A DISMAL day because as I suspected, I had to take Pierrot to the vet early this morning, no peace. But at least things will be done which need to be done, like cutting his nails. Then there was too much mail and a great many small things that I had to do involving telephone calls.

But there was fortunately a wonderful letter from a woman in Iowa City. She did for me what she says my *Journal of a Solitude* did for her. I want to put it on the page here.

I have set aside what I call my sacred time in the house during which I am not interrupted or invited to help on projects or asked, "So what are you doing?" It is a step. Someday I will have structured time absolutely alone in the house, time I can count on and enforce. This is perhaps the most profound thing to happen. It feels like my life has been saved and I wasn't even aware of any danger. Solitude as necessity, demandable, honorable. Not sinful, indulgent, wasteful, undeserved. I feel completely blessed by what has happened to me since I opened that journal of yours.

Isn't that wonderful! What she did for me was, "It feels like my life has been saved and I wasn't even aware of any danger."

Tuesday, October 19, 1993

I KNEW as soon as I saw the airmail envelope from my cousin Janet Mann, who had written me a warm postcard recently to say that she and her mother were enjoying *Encore*, that a real letter meant that Evelyn had died, and that is the truth. I felt such a pang and also so sad that I am far away and cannot invite Janet, who needs a rest desperately now. She has been taking care of her mother for the last ten years. If only she could come here and rest and look at the sea, it would be so wonderful because I think it is going to be lonely. She is the only unmarried child, and her brother and she are not on very good terms. Like me when I saw my mother dead, she had not seen anyone dead before. It was a peaceful death. Evelyn was sitting in an armchair and the doctor had come in and said that her heart was very weak but apparently did not expect the end quite so soon. I hope that Janet will be able to begin her real life since her retirement. As soon as she retired she began to have to take care of her mother, and she has a lovely apartment of her own in Norwich. I hope she can begin a new life if she can first get rest. That is the most important thing.

It is an absolutely glorious autumn day, and the leaves are still in their splendor around here. It takes my breath away. It is like a continual song. It is wonderful to have Pierrot back again. Although I thought there had been a tick embedded, it turned out not to be so, and I got comfort from the doctor about ticks that one does not need to worry too much about them. This kind of deer tick buries itself but dies fairly soon and does not infect the animal. Lyme disease is not a problem with cats; they do not get it. The twenty-four hours without him yesterday were lonely. I felt like a ghost, and the house felt so empty, so it was wonderful to get him at quarter to six. Unfortunately it was dark before I had the talk with the vet, a wonderful doctor for cats, and at first I did not know how to turn on the lights on the dashboard; then I did not remember how to turn down the high beams, and altogether the drive home was enervating. I never drive at night, that is why, and at that hour a little after six everybody is on the road. But nothing happened and we got safely home.

Then dear Pierrot began to meow and tell me what a terrible day it had been for him. They gave him a flea bath, they cut his nails, and I am not sure what else they did, but it certainly was a long day in prison for this poor cat. But right away his tail went up and he trotted into the house but has not been eager to eat. This is good because he is overweight; he has gained two pounds since April, so he now weighs thirteen plus, and the doctor wants that to come off. The one amusing thing was that the doctor gave me as a present a kind of dry food which has no cholesterol; he says the good thing about it is that Pierrot will not like it and will not eat it. Well, I gave him some as soon as we got back and he ate half the bowl of it immediately.

Today I must write to Janet. I have a great deal on my desk, and I must try to think about a poem that came to me in the middle of last night, around three o'clock, which begins "A playful passionate childhood." I began thinking about all the reasons that it was a wonderfully happy childhood that I had and in large part it was because of the Shady Hill School. I used to ride my bike to school every morning and get there at eight, when the doors were opened, and I often did not leave the school until six, when the doors were locked by dear Mr. Lane, the janitor. Meanwhile, I had been climbing the big willows, the great beauty of the school, and had been working in various classes. I was in love with two of my teachers, Katharine Taylor and Anne Thorp, and that was the beginning of the muses, the first muses. Or perhaps the first muse was Agnes Hocking, who taught us all to recite poetry so that by the time I was ten I was constantly trying to get somebody to listen to me recite poetry by Byron, Kipling, whom I was very fond of at about ten years old.

Thereby hangs a tale. It was winter, and coming home from school one day, I saw a five-dollar bill in the snow and picked it up and told Mother about it. She said I must go to every door of neighbors nearby on Agassiz Street in Cambridge and ask if they had by any chance lost five dollars. Luckily none had, so the five dollars was mine, and with it I bought *Collected Poems* by Kipling on India paper so it is a huge book, but very thin. I was crazy about the poems in *The Jungle Book;* that is what I loved when I was a child. So when we went out to lunch sometimes in Boston, there were ladies who loved to get my father to talk, especially Louise Inches on Beacon Street, and I always hoped I would be asked to recite a poem after lunch, and when it was known that this was true, people indulged me and I loved that. It was, I think, a very happy childhood. I had wonderful friends from the beginning, and that was the main reason, that and the school, which I have celebrated in *I Knew a Phoenix* so that I am not going to go into it again here.

It is Susan's book with so many photographs of me as a small child that has made me wake up at three this morning and begin to think about my childhood. I am sure that many people think that genius must probably always begin with an unhappy childhood. Mine was a fulfilled, if that word can be used, childhood, and a great part of it was Shady Hill. But when I think, for instance, of early childhood when we lived in a three-room apartment on Avon Street, I think of the Boutons, a family without a father—he had died—and I called Mrs. Bouton Aunt Mary from the beginning. At first the Boutons had four children, then two died, so there were finally just two, Miggie and Chussie, Margaret and Charlotte, and every Christmas Aunt Mary turned the whole little parlor of their house into a doll's house. I brought over my dolls' furniture. I had two dolls, Eleanor and Nancy, who were Schoenhoff dolls. These are German dolls, I do not know if they still exist, which had realistic faces. They were not the abstract pretty face of the ordinary doll; they were real people, and Mother made them wonderful clothes often imitating my clothes. Eleanor and Nancy were beautifully dressed.

I put many dolls to bed at this period of my life when I was, I suppose, seven or eight. I put something like twenty dolls to bed every night, mostly little dolls, not very important dolls like Eleanor and Nancy, but it took quite a long time. It must have been irritating to my mother. All through Christmas what we did at the Boutons was to pretend that our dolls were a huge family and make them wonderful meals, and the great fun was to decide what we were going to give the dolls to eat and then prepare it. I remember Aunt Mary taught us how to make a kind of sugar and water candy; it looked like peppermint patties, but there was no peppermint. They were very sweet and white and delicious to us. That was one thing.

I was not a good child; I was mischievous. I already loved poetry. Letty Field was my best friend when I was perhaps fourteen and died tragically when she was fifteen. We used to walk around Cambridge, especially in winter at dusk, and recite the whole of Thompson's "The Hound of Heaven," a marvelous poem. I wore knit suits, there were no blue jeans then, and I had an orange suit that Mother got somewhere with short pants and a kind of sweater coat. It enraged little boys, who used to scream at me on my bicycle and chase me and sometimes frightened me very much. Usually I could get away. There was a risky place between my house and the Shady Hill School when it was over at the Norton estate before it moved to near Brattle Street, an entirely different part of Cambridge. The Norton estate was not in a good district, and I was terrified of the dark valley I had to cross, woods and no houses, and people lurked there who did not look savory, and I was always glad when I had gotten past it.

Then I had my other best friend at Shady Hill—Letty was later—Barbara Runkle, who became Barbara Hawthorne when she married. Barbara Runkle and I made up a language of our own called Oyghee. We also were exclusive; for instance, we had a secret hiding place in the lilac bushes on the Norton estate where we buried a tin box with goodies in it, cookies and things. We made a great fuss over this and would never tell anybody where our secret place was.

I also began to attend the First Unitarian Church in Cambridge because the Runkles had a pew there and because I was tremendously moved by Dr. Samuel Crothers, who was then the minister of the First Unitarian Church and a great preacher, very quiet and gentle. I know that I have written about him somewhere at least because he once gave a sermon which is embedded in my life. It was based on the phrase "Go into the innermost chamber of your soul and shut the door." The pause between "soul" and "shut the door" was impressive, and I never forgot it. I have tried to do that all my life, to go into the inner chamber of my soul. It is wonderful to have important things start way at the beginning, and I see as I talk this out that everything in my life really began early. It was not late when I became a poet; I was very young. Most of what I am now I was at eight or nine years old with a great love of my friends, a great need for my friends, and also the love of the muses, which began, as I said, with Anne Thorp and Katharine Taylor.

I expect that most children have periods when they are fascinated by something that is wrong, and I was fascinated, as many children are, I am sure, by fire. It was absolutely forbidden to light the fire. There was a fireplace in our tiny apartment in Cambridge with logs and they could be lit, and I, at least once, did that and was badly scolded and told I must never do it again. Then I did something even worse, which was to make a little fire over at the Boutons' under a high balcony where little Catherine, who later died but was then a baby, was sleeping. Of course, if this fire had been a big one, it would have risked her life. For that my mother did a wise thing to punish me. She lit a match and burned one of my fingers, not terribly, but it certainly hurt. She explained that that is what would have happened to little Catherine if the fire had ever caught and I must never, never do it again. I remember going out that day feeling very remorseful indeed, walking around and not talking to anybody for quite a while.

At Avon Street we could not have a cat, no pets. My mother had given me goldfish because she thought they would be a pet I could have and would not disturb my father, who was then working in the apartment. He did not yet have a study in Widener. Well, it turned out that coming up for air, the goldfish were too loud for my father; it was an irritating put-put, and the goldfish had to be put in another room. Later on we always had a cat; both my father and mother loved cats. And I have always had a cat.

Later, after my nap: This morning from my bed I looked out on a screen of extraordinary maples, all kinds of yellows and golds and oranges with little windows of blue where the leaves had already fallen. The sky looked dark blue in its patches behind the leaves. I do not remember its ever having been quite as dramatic as this, so it was an excellent day to have Peter Pease take me to lunch. The drive to the Stage Neck Inn was nothing but delight because the sea was dark brilliant blue and it was high tide; after we had lunch, he was going fishing. He brought his rod and he fished off the bridge, he tells me. It is always rare when your expectations of a meeting are more than satisfied. Peter is a tremendously rewarding person for an old lady, as I have said in *Encore*, so I am not going to go on about it. What I had not realized is that he is a Quaker. When we talked about the problems of Bosnia-Herzegovina and the terrible bombing which has started again and I said it was like witnessing the extermination of the Jews in the concentration camps because we see it every morning and every night on television and yet can do nothing, he said, "For a Quaker it is a terrible conflict all the time." But I said the Quakers had always been there at every crisis and helped. I think of Harry Green driving an ambulance in France in the 1914–1918 war and later of helping in the Spanish Civil War. Actually he was not a Quaker, but it was a Quakerish thing that he did. And Judy Matlack, who was a Quaker, every summer during the war used to tutor recent immigrants who could not speak English. It was particularly difficult with the Estonians and the Latvians because most of them were more than middle-aged and terribly distraught and were not good students, did not want to learn

English, yet knew they had to in order to keep alive. That summer, I remember, was for her a hard one. The program was held in a mansion along the Hudson, contributed for this cause.

Of course, we talked about a lot of other things besides wars and pacifism within the wars. We talked about Peter's honeymoon, which sounded almost like heaven, the honeymoon which never happens, but did happen in this case. They had perfect weather. They started in Ireland, mostly County Kerry. All the color, he said, was amazing, the greens and blues. And then the enormous charm of the people. From there they went over to London for four or five days of playgoing before flying to Italy, where, due to a neighbor of Peter's who runs a travel agency, they found a small hotel north of Rome on the coast where they had three great meals a day, could swim in a salt pool or the ocean at this place on a high cliff, and where there were few people. It sounded elegant and comfortable, which is rare. It was restful to talk about that, and then I did talk a lot about myself. I cannot help it these days because so much good is happening. I brought Susan's book to show him, and we looked at some of the pictures. Altogether a very good day, but now it is getting late and I have not written the letter I hoped to write.

Wednesday, October 20, 1993

RAINY, BUT the leaves are still beautiful. It is an amazing world, and I am glad I have to go out to get my blood tested because it will give me a chance to see the color along Godfrey Cove Road, which is stunning right now. I am swamped by the mail, but some lovely things happen. One was a letter that came today from San Bruno, California, from a woman named Sarah Tajeldin who tells me she gives a May Sarton Read-a-thon every May. She writes:

> I get many of my high school juniors to read your novels, poetry, and journals. I think I have every one of them and loan them out. Some like *Journal of a Solitude* and *The House by the Sea* which I have multiple copies of. My students thoroughly enjoy them. Even my former students will come back the following May to see if I have any new volumes. Keep writing, May. We are all enriched by your perception of the world.

She asked me then for materials from the Westbrook conference, the book of collected papers to be called *A Celebration for May Sarton*. Connie Hunting told me yesterday that will come out in January. I am longing to see it. What a work of love it has been for Connie to do this!

Nevertheless, I am low in my mind. Not exactly low, it is like being in the eye of a hurricane. I come up to my desk where there is quite literally a pile a foot high, so here I am. I have answered one letter now. I have called the warehouse because Norton still has not sent me my copies of Susan's book, which should have been here last week, so I cannot send it out. Another frustration. And I have lost one of my notebooks, a calendar where I note down what is happening. This is amusing because I had a letter from Bob Merton saying they live in three places: He has an office in New York, the apartment on Riverside Drive, and they have a country place, so things are always in one place or another. For me things are always on one floor or another. I have now been down the three flights of stairs twice to try to find something. I did find it, my little book with the notes I had made. I wanted to know when I have an appointment with Dr. Petrovich; it turns out to be tomorrow.

The good thing about its being autumn is that Pierrot is very often on my bed and affectionate indeed.

To go back to my childhood, which I spent some time yesterday remembering, it is absolutely true that I had a happy childhood although I was parted from my mother a great many times, in the first year of my life perhaps three times when, I believe, she was ill. Once when my father was taking me in the train to friends, I cried so much that he cried. It was uprooting each time. And then we were refugees from Belgium when I was two. Also, I was parted from my mother more than once in England and sent, fortunately, to dear cousins, one of whom it was who just died, Evelyn Mann, of whom my mother was very fond. They were infinitely kind to me, and I have become friends with them newly in recent years and love to think of them. But for the child I was at two who spoke only French and was farmed out to various people, it was traumatic, and thus I have explained to myself why I attach myself so passionately to people almost at once when I am uprooted in any way. I find someone to attach myself to, as if I had to do that. I think it goes back to this terror of the child losing its mother, and all my life I dreaded my mother's death so that when she did die, I had a feeling of relief, partly because she had been so terribly ill and suffered so much, but partly because I knew that the worst thing that could ever happen to me had happened.

I had a letter this morning from a psychiatrist who has on his desk the poem about the psychiatrist which I wrote for Volta Hall. "I keep a copy of 'A Hard Death' and 'The Letter to a Psychiatrist' in a volume next to my desk. I am a physician and I feel these poems, especially 'A Hard Death,' have a special message for health professionals. Please know that

your poems are still cherished and appreciated, and I hope
you will continue to write for years to come." He lives in West
Hartford, Connecticut. It seems strange, I suppose, for me to
copy these things into my journal, but it is because I still feel
great pain that the poems have not been reviewed and probably will not be reviewed. So it comforts me to know they are
alive and being used.

Thursday, October 21, 1993

FOGGY, HEAVY rain all day, yet the leaves remain fantastic in
all the gloom. A Titian day, meltingly beautiful, yet one cannot help feeling depressed. It has been a melancholy autumn
so far. I had to see Dr. Petrovich, my heart doctor, this afternoon, and with afternoon appointments there seems always to
be a long wait. I waited nearly an hour and was at the point of
feeling the tension too much, and I had better go home, when
finally I did see him. He was pleased with me, as I have
gained a little weight. He thinks that I should be walking
better than I do, and I think I must try to do so. Lately I have
felt I can handle myself a little better, I have not been quite as
shaky, though I certainly was when I stood up after sitting
nearly an hour in that office.

This morning Karen came and took me shopping. She is a
life-giving and life-enhancing person, a magnificent survivor
who has had terrible cancer of which she cured herself. Now
she teaches yoga and looks absolutely splendid and glowing. I
am grateful that she has offered to take me once a week to do
shopping; it is always a restorative time.

The big event in the doctor's office was that when I

walked in, there was Alice Murphy, Beverly Hallam's mother, who is now over ninety and has Parkinson's disease, but the most adorable woman. To see her is to feel that one is already in heaven, and I mean that.

Now there is the great joy of packing the books to send to friends. A few every day. I have sent six so far in priority mail envelopes, which do not require packing. In addition, that means the book will be delivered in two days. This project is a big event and great fun for me.

Friday, October 22, 1993

I WAS not going to put anything on this today until I had seen Larry and Eda LeShan, with whom I am having lunch, for this will be the great event of this autumn. The sun is brilliant. I am glad for their sake, for even though it is windy, it is Maine at its best today.

I was not going to put anything on the cassette, but then I read a letter which amused me so much. It is from a woman who lives in Florida and retired early to go back to school to study veterinary technology. She is forty-seven and says:

> During my first semester, a new friend loaned me a book she thought I'd enjoy, *The Fur Person*. I guess she thought I like cats. I only had nineteen at the time. I fell in love with the book as I am sure many people have.
>
> A year and a half later I officially started a shelter just for cats. I named it "The Fur Person Retreat" (I hope you don't mind) because I was so moved by Tom Jones's definition of a fur person. As a matter of fact, I cry every time I read those pages of the book. My mis-

sion is to provide a home that reflects Tom Jones's ideal, one which provides dignity, reserve, and freedom. For those cats that wish a permanent home elsewhere, I try to find fur persons that will continue to treat the animals as I try to do. I chose the word 'retreat' because a retreat is a place of rest and renewal, something I hope I offer to all my cats whether they are with me for life or for only a few weeks.

I love to think of somebody reading that book and doing all this. The only mistake is she seems not to recognize the fur person; the fur person is the cat, not the owner of the cat. This extraordinary Elizabeth Karsten has, she said, "adopted seventy-two cats during 1992–93 and about one hundred and fifty since I started three years ago." She finds homes for them. She ends her letter which delighted me even more with "I HOPE TOM JONES WOULD BE PROUD OF ME." Naturally I sent her the card with Tom Jones on the terrace, I mean with Pierrot on the terrace. What's the matter with me?

Saturday, October 23, 1993

I WONDER how best to use this wonderful day when I have no appointments except for Sally, whom I am hiring to make me some kind of dish every weekend so I do not have to cook seven days a week, and today at three thirty she will bring a meat loaf.

But the thing I want to think about a little is the reunion with Larry and Eda LeShan at last. We have been trying for years, I think it must be pretty nearly four years since we have met. When I stay with Rene Morgan on the Cape, I often see them, and I did four years ago for a wonderful afternoon, but that was soon after Eda's stroke, and she was frail. So I could not believe it when I saw her in the lobby of Stage Neck Inn looking wonderfully well and Larry so distinguished. I felt honored and happy to be with them. We embraced each other and kept saying, "It's a miracle," because in a way it is. We are three survivors. She had a stroke, he very serious heart trouble, and I an infinity of things wrong with me, including a small stroke in London in March. We talked for two hours about everything under the sun and exchanged books. I brought *Among the Usual Days* and Eda brought her new book, *Grandparenting in a Changing World*. I read one chapter, and it is full of her vivid understanding and ability to make me feel that even I, who am not a grandmother, am right there.

So we talked about everything. The general atmosphere, apart from our joy in each other, was the gloom caused by the state of the world and the state of the United States. It looks as though the planet were dying, and indeed, if it does die, there would be nothing suddenly, no books, no art, no architecture, nothing left. No plants, no animals. I felt a terrible shudder inside me because I had so counted on my work going on and being like my children, so people with children must feel this even more, that there will not be any earth. Every time I see one of the animals which is nearly extinct, and there are twenty or thirty such species dying out every day, and more insects even than that, when I think that there will never be again a certain parrot, a certain mouse, whatever it may be, that they are gone forever, it is hard to take in.

But we laughed a lot, we always do, laughed at ourselves, the horror of lack of memory. When I started to sign the book for them just before I went to meet them, I had one of these total blanks. What are their names? So we laughed about that. They told me instances of their forgetting. One of the wonders of Eda is that she has suddenly become an "animal person," which I do not think she ever was in New York. It is too difficult to have an animal there, and the LeShans travel a great deal. But now she has a kitten whom she adores. In fact, they were going back right after lunch in order not to leave the kitten for another day. I have forgotten the kitten's name, of course; he is a marmalade cat, I know that, and sleeps on her bed, which forces her to sleep in uncomfortable positions so as not to disturb him. It is very much like me and Pierrot, and I said, "After all, cats are the only untamed pets that we have. You cannot tame a cat." I feel this every day when I want to spank Pierrot when he does his awful spraying. But there is no point in doing it; he hasn't the slightest guilt. He just goes outdoors, never holds it against me, comes purring back when he feels like it. In a way, that is the charm of a cat. They cannot be spoiled; therefore we do spoil them and enjoy being able to spoil something without guilt.

We talked about the frightful inability to do anything about Bosnia. It gets worse and worse. We know that the extinction of a race is going on, that it is really happening, and this is extremely destructive to the soul of man. We are all dying a little because of this.

Larry was very moving about what Eda has done since her stroke to help him with his work. It is a new talent that she has discovered. He is a great healer for people coping with cancer and believer in the importance of one's mental attitude in healing oneself; he has been successful with many patients who thought they were dying and are now alive. He does, if I understand, have seminars that last a week in which eight or ten patients concentrate on techniques for handling themselves and for getting well. Eda has written a monologue spoken by a woman dying of cancer and what it feels like. Larry was eloquent in his description of it. There usually is a discussion period after each activity, a film or whatever. After Eda's

Pierrot on the stone wall.

monologue was shown, there was such a potent silence in the group of twelve that Larry said there would be no discussion. Of course he was right. They had been so moved that they did not want to talk about it.

So there is Eda, having had her stroke, doing the impossible, as she has always done, as they both have always done. The only bone of contention was Betty Friedan, but I hope I persuaded them to read her new book, which I still think is extraordinary and not as negative as perhaps they thought. I can understand Friedan's irritating people, only there is no point in letting it irritate when the book has so much to offer. The LeShans were eloquent about some of the things she says about nursing homes and how much is happening since Friedan began investigating. In Massachusetts, for instance, it is against the law to tie somebody into a wheelchair, which was done so much before, or to sedate them so they are controllable. Wendy, the LeShans' daughter, works in a nursing home on the Cape in Massachusetts and said that it is extremely well checked on. They are invaded, if you will, by state health people, I think every three months, and they have to be right on their toes not to do any of the things they are not allowed to do. The fact is that you can have everything good done for you and still not be happy, and I think the biggest danger for single people like me going to a nursing home is simply that you go to an environment where you do not know anybody. Eda's father died in this nursing home, but he had his granddaughter there as a nurse, so he immediately walked into a family atmosphere. But if I went to a nursing home, there would be literally nobody. I hope my friends would come and see me, but it must be hard.

On the other hand, Anne Woodson's mother and very difficult stepfather are in a nursing home now on Medicaid, and it is a good place, Anne says. They are happy with it, and her mother is comfortable there. It is the relief of not having to cook meals, for instance. Her mother cooked when she was ninety, I think, and this is difficult. He is not an easy man to do anything for.

Eda told a wonderful story about the helplessness of men apropos of this. A friend of theirs whose wife was in Philadelphia, he lives in New York, called her up and said there was no mouthwash in the bathroom. Desperate. It never occurred to him, as she pointed out, that all he had to do was to go to a drugstore and buy some, which he had never done before. So he is learning.

And I am learning a great deal every day and finding all that I do more justifiable. I think one of my problems has been that anything which was not writing at my desk did not seem like my real life or valid work. I now realize that keeping up the house is quite a job, and it is not a bad thing that I can do it and do it as well as I do.

Well, it was a full two hours. We covered a great deal of ground. Mostly we found each other again. I felt Eda was looking extremely well, and she was amazed at how well I looked. That in itself was a shot in the arm for both of us. They discovered that there is an elevator at Stage Neck Inn whereas I have always climbed the interminable stairs to get to the bar, where I often have meals when I dine out. But it is a help to know there is an elevator, so we went down in it. They are crazy about Stage Neck and were impressed by the kindness and the comfort. They used the swimming pool; Larry had two swims, one when they arrived after having driven through a terrible northeaster to get there and were exhausted; he swam then and swam again in the morning. They brought me clam chowder from the Cape, which I am going to have for lunch, and apple strudel from Zabar's in New York, which I had a little of last night with one of my favorite meals, which is asparagus on toast with a hard-boiled egg mashed up and lots of melted butter over it.

I must admit that after two hours of intense talk I was done in, but I managed to go to the post office and mail a few books.

I am trying to gird myself to get back to the novella which has been laid aside so long, and I found something in a rather remarkable book I am reading among all the things I am reading, *Long Quiet Highway* by Natalie Goldberg. The subtitle is *Waking Up in America.* One of the things she does which interested me enormously is to describe her Zen training and what it is to sit as they do and why you do and what happens when you do. It is interspersed with a lot about writing, and this is one of the things that interested me. Natalie Goldberg has published novels as well as this book of memoirs. It is the same for writing, the same as what Zen teaches you—that is, not to give up no matter what the situation.

> Get in there, stay in there, figure it out. It is the same for writing. Some people write for fifteen years with no success and then decide to quit. Don't look for success and don't quit. If you want writing, write under all circumstances. Success will or will not come, in this lifetime or the next. Success is none of our business. It comes from outside. Our job is to write, not to look up from our notebook and wonder how much money Norman Mailer earns.

I recognize that so well. I came to bed last night tired but full of excitement because Doris Grumbach's new book is here. About that I shall talk a little later. I am glad she confesses to her anxiety about reviews and dreads the envelopes that come from Norton with photocopied reviews in them, and she admits that some were not very good on her. I thought, wonderful first book of memoirs, first journal, if you will.

Monday, October 25, 1993

I AM edified to see Doris Grumbach's new journal, *Extra Innings* (she calls it a memoir), which I am reading now. There is a difference between a memoir and a journal. A memoir supposes, I think, distance, time; the whole point of a journal is the day-to-day struggle. Quite a lot of Doris's book, which is fascinating, is the day-to-day things. Then there are, as there are in a good journal too, short essays on death and dying, things like that. I am impressed with how religious Doris is. She talks more about that than she did in the first journal or memoir. It is moving. I envy her that certainty, that belief that praying when her daughter, for instance, was having an operation for a brain tumor helps. I have always thought that praying mostly helped the person who prays and that perhaps that was the point of it. But then I think of all the people who have said that they prayed for me, and how grateful I always am at the idea that they are thinking of me and lifting me up in their thoughts.

I do feel driven and, as a result, unhappy. More and more I have come to believe that what I must try to learn is to do only what I feel like doing on a given day. The next day, perhaps, I shall feel much better and more able to cope with a letter which simply irritated me beyond belief one day; perhaps I can read it the next day in a more tranquil state of mind, not expecting anything much and therefore able to answer it in a civilized manner. Let us hope.

Right now what I want is to find out what I earned last year, and so I think I am going to do that right now.

Tuesday, October 26, 1993

AND A beautiful sunny day, although a nor'easter is on its way and I wonder whether Dorothy Wallace will have a safe drive. But they have decided to come anyway, and I think the worst will probably be tomorrow afternoon. It is such an event to have Dorothy Wallace come. I celebrated her eightieth birthday this year with a poem which begins "Here comes the sun," so let us hope that tomorrow there will be some sun if she will bring it.

I am deep into Doris Grumbach's journal—I have now been down the stairs and climbed up again in order to find the titles of Doris's two "memoirs." *Extra Innings* is the second one following on *Coming into the End Zone,* which I found extremely fascinating. This was the journal when she dreaded so much getting to be seventy. It will be interesting to compare *Extra Innings* with Frances Partridge's new diary, called *Other People.* Frances Partridge is now ninety, but still the extraordinarily life-enhancing and life-enjoying woman that she has always been. At ninety she will give a dinner party for four, and they will talk until nearly one in the morning. I could never do that now at eighty-two. Most extraordinary woman.

But the reason I am bringing up Doris is that yesterday evening reading her journal, I came on a passage where she says that she cannot work if there is any disorder on her desk or anywhere in the house, so before she gets to work, she has to make order. This is the ideal thing. If I could do it, I would, but I do not know whether ten letters a day come into her that have to be answered, but they do to me, and I am ten years older than she is now. The pile grows and grows. I finally have to write the important letters whether the pile is diminished or not. Finally it becomes psychologically impossible to deal with it, and that is what happened yesterday. I spent two hours going over the pile at my right and throwing away, but there still is a whole box now at my feet with things that should be answered. I simply do not have my own life now, and there is nothing creative in it. That is why I am depressed. The only thing I do is attack this impossible pile of mail. When I get a really good letter, I always answer it, and I always will, but a great many of the letters I get are kind and generous letters but are not what one might call "good" letters. Therefore, one does not want to answer them when the effort becomes even greater.

But imagine. If I could start the day with a perfectly clean desk, that would be my idea of heaven, whereas it is Doris's usual thing, like my washing up the breakfast dishes when one of my minions, the women who help me, is not here. I have not yet managed, this is what is really shocking, to write to Erika Pfander, who produced *The Music Box Bird*, to thank her and to tell her how very remarkable I thought her direction of it was. Instead of going any further into this journal, I must try to do that.

Now that I cannot travel it is fun to have letters from friends of mine who do. My friend Diane Amiel celebrated her fortieth birthday by going to Rwanda to see the gorillas. They are so friendly that she was able to sit three feet from a mother and her one-month-old baby while nursing. She says they are gentle creatures and have no fear of humans. So I get my travel experiences these days by reading about or hearing about other people's travels.

Sylvia Frieze and her husband have been in the Adirondacks, and I am dying to hear about that.

It is now the afternoon. I had a wild morning getting

stamps. I spent sixty dollars. And then I took the lovely drawing that was made of the stage set of *The Music Box Bird*,
signed by all the actors, to be framed—as simply as possible.
It was forty dollars, so there goes one hundred dollars down
the drain.

But I am relieved that I did not earn quite as much money
this year as last as the income tax approaches. Now I feel I
want to read a poem that I used to know by heart and recited
many, many times to myself by Siegfried Sassoon:

> '*When I'm alone*'—the words tripped off his tongue
> As though to be alone were nothing strange.
> '*When I was young*,' he said; '*when I was young.* . . .'
>
> I thought of age, and loneliness, and change.
> I thought how strange we grow when we're alone,
> And how unlike the selves that meet and talk,
> And blow the candles out, and say goodnight.
> *Alone* . . . The word is life endured and known.
> It is the tillness where our spirits walk
> And all but inmost faith is overthrown.

I always feel this when people have just left. There is a kind of
parting of the air, whatever it is, as if I were going through
something like the parting of the ocean, some extraordinary
aloneness that is frightening for a little while, or at least feels
very empty. Then I realize I am coming back into myself, my
real self, and then I am happy. These days the problem is that
I am not with my real self very much. They are almost all days
of small, unimportant things that nevertheless have to be
done. It is exhausting because there is nothing creative in
these little things, in the errands I did today, for instance,
where I had to get out of the car six or seven times and drive
around. I also got three copies of the play that have come and
have just wrapped it to go to Maggie Lewis, who thinks a little
theater in Sag Harbor might be interested. I am glad to have

the copies now. I may lend one to Dorothy Wallace tomorrow if she wants to read it and send it back to me. Now I have four copies in all, and I will not get back the one I send to Maggie Lewis.

It makes me laugh that I tried to clear my desk yesterday, spent two hours at it, and now it is worse than it was before. I need all kinds of things, like a big jug that I could put all my pens and pencils in. Perhaps something will come to the house that would do that for me.

It is a down time, although a great deal that is good happens. I had a darling letter from Bill Brown, who is back at his painting and feels wonderful and loves Susan's book. I was relieved to hear that he really loves it. Lots of good things like that happen, and yet I am not here.

Thursday, October 28, 1993

YESTERDAY WAS one of the most rewarding days of this year. We were in for a real nor'easter, so it was a melancholy, rainy, windy day, but into it came Dorothy Wallace and a friend, Claire, who drove her and who is a composer, to pick me up and take me to lunch. Dorothy Wallace, who is just a year younger than I, was a student of mine in the Radcliffe Seminars for a course in short story and a second one in creative writing. We became fast friends, and during the forties, as she reminded me, quite often had lunch Chez Dreyfus, which no longer exists, in Cambridge, and talked about everything under the sun. Dorothy has been a tremendous support psychologically ever since then. She is a true believer and a very dear one.

First of all, it was wonderful to see her coming slowly

down the path strewn with leaves in the rain, her lion head, now white hair cut simply so it is soft but does not look done by a hairdresser. Yesterday in the pouring rain Dorothy brought the sun.

She wanted to show her friend Claire a little of the house, the flower window and some of the books that Dorothy too has not seen that have come out in the last year, the books about me. This was fun to show her, as she observes everything and enjoys everything in the most wonderful way. But doing all this, and then signing some books for them and giving one of the new ones [*Among the Usual Days*] to Dorothy all signed, meant there was not much time for talk. Finally we got to Stage Neck, had a table watching a rough sea and great waves pouring in on the beach, and then finally began almost two hours of brilliantly amusing and thoughtful talk among the three of us. It was one of those occasions when conversation flowered, one could say, or one could say we were playing ball and the ball was passed from one to another with great skill, and we laughed a lot.

I was surprised to hear that Danny, I think Dorothy's youngest child, youngest son anyway, has moved to Salt Lake City of all places, and the reason is interesting. It is because their twelve-year-old son has the makings of an Olympic skier, and we talked about whether this was a good choice, to uproot a whole family and have them entirely concentrated on getting this boy onto the Olympic team. I am against it, and I told Dorothy the story of Dr. Weille, the famous nose and throat man whom I used to go to often. His daughter went to the Winsor School and could have been an Olympic skater, but when it turned out how much this meant in time away from her studies and in concentration, the head of the Winsor School went to Dr. Weille and his wife and said, "We feel that she does not belong in this school if she is going to be a champion skater. It is impossible to do both well." Much to my admiration and surprise, Dr. Weille and his wife made that difficult decision not to push her to be the star that she might have been for the sake of a real education. The thing about starring in sports is that it ends so soon. One is not much good after age thirty in almost any sport, and then what happens? If you are a very extraordinary person, you find another career, but this is quite rare. Too often someone in his sixties is referred to always as "You know he was an Olympic skater," and what has he done since?

We talked about everything. Dorothy has always been a liberal like me, so there is no point in discussing politics. I wanted to hear about some of her children. She has five, but I only succeeded in hearing about Danny and Connie, whom I once wrote a poem about, who plays the cello. It is called "Girl with a Cello" and has been much quoted.

There was one thing that was hard about yesterday, otherwise a glowing day. It was more than two hours that they were here in York, and I never felt that queer drained feeling that I so often experience when people are here with whom I have to converse intelligently. I felt exhilarated and happy and grateful to Dorothy for all she is and has been to me. Such a wonderful woman! When we had ordered drinks and watched the surf for a while, great surf, Dorothy said that she had found a poem recently that reminded her of me. She said that she knew that it was a famous poem, but she had only just discovered it. Walter Savage Landor, and I find it now in *The New Oxford Book of English Verse:*

> I strove with none, for none was worth my strife.
> Nature I loved and, next to Nature, Art:
> I warm'd both hands before the fire of life;
> It sinks, and I am ready to depart.

Dorothy talked quite a lot about this, much to my delight. She felt that it was appropriate to think of me in relation to this poem, and she more than once said, "You do warm both hands at the fire of life," and I am glad she feels that I do because I guess I do. But am I ready to depart?

That is the other question and brings me to what I am reading now that I have finished Doris Grumbach's book. I began to read Frances Partridge with the greatest pleasure, as I expect to, for she is probably the best writer of diaries alive today, and she is now ninety. What may be her last diary has just come out, *Other People, Diary '63–'66*. I finished Doris's *Extra Innings* the night before last and last night began Frances Partridge. There could not be a greater contrast between these two women, who are both excellent writers. I feel more attuned to Partridge, I suppose because she is more like me, a warm, outgoing person who is fond of people and sees a great many. This journal, for the first time, no, really for the second time because there was one after her beloved husband died, followed on the tragic death of her son, whom she adored and who had recently married, a few days or perhaps a month before. She is struggling in this journal to go on living. In fact, she contemplates suicide quite often; then she does all kinds of things to try to come out of the awful burden of grief which never leaves her.

One of the things that interests me most in reading these first few pages when she is quite a lot of the time traveling in Italy with a friend, a male writer, is that she is simply trying to forget, simply to be somewhere else. She more than once talks about the sense that she has of being disfigured by grief so that she feels she is no good to other people because they must see this as if she had been brutally beaten by someone. This is what grief does and makes her, she feels, unapproachable and not a social possibility. It is interesting. I feel very much like that when I am depressed, that I must not show myself, as it were. Of course, that is somewhat why she chose the title for this journal, which is *Other People*. She tries to think about other people very hard and not about herself, and she keeps extremely busy because as soon as she is not busy, the grief comes in, the terrible grief.

This is not a fair comparison, but this situation I am in of being both in some ways very successful and in other ways denied what I most want and what I think I deserve means that I too often feel somehow unequipped for life. I resent it when someone feels that it is not true, what I am saying, or says, "But remember there are so many people who read you." That is true, but what if you were a great tennis player and you never got to Wimbledon and nobody ever knew that you were a great tennis player? You would mind. I mind very much that the poems have not been recognized, and when I came back from that wonderful lunch, exhilarated, happy, loving Dorothy so much and so glad to have had a reunion at last, maybe not for five years, I picked up the *Women's Review of Books,* and the leading article is a review of a new anthology of twentieth-century women poets edited by Florence Howe, and I am not in it. This seems almost incredible to me. She has put in a lot of people whom she did not know before, I guess, like Genevieve Taggard. I have forgotten some of the other names. And I am hurt. I am terribly hurt. It corroborates what I have kept saying, that I am nowhere as a poet. This matters to me and is hard on me, but at the same time I realized last night, when I started to read Frances Partridge and was utterly absorbed in it and glad to have it to read, that failure or bad luck, whatever you want to call it, has always stimulated rather than killed me. I would have stopped writing poetry after that terrible review thirty years ago of Karl Shapiro's.

Anne Lindbergh, after the famous review that Ciardi wrote of her poems, never published another book of poems. That did it. She was, if you will, murdered. That was particularly cruel because he had chosen a poet who was both well known as a writer and adored and yet could not be called a first-rate poet, so he could attack her and know that she would not be defended by anybody famous. That was what happened. He got hundreds of letters from fans of hers which he could then answer by pointing out that she really was not a good poet and have it his way. I think it is one of the dirtiest things that has ever been done in literature. It was so mean because she was so defenseless, and she is a great woman.

So I am swallowing that piece of bad news and hoping to get through to a point where pretty soon I can begin to do something creative. Otherwise I will be, I am sure, in an even more serious depression. I had a wonderful letter from Norma Allen, to whom I have sent *Among the Usual Days*. She is one of the few people who have answered among the ten or twelve to whom I have sent it. She said she had a full day at the clinic and came home to find "the beautiful book you sent. I sat down to just take a small taste of *Among the Usual Days* and stopped tasting at 2:00 A.M." That is encouraging.

At the end of autumn, when almost everything has gone, when especially the maple leaves are gone, fothergill, that wonderful little bush that I got from the Arnold Arboretum some years ago, suddenly turns a vivid yellow. It is lovely. I have two fothergills, two bushes under the pine trees. The other thing that is sometimes glorious, but suffered from the drought this year, is the Korean dogwood, Kousa, and that is beautiful now but not as brilliant as it has been in some years. In the woods the beech leaves are the great joy, their extraordinary yellow which I call Chinese yellow. It has been a remarkable autumn, and now it is almost gone. I dread the dark, after next week I think it is, when it will be dark at four and you feel life closing in and the crows cawing. I have never seen as many crows as there are around now, huge birds.

Well, it is a great thing that I remembered "fothergill" because I have not been able to fish the name of that bush out of my memory for days, perhaps even weeks, and suddenly it came to me as I was getting up from my nap. A nice little gift.

ONE OF the ways I travel these days has been memories, memories of all the wonderful places I have been, like Assisi with my mother. That was in 1932. The peace of it! I will never forget the beauty of the Umbrian plain, the extraordinary peace. I have been reading a description of it in the journal by Frances Partridge. It is strange the way she, and I suppose this is a typical part of the Bloomsbury ethos, treats the rituals of the Catholic Church. She is derisive, and this I mind. She is not in any way a mystic, but she is a wonderful friend, and in this book, where she herself is in real pain, extreme pain and grief because of the loss of her son (he was young, and it was a terrible business that does not take place in this journal, so I cannot remember what happened, but I know that it was sudden and awful) and she is struggling all the time with a wish to commit suicide, she keeps saying to herself that she must think of other people. The title of the book is *Other People*. This she does in a most remarkable way. She must be an exemplary friend. Also, she has, at ninety, incredible energy. She can give a dinner party for four or five people, and the conversation is so good they stay till one in the morning. This would finish me off completely. I would not be able to do anything for days.

The state of the world continues to be so depressing that it is hard even to look at the news. One simply does not know what will happen in Haiti. It is not possible for us to send fifty thousand troops, which is probably what it would need to pacify the country and to get rid of the dictators, both the police and the army, who are against the people and who terrify everybody. It is a land of fear and horror.

The same thing is true of Bosnia, where things are worse again. It is so depressing, and I think what is really depressing is that every day we face the inhumanity of man toward man, and it comes into our houses, into our rooms, and is right there under our noses on the television set every day. How does one handle this? I envy people who believe, as Doris Grumbach does and says in her journal, in prayer and the efficacy of prayer, but my feeling about prayer, and I have stated it in other journals, is that prayer is extremely valuable and should be done as much as one can although I do not believe in a personal God. I think what prayer does is to lift one out of the extremely personal into some larger sphere where one is a little more than oneself, and where one feels, perhaps, part of a greater universe.

I am now pursued by little verses, I cannot call them poems. I did start one during my nap today, and when I came up to my desk, I found one that I had written yesterday about how I travel now in my imagination. This I might be able to do something with. We'll see.

Meanwhile, the sea is cerulean, the field is sort of dusty beige, not attractive, and one prepares for the dim colors of winter and then hopefully for some snow.

One of the things on the news these days is the terrible fires in California. It is unbelievably awful, so many people who see their house go up in smoke literally in a few minutes because of the high Santa Ana winds, and yet most of these people say they will rebuild. They love the site, they love the view, yet it seems crazy to rebuild when in fact they are on the San Andreas Fault so there is always the imminent possibility of an earthquake. I know several friends in various parts of the area, but no one directly involved except Jean Burden, the poet, in Altadena, and there there has been a lot of trouble. I must write a word to say that I am thinking of her, which I had better do right now.

Saturday, October 30, 1993

SUSAN'S BIRTHDAY, and she reminded me this morning that three years ago today she went to the head of her school and asked for a half year off in order to come and take care of me because I was so ill I thought I was dying and so did the doctors. She came, and as I have told in other journals, she saved my life. Now we are like mother and daughter, close and loving and greatly enjoying our friendship. So it is exhilarating to be celebrating Susan on this awfully dismal day. An absolutely gray sea with no light reflected from a flat, totally gray sky over the brownish field. It is grim, and I woke up exhausted. I do not know why I am so tired, but it is frightening. After I had made my bed and gotten dressed, which is always these days rather an effort, and put on a red sweater to cheer myself up, I suddenly felt so tired I had to go and lie down. Luckily the cat came in and ate a little and came and purred on my lap. Now I have managed to come up here and to think about everything on my desk that should have been answered.

I GOT a charming fan letter from Eric Baumstead in Joliet, Illinois. He thanks me, amongst other things, for introducing him to other writers, and he actually got hold of Deborah Pease's *The Feathered Wind*, I must tell her, which he greatly enjoyed. But he asked me, and this was a gift, this kind of question, whether there are any interesting journals by men. "I did read Cheever's," he adds. Then I suddenly realized that the great journals by men, in the twentieth century, were by the French, Mauriac, and especially Gide, with his voluminous journals, and Julian Green, who has written both in English and French. I was certainly much influenced by Gide, whose Pléiade edition I annotated; it is thousands of pages long and somebody stole it, so I do not have the annotated version, but I did buy it again because it is an extraordinary book.

Also Eric Baumstead told me that he had written to Gwendolyn Brooks, he says, "about you and *Encore* as well." Apparently he had a creative writing class with her in college some twenty-five years ago, "and that opened my eyes to Haiku and deepened my interest in short stories." I met Gwendolyn Brooks some years ago when we both read poems at Clark University as part of their celebration of a hundred years. I felt immediately at home with her, immediately drawn to her, and felt that I had made a new and precious friend at the end of that weekend. But here we are, she in Illinois, I in Maine, both very busy, and although she generously wrote something for my *Festschrift* and later agreed to let it be used for the *Collected Poems*, we have not been in touch. So this was lovely, to think of this man I do not know writing to Gwendolyn Brooks about me. These are the small miracles that happen.

I had a brilliant short letter from J. L. Haddaway, Edythe's daughter, who is now writing poetry and very successful in it, toward an M.F.A., I think it is called; then she will be getting a doctorate and will teach creative writing. I enjoyed her letter because it was succinct and said so much about my work in two paragraphs.

I keep jotting things down for poems and then I do not ever finish them because when I come up to my desk there is too much else. It is quite true what one of them talks about, that traveling for me now really has to do with imagining, remembering the wonderful travels I have made since I was a child, and also the pleasure of reading about other people's travels, which is very great these days.

Now I must write to Bill Brown, who is so large a part of the new book *Among the Usual Days,* and who wrote me a dear letter praising the book but not telling me specifically the things he liked. It is hard to do that with so much material, but Susan and I are both disappointed that people do not write in greater detail.

Monday, November 1, 1993

I HAVE a bad head cold which makes my voice sound strange, and what a nuisance it is when I have so much I want to do, including some heartening things. A wonderful thing happened on Sunday while Susan was here. We were celebrating her birthday. In the mail I had a letter from *Poetry* magazine saying that I had won the Levinson Prize, one of the prizes that *Poetry* magazine gives at the end of the year for poems that have been published during the year. This, I am happy to say, was for the poems they published in December 1992, poems written during my seventy-ninth and eightieth year and will be an important part of the new book. So this was triumphant news! A thousand-dollar check. And I had been so depressed about anything ever happening to my poetry! This filled the balloon again which had been lying flat on the ground.

This morning I hear from Carol Houck Smith, the editor for the new book of poems, which is called *Coming into Eighty,* that she is very pleased and Norton is going ahead with them. She gives me a wonderful hope or, I don't know what to say, wonderful idea that I might try a short book about Pierrot, and I think I could do it because there is quite a lot of material, I realize thinking about it. It would be relatively easy compared to trying to finish the novella, which I still want to do but which means digging very deep into my past into things that are painful and difficult to deal with, whereas Pierrot has been chiefly a joy and a luxury, and a true "fur person" though he has never been the soul that Bramble was. No cat will ever replace her because she was the great soul, and Pierrot is not a great soul. What he is is a great beauty, so he gives me immense aesthetic pleasure. He is a kind of super luxury cat. So a new cat book is something to think about right away, and that is a challenge.

The weather the last three days has been lugubrious. There is heavy, dripping rain, and yesterday was the first day to be dark at four, as we have now put our clocks back. As the dark came in at four yesterday, and Susan was on her way back to New York driving through the rain, it seemed dismal. This cold does not help. I am blowing my nose like crazy, and I must go out today. I want to deposit that thousand-dollar check, which will make me feel rich at a time when I have been feeling rather poor.

Also, I think one is terribly oppressed and badgered by the huge numbers of requests for money, all of them important charities, but one cannot give to everything, so I spend five or ten minutes every morning throwing things away that I cannot answer.

Susan and I had a wonderful time. I like to give her things from the house because she is involved with and loves everything here so much. So I gave her a little coat that my mother had made for me when I was two and a photograph of me in it. It is white with little embroidered flowers around its edges. Now it is safe. All these fires in California make one realize how quickly everything could go, and I feel that I must give

certain things away now so they will be safe. Anyway, I loved
giving Susan that and also a bound copy of *The Fur Person*,
the first edition, which I had given to Judy, so it has a special
meaning for me, and in it I discovered a whole set of photographs about the fur person, Tom Jones, including one of him
lying in the window box at 14 Wright Street, where he loved
to lie.

Susan brought a video for us to see which had been highly
recommended to her and which was called *Eating*. We could
not make out what "eating" was, but we soon did. It was a
fortieth birthday party with a group of young women helping
the forty-year-old, who felt she was over the hill, celebrate, if
you can celebrate, that birthday. All were on diets, nobody
would eat any of the cake, and the emphasis on the figure and
on not eating and on eating and so on was really quite disgust-
ing. It is an ironic film and certainly does not make one happy
about the state of civilization.

Speaking of food, Sally, whom I am hiring to cook one big
meal for me every weekend so I have three or four evenings
when I do not have to cook, this week made, as I asked her to,
a birthday cake for Susan instead of a big meal for me, a most
exquisite lemon cake, really a triumph. Susan, who does not
like sweets and usually will not eat them, was crazy about
this, and I was pleased. Everything about it, its texture and
design, was elegant and delicious, pleasing the eye and certainly every sense imaginable. I still have some in the fridge;
she took some, but I have a treat ahead which I may try to
keep for Anne and Barbara, who come Thursday. I hope this
cold will subside by then.

There is a little more space on this tape, so I must put in
the letter that I got from Joe Parisi, the editor of *Poetry* magazine, because I have had so little of this kind of thing, almost
none in my life. Years ago *Poetry* magazine gave me one of
their prizes, a lesser one, for some political poems, and that

delighted me too, but this is particularly wonderful at eighty-one. Parisi says: "I am very pleased to be able to tell you that Poetry has awarded you the Levinson Prize for your poems in the December 1992 issue. The Prize in the amount of $1,000 is the oldest and most prestigious of the magazine's prizes." Then he gives me the address of the widow of the donor, who happens to live in Cape Elizabeth, so that I can thank her, and I was happy to be able to do that. I did do it yesterday, when I felt ill and queer, nauseated, and did not know whether I could do anything, but I did manage to write to Joe and also to Mrs. Scott and to send the *Poetry* letter to Eric at Norton and to Carol Houck Smith suggesting that they put an ad in *Poetry* magazine in honor of the prize because there had been nothing, no ads, nothing.

Wednesday, November 3, 1993

AT LAST a sunny day, but I feel worse than I did when I went to the hospital in August when they thought I had pneumonia. I still have a sore throat every morning. Now I am on an antibiotic; I continually say to myself, "You must keep going so as not to have to go to the hospital this time." I am determined to stay home, where I have my life and where I get an enormous amount of help from friends. Sally, who made the marvelous cake for Susan's birthday on Saturday, saw that I was not feeling very well and called yesterday to see whether I needed help; I was so grateful to have somebody drive me. I had to have a blood test because I had taken aspirin with Coumadin, which I had not realized is dangerous, and then picked up the antibiotic, which I have been on for twenty-four hours; it does not seem to have done any good yet.

Otherwise there is nothing to say. I got angry because Pat Robinson does not realize that when she is gardening and I am resting, it is exactly as if she were in the next room because it is so silent here otherwise. I was trying to rest and she was talking to Maggie and I got into a fit of crying and behaved very badly.

Friday, November 5, 1993

ABOUT THE gloomiest day I can imagine here. It is raining, was totally dark at four, and *No More Masks!*, which I ordered to confirm I was not in it, does not have a single poem of mine. This is a terrible blow all over again, and I cannot understand it. One of the editor's criteria for choosing was poems that said things about women that have not been said and surely my sequence "My Sisters, O My Sisters" which has been much quoted would have been a perfect selection. It is an indignity and hard to take, but one has to take it.

So I try to think of all the good things that have happened, and they are many, but I am low in my mind partly because of the cold. The antibiotic has made me nauseated and not myself. I guess that is what it always does.

I only managed today to write six thank-you notes. This is the kind of day which utterly depresses me because I cannot see it as a lifework, only an existence to thank people, as I have been obliged to do lately almost all the time.

Right now the florist is bringing flowers from somebody. It will be lovely to have flowers because it really is dismal here, and yet again, they must be acknowledged.

Saturday, November 6, 1993

THE SUN is out, but I am having a very hard time. The antibiotic is sickening. In the middle of feeling miserable, it has been a tremendous gift to have Jean Burden's book *Taking Light from Each Other*, which she sent me after we had a telephone call because I was worried that the fire storm in California might have affected her. She lives in Altadena, one of the places mentioned. Her book is extraordinary because for me, at least, almost every poem hits me where I live, and one of them especially, which I have asked her permission to quote here called "Lost Word" because this happens to me four or five times or more than that every day.

Lost Word

I do not believe in a God
who bothers Himself in the trivia
of this planet, but
Lord, could you find me this word?
I know it as well as my name,
but it is running backwards into darkness
as I lurch after it.
It stands for the small mammal
that ate raspberry parfait
at the back door in Big Sur; the huge one
that climbed through Eric's window,
and clawed at his cats;
the old one that made a shambles of his kitchen.
I say *possum, skunk,*
porcupine, knowing it is not any of these.

The word, Lord! You are supposed to be good
at words. Remember the Word? It is midnight
and I yearn for the elusive thing. I sleep
and waken. It is coming closer. It skitters by
avoiding my eyes. I scurry from attic to cellar
of my mind. It is not there.
Weasel, squirrel, badger, rat.
I am not asking to see the dark side of the moon, God.
Only one word. Will you give it to me with Your light?
I roll to one side. The beast
turns its black triangle of a face
full on me. Ah, *raccoon.*

A great event yesterday was a rare letter from Bill Heyen
because Bill Ewert talked to him on the telephone and read
him my Christmas poem, and apparently this moved Heyen
enormously. He says, "I was hit hard. Your heart concentrates
into a sound that could melt stone. What a poem this will be to
receive for Christmas! Bless you for blasting through all the
Hallmark dreck and the Muzak of the holidays. When Bill was
done reading, I could hardly talk." I admire Heyen so much as
a poet; he is one of the very few living poets whom I know and
am in touch with at all, so it made me feel better about not
being in that anthology.

. . . but I do wish I felt stronger because there is so much I
want to do and there is so much on my desk. I did manage to
write five thank-you notes. Liz Evans sent roses to celebrate
all the books that have come, and I really must try to write to
her today, as well as Paul Reed, who wrote me a lovely letter
about *Encore.*

CREDIT: SUSAN SHERMAN

May, with Bill Ewert, signing her Christmas broadsides.

Sunday, November 7, 1993

AT LAST. For ten minutes I have been trying to get this machine to work and now at last it is recording.

A most depressing day. I am trying to figure some way to get out of this depression. One of the ways is certainly to think of friends, of wonderful times that there have been. I was thinking suddenly of Mark Turian and Meta, their marvelous house in Satigny near Geneva. This house looked like a very large, very old, perhaps eighteenth-century apartment house, an enormous castlelike building with vineyards behind it going up the steep hill. They were the most adorable people. A great burly man, he had a wonderful sense of humor, was childlike, always terribly worried about the weather; I am sure all people who grow grapes are. It might be a great year and then a frost would come or something else would happen. You are so much in the hands of something you cannot control. One of his inspired sayings I always remember is when Meta, his wife, found a mouse in a linen drawer one day, Mark said, "That mouse was an entrechat." As you know, an entrechat is a leap in ballet. It also means, of course, between cats. This was typical of Mark. He would go on thinking about something like this for days and come out with all kinds of marvels that he made up. He did most of the cooking, mostly soup, as I remember, for supper. Sometimes we went out to eat the famous fish from Lac Leman.

I always remember arriving there. I would have climbed the three flights of stairs, Mark bringing up my luggage, my typewriter, I always had much too much luggage, and there I would land in an enormous room the whole breadth of the house. In that room was a great table looking out over the vineyards where I could put my typewriter and papers, and on that table magnificent flowers, a basket of fruit, and a basket of wonderful chocolates which Meta knew I had a passion for, the Swiss chocolates. It was like fairyland, like being a princess.

We would go on little excursions, but mostly it was the wonderful routine of writing poems, which I did, I wrote a lot of poems there, and then having lunch somewhere, perhaps out, and then having a rest, and then in the evening talking together and being glad to be together. Memorable times.

What has got me down are two things. One, of course, is Florence Howe's anthology, a bitter blow which has somehow shaken my faith in my poetry all over again, although I do remember the prize from *Poetry* and say to myself, "It *is* appreciated. Somebody thought it good enough to give it a prize." The other thing is the fact that Norton, which has published three books of mine this summer, has not given me a single ad. I think it probably can be explained by what Eda LeShan wrote me the other day. All the publicity people now are young. The new publicity person or the advertising manager, as she is called at Norton, may not really have any idea about me. I am not a best seller, but I have gone on selling. Norton sells a lot of my books, and once, some years ago when they decided they would find out what their authors actually were worth in money, they told me that they had taken in a million dollars on me over the twenty years or so that I have been an author of theirs. That is quite a lot. It seems to me that they owe me, at eighty-two with three books, an ad, and I am going to fight for it, but I hate fighting.

The great comfort is Pierrot, without whom I am sure I would now be dead.

Today the sun was out, although I still feel ill and have this strange pain in my left arm and left side over the rib cage where my breast would be if it had not been removed for cancer. They tell you that heart pain is never on the left side but on the right side, so I have to try to believe this is not my heart. I try to make myself think of other things, and one of the things I am trying to do is to make a little anthology of poems only four lines long, of which there are a great many. But as always happens, I cannot find what I am looking for; now I cannot find a wonderful anthology that Ellery Sedgwick gave me years ago. I cannot imagine where it can be. It simply disappeared. These things are frightening. It makes me feel bewildered and very much at a loss.

It was good this morning to hear Clinton help celebrate what may be the twentieth year of "Meet the Press." He did an extremely good job. It is so extraordinary to think of how much he has to know about so many things; he was quiet and sure of himself. It was impressive. At the end he was modest and said, "I try every morning to think I will do the best I can with the day, and that is all I can do." And I guess that is the best I can do too.

Tuesday, November 9, 1993

ONCE THE leaves have gone I see a great arc of ocean from left to right. It is an amazing sight, and this morning, because I had to take the rubbish out, I went out just after dawn. The sky was perfectly clear and brilliant orange and, above that, bright blue with a little half-moon. It was a transporting sight, absolutely beautiful. So there are compensations to the November weather.

Luckily I have heard only one shot so far, though I was terrified to see two fawns in the big meadow off Godfrey Cove Road when I went in town to cash a check at twelve. Luckily there was not a car in sight, I mean a parked car or anything that suggested there were hunters around, but there well may be now.

The event of the day was at last to hear from Margot, who has been in Virginia, the lucky woman, with a friend, and speaking of how exquisitely beautiful it was, they had very good weather. She did mention Susan's book and was, of course, I say "of course" because I knew she would be, somewhat dismayed. She feels that so much is given there, but actually there is no story, and the connection between me and the people to whom I wrote in that book is simply not there. That is the biographer's art, to bring life to and make flesh out of these initials, JM, and so on.

It was quite a blow when I opened *Time* this morning after I came back from the mail and found an obituary of Maeve Brennan. She was seventy-six, I see; I knew she was a little younger than I am. I knew her because she was at the MacDowell Colony one year and fell in love with the region and so rented a house in Nelson and was there one whole winter, adopting cats all the time and always out of money. I remember being glad that I could lend her five hundred dollars, though I did not have very much then and I knew I would never see it back. She was a life-giving person, and I greatly enjoyed the evenings we spent together talking. She used to write in "Talk of the Town" the letters to the editors from the long-winded lady, and they were remarkable, all about New York and the New York scene, of what was going on in the streets. She was a good short-story writer but produced little. This moved me very much: The obituary ends by saying she set great store by W. B. Yeats's statement "Only that which does not teach, which does not cry out, which does not persuade, which does not condescend, which does not explain, is irresistible." This is very much what I believe and hope that I do myself.

I am not, like Adrienne Rich, a moralist. This came to me when I read the marvelous review of her last book in the Sunday *Times*. It made me think about her and about myself and how different we are. I suppose if you wanted to take an alter ego in the past for Adrienne, it might be George Eliot; for me, it might be Colette, who also is not a moralist but was a woman who glorified life itself, as I try to do. Connie Hunting has said that my poetry is a poetry of praise. This is unfashionable, which explains in part why I have gotten nowhere.

To go back to the letter from Margot Peters about *Among the Usual Days*, she feels that her thunder has been stolen as biographer; I do not think she is right, though it is understandable. She is concerned to see a large book about me come out when she is writing the biography. But this is a book of essences, and so much is not even approached in it, nothing to do with the life as it is lived, the relationships with the people which are so important. There is no story, if you will, and I think in some ways Susan's book is rather hard to read for that reason because it is a matter of essences.

My awful depression seems to be lifting a little. Maybe it is having the enormous expanse of blue ocean that I saw this morning, but something has made me try to look at what is good, and there is much that is good.

Today I managed to write almost a page of what may turn into a book called *My Friend Pierrot.* I realize that it is going to be more about me than it is about him, or it will be about us together, but there is not that much to say. It is our living along together which has its enormous charm, and that becomes somewhat repetitious. There is nothing as dramatic, for instance, as when there was a terrible cat fight when Bramble was alive. It occurred in the middle of the night when it was zero and I had the flu; I suddenly realized there was Tamas on the bed, that the answer was Tamas. So I got him to go down with me and I said, "Tamas, go and get your cat," opened the door, and in a second he was back with the cat waiting at the door to come in. The enemy cat had been driven off by his barks. That was a dramatic moment.

There is the time when Pierrot experienced stark terror perhaps caused by an owl, a thing I will never forget and have never seen again and which I shall certainly describe in the book. There is quite a lot, after all, when I come to think of it.

Sunday, November 14, 1993

I WANT to remember November 5, the day Anne Woodson and Barbara Barton came here for one of our yearly visits, or twice yearly now, I guess, but which I had no energy or time to record. How wonderful it was to see them, who go back to the early days of Nelson, when Anne used to do a great deal for me there and even painted a wonderful painting there. Anne and I have known each other for a good thirty years, and more than twenty since Barbara and I met, a rich friendship with them both which has brought me great windows on the natural world. This time they said that they are sure there are two bears down by the summer house deep in the woods below their house because the bird feeders are all upset, ravaged and torn up. At the same time they are quite sure that a moose has been at the summer house because the screen was broken down and only a moose would be high enough to do that. Of course, there are raccoons to eat things too, and a small furtive animal whose name I forget.

So I heard all this with great joy, and we talked about everything, as we always do. The dearness of them is palpable to me always, but even more when they are here and insist on doing all the washing up—we always have lobsters. Anne sees something that needs doing around the place; this time she noticed that one of her birdbaths that she creates had broken off at the end, making it hard to keep full, and lo and behold, she brought a new one for me. So many people have mentioned the birdbath, people who had to fill it all the time when it was broken. So that was a great day here though a big effort for me, because they were here four hours, which is longer than I can last these days.

Second Entry on Sunday, November 14, 1993

A BRILLIANT day again but depressing because I feel weak. It is difficult to do anything. This morning, however, I have managed to write the checks for Joan and Nadine, who come during the week to help me out, and that is something done. Now for the first time in several days I am talking to the cassette, which fortunately Susan has helped me to install because I always get something wrong. It shouldn't be so difficult, but I balk at machines.

Susan pointed out this morning that the remote control for the TV which lets me block out commercials is run on batteries and has lost its power. So she has actually taken it apart and gone down to get the batteries only to find that there were three and she had only seen two when she took it apart, so she has gone back. The amount she does when she is here is staggering. All these things that nobody sees because they are not here, except Maggie, who is coming this weekend and will undoubtedly find other things that need to be done in the house.

I do enjoy the house enormously although it is a big house for one person. Nevertheless, I use almost all of it except the guest room a great deal of the time.

Yesterday Susan Swartzlander came with the professor

from Grand Valley State in Illinois who is teaching *As We Are Now* to interview me—for them to interview me; there were eight people here all told—for a video for students about *As We Are Now*. This is I think my best novel, and if not the best, certainly one of the three best; I would put *Faithful Are the Wounds* and *Mrs. Stevens* among them. As I am sure always happens with equipment of this kind, because we had to be both photographed and heard, it took them a long time to get both the audio and camera set up. And then we had to repeat the first part three times, which Susan, who is not used to interviewing, was nervous about. I found it difficult to redo because I had talked for three minutes quite fluently about the book and how it was based on a real place which I saw because Perley Cole, the old farmer who worked for me in Nelson, died there and I went to see him and found out what dreadful people were running it and how unwholesome and cruel the atmosphere was. I found out that it had never been visited by the New Hampshire Health Service so nobody knew how bad it was. And I did, through knowing somebody who had some influence, manage to get it closed to people as ill as Perley. He was dying of cancer. I still mourn because I finally managed to get him out and into a good place. Oh, the difference! The airy, sunny room was where he died, but it was too late because he did not want to be moved. He was too ill. They came and got him in an ambulance.

This is not in the novel because in the novel I had him die in the ambulance, but I was able to go and see him in the new place the next day and bring him a pair of pajamas for his birthday and then that night he died. He kept saying all the time, "I never thought my life would end like this." His wife was in a different nursing home; they were not together, and he was in a state of not only misery but rage.

But I was touched by how enthusiastic Susan and her whole group were, and the delightful professor who is teaching it and who was extremely warm in his appreciation at what I have done for them.

What I dread is the week ahead. I have too many appointments, every single day, and tomorrow I have to go twice to the hospital—at eleven for an X ray of my arm and an X ray perhaps of the rib structure on the left because Dr. Gilroy thought that what had been causing the pain in my arm and just over the ribs may well be a recurrence of cancer; that is the side on which I had the mastectomy. It made sense to me, and I shall be interested to know what comes out. Interested, but when you are eighty-one and as ill as I feel and have felt for the last four years, death is a friend, especially when one knows that pain probably can be taken care of now, and when I think of dying in this beautiful place and seeing the sun rise every morning I think how lucky I am and also how lucky in having Pierrot, whom I am anxious to write about, but then there is the frustration of feeling ill. It is hard to walk even a few steps, and I am in pain all down the left side. I want to write about Pierrot, but writing takes effort and I do not have what it takes today.

Tuesday, November 16, 1993

AFTER A strange foggy day yesterday we have a brilliant day today, rather warm. I got up at half past six to take out the rubbish and saw the expanse, much more ocean than I ever see until the leaves have gone. It is exciting. It is a wonderful way to start the day with that orange sky and that luminous blue sea halfway around me as if I were wrapped in the sight of ocean.

It has been a hard time because of the lack of advertising for the three books Norton has brought out this year. I have gone into an angry rebellion about it and tried to do something. Yesterday Susan read me a letter from Eric Swenson to her—she had written him begging him to do something for me—in which apparently he explained that no one can now afford a full-page ad in the *Times*, which I used to get quite often, unless the book has an advance sale of eighty thousand or is expected to sell about that. He says they think that mine may sell thirty thousand, which is good for me. What is not good for me is that they did not advertise *Encore* before *Among the Usual Days* and that they will be advertised in one ad this coming Sunday and then again before Christmas. The problem is that even my most fervent fans will perhaps not be able to spend forty-five dollars, which the two books cost. If there had been an ad on *Encore* three months ago when it came out, then everybody who loves my work would have bought it without knowing that there was a sequel to come and then would have been surprised and delighted to find it. But the truth of all this is that I must give up all thoughts of success in the ordinary sense. I have not had it. Nobody believes this and everybody says, "Think of all your readers." Yes, but the great number of my readers are ordinary people, perhaps that is a compliment. But right now I feel that in spite of having a great many people read me, I am a failure as a writer. There is no getting around that. What I have got to do is make peace with it and go ahead and try to write the book about Pierrot, which, if I can get into it, will be a tremendous pleasure. Yesterday I had a letter from Carol Heilbrun about what it was like to bring him here, the traumatic time that they both had, and that is what I must get at today and try to write.

I am reading Dorothy Bryant's *Anita, Anita*. Anita was the mistress of Garibaldi at the time when he was in Brazil in exile. A heroic figure of a woman. And I consider Dorothy Bryant one of the most brilliant writers of fiction in America today. She publishes herself because she got so fed up with all the things that are making me angry now about publishers. She has written a whole string of remarkable novels and, I think, three plays, one on the Flaubert correspondence with George Sand which had a great success in Berkeley, where she lives. The trouble with *Anita Anita,* which is extremely well written—I am staggered by the research that must have gone into it—is that it is a violent story in which a great many brutal things are recorded, terrible battles, people being shot by cannon or exploded in their ships, the whole tenor is violence, and I must admit that it is extraordinary to find a woman who can describe it as well as she does, but it also is not exactly what I need right now when I go to bed; I dread another terrible battle and slaughter every night, so it may be that I shall not finish it. But Bryant is a brilliant writer. There is no doubt about that. How vivid she makes it all!

Monday, November 22, 1993

IT IS a magnificent day again, and every day lately I have rejoiced at the splendor of the sunrise. When I get up to feed the cat, usually about six, before the sun rises, the whole sky is orange. It is amazing. Every day I think what a marvelous place this is and how lucky I am to have the constant presence of beauty in my life, and I certainly do because the house too is beautiful and all the things that are here that represent my parents' lives and my life and the lives of friends make it

The presence of beauty in my life.

precious. But I am in a tailspin about my life. It is too much for
me to handle, and I think that at my age and as ill as I am—I
now have a bladder infection, of all things—I really should
not be asked to do so much.

Today, for example, comes a long memoir from a young
woman whom I knew maybe twenty years ago very slightly
because she worked for Katherine Davis, whom I wrote to
fairly often, as is visible in Susan's book. She has been in
psychiatry and has been influenced by my journals and has
kept this memoir for her psychoanalyst, who turns out to be
somebody who knew my work well. This happens fairly often
and is rewarding to me, but here I am now just before
Thanksgiving and in a day or so two hundred Christmas
poems to send out and here is a long, maybe forty- or fifty-

page, typed memoir that I am expected to read and answer, and there is one other thing of the same kind in the mail today. People simply do not realize, I think do not add up, how old I am. Of course, the journals suggest somebody who is still very much alive as I am, but lately I have felt I cannot handle it and do not know how to manage. Maggie was here for the weekend, always such a blessing, and this time she did an infinite number of things including sharpening all the knives towards Thanksgiving. This morning I heard that Sally can do the Thanksgiving dinner. This is a relief because she had flu last week and we were not sure whether she could.

At five o'clock yesterday we discovered that the cellar was full of water, and as it had not rained, I was terrified that it must be the septic tank again, and there is supposed to be a whole new sewage system put in, but they have not come. I have tried to use as little as I could of water. All of that is part of running a place, of running a house, but curiously enough, when I cried trying to explain to Maggie why I feel so depressed and unable to cope, I realized that the things I do around the house, like rearranging flowers or feeding the cat or washing his dishes, are very satisfying and that, at eighty-one, would be the way to live if I could. But the thing that destroys those simple satisfactions is that I can never take the time to do them well because "I must get up to my desk," and up at my desk the disorder is terrifying and makes disorder in my spirit. Yesterday I misplaced my new address book, which has all the addresses I need most in it. It was underneath the desk; Maggie finally found it for me. Also the best pair of scissors in the house had disappeared. These are the things that make me feel incompetent. The loss of memory and then the fact that I am so slow. The telephone rings and it takes me ten rings to get from the library to the phone and often people do not let it ring that long. The one great comfort is Pierrot, and without him, who knows?

Now I think I may ask Judy Harrison, my secretary, to take some dictation and try to dictate a few letters if she comes this week before Thanksgiving. I must write to Norma, who sent me flowers for Thanksgiving and stamps, as she often does, with a wonderful letter about Susan's book. When Norma wrote this letter to me, she "had just come off nine hours of working at the clinic, where I saw about fifty patients. Too many. My head is spinning. Nothing serious that took mind, that took much expertise. I did see a very nice dislocated shoulder in a Marfan's syndrome (hyperdistensible joints) and was able to replace it after giving the patient IV Valium." She thinks that I am restless, which is really not true. I guess she thinks that because I have been to Europe from the time I was nineteen until I left Nelson and even after that I was in Europe every spring practically and divided between my European self and my American self, so I suppose that does suggest a certain kind of restlessness, but I have lived in this house for nearly twenty-two years now, I lived in Nelson for fifteen. There are not many people in America who have lived in the same place for that long.

Tuesday, November 23, 1993

AGAIN THE marvelous orange light early in the morning when I went out to take out the rubbish. I enjoy this though I dread making the effort, but when I get there with that tremendous early-morning world around me, it is thrilling. This has been a wonderful day. How rare it is when something one has greatly desired to possess finally arrives, and this morning a book that

I had and lost maybe forty years ago or more when we were living on Wright Street, Judy and I, has been sent to me by Dorothy Wallace and arrived today. It is Maurice Goudeket's *Près de Colette*, this wonderful telling of his life with Colette and celebration of Colette. It is a rare book, and I think its rareness is in the title, which is perfect, close to Colette, near Colette, I do not know how to translate it exactly. They lived together for twenty-one years. Goudeket was Jewish and taken by the French police under the Nazis to a camp in France. They were terrible years, when Colette did not know where he was or whether she would ever see him again, and then I remember her description clearly of when he was there at the door. "Suddenly life began again."

This is a wonderful day. Not only did this much-wanted, much-desired book come into my possession, but there was also a letter from Parker Huber, whom I see once a year for a long talk as to where we each are. This time I gave him *Among the Usual Days*. I knew he would be one person who would appreciate it and who would read it slowly and enjoy it. He does what I always hope people will do who read it—that is, he quotes some of the things that he most likes.

But the thing that moved me this morning was the first two paragraphs of his letter. He says:

Such a joy to be with you 8th November. I was lifted on high. I went to Ogunquit Beach to walk and give thanks for you. Then, I saw you as a child on that same beach in *May Sarton: Among the Usual Days* and realized why that magnificent stretch of sand calls me so. It is my annual pilgrimage to see you and the sea. I was struck with the thought that I could perform this ritual in honor of you and our friendship forever; that it need not be dependent upon your being here; that I can continue to give thanks to you wherever you are and in whatever form you are. Know that I shall be doing this for you for as long as I can. That made me feel very good inside. I thanked the sea for that gift.

Well, it brings tears to my eyes because I think a lot about dying these days, the death wish is rather strong, although having one day to myself yesterday lifted my spirits beyond absolute despair, and now I have another day here alone with no appointments and it does seem like heaven.

There was another great event in the mail. What a day! That is the first copy I have seen of my Christmas poem, which now means that in a few days I will have two hundred of them to send out, and already the people to whom I want to send it are accumulating in my mind. I was distressed about the poem. It seemed impossible to write a Christmas poem this year, but now that I see it beautifully done in print I think it is very moving and I am glad that I can send it out.

Parker is an original human being. Every Thanksgiving and every Christmas he climbs Mount Monadnock to thank the Lord, I guess, for all his friends.

But I think I was about to read my Christmas poem when I began to think that I had not said enough about Parker, who has said so much so feelingly about me.

Christmas 1993

Bullets rain all day
On Sarajevo now.
The children do not play
Too cold in the snow.

We witness in black rage
What we cannot prevent
Or calm or assuage—
Comfort cannot be sent.

Another Christmas come
We know we are not able

To bring the homeless home
Hunger eat at our table.

How summon Christmas from
The welter of our grief
And from the nothing done
Create saving belief?

Wherever we do live
And help the helpless there
We touch the precious love
The hope beyond despair.

What we can do, then do!
The story told in Hell
Two thousand years ago
Leads us to Heaven still.

I am quite pleased with it.

And now there are a great many things on my desk which
I must try to answer today. One of them is dear cousin Alan
Eastaugh, who is arranging to have sent from London a case
of burgundy and claret to Juliette Huxley for her ninety-sev-
enth birthday, which comes December 6 and makes me think
I must write her a birthday letter, but not today. Very soon.

Wednesday, November 24, 1993

AN OPPRESSIVE and devastating day because there is a mean
review of both Doris Grumbach's new journal *Extra Innings*
and my *Encore* in the *Women's Review of Books*, which has
never reviewed me, and this is, I think, fairly typical of their
general style—extremely serious and even pedantic. It is diffi-

cult to take because it suggests in the first place that the writer of it whose name is Milton did not even know that I had written quite a few journals and suggests that like Doris, *Encore* is a second journal, the first one being *Endgame*, and she is very critical of me as a journal writer, suggesting that there is no larger ambience, no world around me, that I am extremely full of myself. But the thing about *Encore* is that it was the journal of my eightieth year, when so much good did happen. I had struggled for fifty years and written fifty books, of which she seems to be unaware, without ever making it in the literary world, that this long struggle finally in my eightieth year seemed to be coming out like a game of solitaire, and I was extremely happy about it; I think it is normal that I was. It is not strange, and I am sure that most of my readers, those who have been following me since *Journal of a Solitude*, rejoiced that at last a little of the pain has lifted.

I have thought a lot since I read this review, about what it is about a bad review, why it is so hard to take. In a way I admire writers who say they never read their reviews, although I do not believe them. Very often it turns out that the reviews have been read for them by a husband or a secretary or somebody they trust. I want to know; I guess it is curiosity. But the effect of a bad review is very much like being physically bruised. Somebody socks you in the breast, and you know it is not fatal, that you are not going to die of it, and it may be the reviewer did not feel ill will, but the bruise hurts. And the bad review creates a bruise whose pain has to be gotten over in one way or another.

Today I was not good at getting over it. A long, difficult day, the day before Thanksgiving. Flowers arrived. One of the things this reviewer minded was the flowers, that so many people sent flowers. She says, at one point, "too many flowers" apropos of Susan bringing roses. That is mean. Somehow or other she resents the fact that in that particular journal I am very much at the center of a lot of praise which I must believe I deserve and had waited a long time to hear.

She never takes into account what it is like to be eighty and how different it is from Doris's seventy-five, when she wrote her new journal. But the biggest difference between Doris and me is that she is well and I am ill.

The effort of simply getting to the next day is enormous. Luckily the routine and the rhythm of my life do help me, there is no doubt about it. Right now it is half past four and I know that in forty-five minutes I will be going down and getting ready for my supper, making my drink, listening to the news, and that framework is comforting and keeps me going.

But life right now is joyless. There is nothing that I look forward to, and that is bad. Yes, I look forward to reading, and I have got Goudeket's *Près de Colette*. I look forward to getting into bed and going on with this adorable book. So there are compensations. Another is that nothing has to be done; it has to be done in my mind because of my conscience, "I must write this answer," but it is not as if I had a job which required me to appear at four-thirty and be brilliant. I can choose what I am going to give and when I am going to give it, and that is a wonderful dispensation to old age.

After the shock of reading that review and lying down with the cat and trying to get over it, crying and then trying to sleep and then waking up again crying, I finally decided to call Doris just so we could be our real selves and be friends again. I wanted to tell her, how shall I say, that I did not mind, that I loved her book and did not mind being the fall guy or the one who was hit most although the review is not entirely generous to her either. I am delighted to hear that her book on solitude is going to come out, that Beacon is bringing it out. She spent a month in solitude and wrote about it, and it will be interesting, I must say, to read this. It also amused me because I have spent forty years in solitude, though not absolute solitude, but solitude as a way of life, and that is rather different. But we shall see; it is bound to be fascinating, and Beacon has paid her a very large advance, which is always nice to know, far better than Norton offered.

I really should write to Juliette, which I have not done for a long time, because her ninety-seventh birthday is on December 6 and I decided that if I did not write today, it would simply get lost in the crush of sending out the Christmas poem. I thought, I am going to write to her now for her birthday, but I felt distant and unmotivated because somehow knowing that I cannot get over there and I shall never see her again makes it hard to sustain the intimacy, particularly since she cannot write, has not written to me now for three years. Thus I write into a kind of void, although I know it is not really a void. I know that she is there, and if I call on the telephone, she sounds as though she were in the next room, delighted to hear my voice, tells me I should do it more than I do, but it is always a great effort, that leaping over an ocean of time as well as the real ocean. And when she goes, how empty my world will be.

Thanksgiving Day, November 25, 1993

A BRILLIANT day after heavy rain last night and snow in some places. Susan had to drive through snow in Massachusetts and did not get here until eleven, when I was, I am ashamed to say, fast asleep. But it had been a long and difficult day yesterday. However, now all the delicious bowls and pots that Sally has filled with goodies for us are here in the house, and it looks like a wonderful Thanksgiving dinner which neither Susan nor I have had to work at.

The best thing about this Thanksgiving for me is, curiously enough, the photograph of an enormous turkey called Tom who weighs sixty pounds and belongs to Gracie Warner. When I saw the photograph of this gigantic turkey, I was sure they were going to have it for their Thanksgiving dinner, as they so often have to eat animals they have had as pets—for instance, the pig every year. But thank goodness this Tom is a pet and is not going to be eaten but gloriously represent the sacred bird at their dinner, and I have him on the table here so that we can enjoy him. One turkey that did not get eaten. We ourselves are having a chicken, not a turkey.

That review has taken it out of me, but I am sure that when people come, I will revive.

Friday, November 26, 1993

A BRILLIANT, beautiful day, but extremely cold. In fact, I am amazed that the cat goes out at all. You can feel him shivering before he makes up his mind, but then he suddenly decides he has to go, and after I have stood there for five minutes, he does finally go out. How wonderful that he now has a cat door in the cellar, thanks to Maggie Vaughan!

We had a delightful Thanksgiving Day, and a great deal of it was due to Sally, who cooked it for us. She brought it around Wednesday night. Everything. The most wonderful sweet potatoes with pecans and just a few little marshmallows on top which were simply delicious. The perfect creamed onions in the perfect cream sauce which is so difficult for me to make and have stay as it should stay, and stuffing that was superior, cornbread and chestnuts. I had asked for chestnuts but would not have thought of using cornbread, but it worked extremely well. The whole dinner was an Epicurean delight. She had made a special sort of conserve of cranberries with perhaps some orange; I could not quite make out what it was, and there must have been ginger in the sweet potatoes, I think. And as for the bird, it was delicious because it was not dried out at all. We had only the juices as gravy, and it was superb.

I suppose like everybody else, I feel a kind of relief that Thanksgiving is over. It is, however one does it, even in this easiest way, quite an effort, but it was lovely to have Judy Burrowes with us, who had nowhere to go this Thanksgiving because her mother has died and her father is in a nursing home. She looked lovely and I think enjoyed herself, and without Susan nothing would have happened because she organized and served so beautifully and carved so beautifully. It was a relief to me not to have to do it. And then, as we have now for four Thanksgivings, Edythe Haddaway had brought a specialty of hers, a light lemon pie which is rich with cream and real lemons—made from scratch, delicate and delicious. I look forward to having a second helping tonight.

Susan and Edythe got into quite an amusing exchange which made us all laugh just because everything they said to each other seemed to make one or the other of them laugh, so this was quite a delight and I was happy to have my nap at three o'clock and not to have any supper. I had had a huge meal, and I eat very little usually.

And now I am in the thicket of Christmas and beginning to send out the Christmas poem. I have sent out ten over the last couple of days; there are two hundred. But it is wonderful to think of all the dear faces and to remember when I met people. I am only afraid I shall not have enough, so the thing is to get it off to the most important people right away.

Susan was tremendously impressed by Carolyn Heilbrun's speech that she gave at Westbrook as part of the eightieth birthday celebration and which has just been printed now in a book of distinguished women's speeches. I was also delighted and moved by it. Susan thinks it is the best thing that has ever been written about me, about the whole work, and I think she is right.

It is very cold today. We have a little breather because tomorrow is our joint book signing here in York, but today we are going to have a lovely dinner that we do not have to cook and then tomorrow will be the day, again a great effort.

Sunday, November 28, 1993

AFTER SEVERAL beautiful days we are now having an uncommonly harsh one. It is gloomy, with wild rain and wind, and I am afraid at any moment the lights will go out. The sea is pouring into the shore in great fountains of foam, but it seems a laboring day, a day of trees laboring against wind and of me laboring against the depression caused by the darkness and by Susan's leaving today; her having to drive to New York in this weather makes me very anxious.

Yesterday was our book signing at Books Plus in York, and as usual Liz had collected a marvelous number of my books, even to someone who bought *The Poet and the Donkey* for a child. I do not know that the child will like it, but I hope she will. The thing that is most moving to me always is that the people who read me are often such dear people. I love to see their faces and to say a word or two, exchange a word or two with them as I sign books, and people bought a great many books, I guess for Christmas presents. Almost everybody had three or four books with them, and that included Susan's expensive one and my *Encore,* which is after all expensive too. The most touching couple was an elderly couple of whom the wife has the same eye trouble as Susan's mother, macular degeneration, and her husband said, "We've made a whole new time of our marriage because I read aloud to her and so we have a great deal of fun." He bought the *Collected Poems*—I was so glad—to read to her and I think also Susan's book.

There were small children, there were young people, there were older people, it was a various and loving group and a delightful group of people to come into contact with for a brief hour, but of course, I was exhausted at the end. I knew I would be, but it was worth it. It was not a bad exhaustion.

I wanted to find a poem of Yeats's to end this tape with and have just been roving through all the ones I have loved for so many years and suddenly came upon this, which is a comfort to me after that horrible review.

A Coat

I made myself a coat
Covered with embroideries
Out of old mythologies
From heel to throat.
But the fools caught it,
Wore it in the world's eyes
As though they'd wrought it.
Song, let them take it,
For there's more enterprise
In walking naked.

That's good.

Monday, November 29, 1993

I HAD to go to the hospital to give blood because I am still taking Coumadin and it has to be tested every two weeks these days. It was a beautiful, sunny day as I tottered over along the cement sidewalk, which is hard on me, into the hospital. I thought it was rather like coming into a village, a friendly village where many kinds of people pursued various crafts and were all knowledgeable and especially kind so that walking into the hospital was like walking into a serene and helpful space for me, for I am still depressed.

I went after the hospital to sign some books for Liz at Books Plus, where we signed on Saturday. There were a whole lot of people who had called in from as far away as California, God knows where, Texas, to get her to send them books and to get me to sign them. So I did that. It did not take a full hour, but I was spent at the end and came limping home to make myself a good cheese and tomato and bacon sandwich and read the *Times*, which on Monday is not very exhilarating, and then had a good nap with the cat.

I did manage to answer an express letter which contained a return express envelope, and at least that is done. It was hanging over me that I had to do it this afternoon. When I was about to sit down at my lunch, Carol Heilbrun called, such a welcome call. She had been away over the weekend and so had only just seen the review in the *Women's Review of Books*. She was sympathetic about it and also told me, what I did not know, about really terrible reviews she had at the time of her book on androgyny, which was ahead of its time and which I guess shocked some people. She said she had some very bad reviews on it and on, I think, the book that followed it. So she was comforting about how one just has to forget it, but it is hard to get over it at the time. She suggested that I write a humorous letter to the editors; this is hard for me to do, but I have been thinking about it as I had my nap, and if I could do it, it would clear the air. I would not, as I have for the last three nights, wake up at 2:00 A.M. and not get to sleep again. We shall see.

I called Judy and she will come on Wednesday, which is good as I will have a cassette for her then. This one should come to its end.

Friday, December 3, 1993

I HAVE not been recording because I am so busy with Christmas. It is funny how it suddenly seizes on one, and for me it is partly the pleasure of sending out the Christmas poem. It is not a great poem this year; it was hard to do, for one thing, because of its being such a depressing Christmas in so many parts of the world.

I have not spoken of two important lunches. On Thursday I saw Nancy, my former secretary, Nancy Hartley, for the first time in I should think three or four months, and it is always so very good to see her. She is such a wise and, somebody said, such a sane person. So we talked about some of my problems, about my depression, and I think she understood that in some ways I feel very much exposed by Susan's book, which is a wonderful book, but in some ways perhaps I wish that it had appeared after I was dead because I give away so much more.

People always talk about how much I give away, but in Susan's book I give myself unprotected because these are letters to friends originally meant for one person only, and not a journal, which I am aware many people will read. So although I seem to give away a great deal in the journals, I also have kept a great deal private, and now some of that is out there blowing in the wind, and it is painful. I think it is hard for Susan to understand this, naturally enough, because she sees that it is a beautiful book and knows what an enormous amount of work went into it, and she is proud of it and proud of me for my part in it, which is, of course, the whole text. Anyway, Nancy and I had a good time, and I gave her her birthday present, which is a wonderful kind of dark chocolate with pecans that I get from Georgia.

The other momentous luncheon was one with Beverly Hallam and Mary-Leigh Smart. Mary-Leigh owns my house, as I have said before, and we see each other too rarely because we are all three extremely busy. They do an enormous amount for the art world in various ways. Mary-Leigh is on the board of almost every museum in Maine and maybe other places too, and Beverly is a well-known painter. Beverly's mother, Alice Murphy, who is an angel and an extremely beautiful woman, is ninety-three and was lonely and they did not know quite what to do. I suggested they try what I did, which was to go to the hospital, which provides a list of nurses who would like extra or part-time work, and so now Alice, bless her heart, has three delightful young women who work for her and is alive again and feels cherished; one of them is learning to knit as Alice is teaching her. So this is one solution as nobody wants to be put away in a nursing home.

I feel it very strongly for myself that I must somehow manage to be able to pay people to help me here and eventually possibly get one of those chair lifts that go up the stairs. This might be a solution when I cannot climb the stairs anymore. The thing that happens now, which is common in old age, is that I so often forget things that I need that are upstairs when I am downstairs or downstairs when I am upstairs; some of the juggling that I have to do is to ask myself constantly, before I go downstairs, what do I have to take down; before I come upstairs, what am I going to need upstairs that I had better take now so I will not have to go down again?

Saturday, December 4, 1993

THE GLOOMIEST day that it is possible to imagine, there has been heavy rain all night and all through the day, and I almost did not go out to get the paper. Then I made myself do it. But I am feeling less depressed and I think, curiously enough, that a book which I had despised without having read it because it was on the best seller list—*Care of the Soul* by Thomas Moore—is helping me. Dear Amalie Starkey out in New Mexico sent it to me, and I have been reading it and finding it helpful. It is Jungian, so Thomas Moore uses myths a great deal and makes us aware that the shadow is part of everything, that there is always a shadow. One of the first things that impressed me early on in the book is this: "A thirty year old woman comes to me for therapy and confesses, 'I have a terrible time in relationships because I have become too dependent. Help me to be less dependent.' I am being asked to take some soul stuff away."

He then asks, "What is it you find difficult about dependence."

She says, "It makes me feel powerless, besides it isn't

good to be too dependent. I should be my own person."

Finally he says to her, "I wonder if you could find a way to be dependent without feeling disempowered. After all we all depend on each other every minute of the day." And so the talk continues. Finally he decides that he must find a way to champion dependence a little bit as she is so sure that independence is what the soul demands, and he says, "Don't you want to be attached to people, learn from them, get close, rely on friendship, get advice from someone you respect, be part of a community where people need each other, find intimacy with someone that is so delicious that you can't live without it."

"Of course," she says, "is that dependence?"

"It sounds like it to me," I reply, "and like everything else you can't have it without its shadows, its neediness, inferiority, submission, and loss of control."

That really spoke to me—it is pages 6 and 7 of the book, by the way—because I have been feeling frightened by my dependency on Susan when she is here in the summer because when she leaves I feel abandoned, and now I begin to see that that is all right. Let me accept that I am very dependent on her when she is here and that it is a good thing, a part of our relationship as it is.

I managed to wrap the Bengal tiger cub that I am giving Heather Miriam for Christmas. Heather Miriam went off with a stuffed unicorn of mine once when she was four years old and did not know any better and I had to get it back because it had been given to me by somebody I love and they would be disappointed if I did not have it, but I swore to myself that I would find for Christmas for her a wonderful stuffed animal. Lo and behold, from the National Wildlife Federation I saw a photograph of a little tiger cub with quite a long tail who growls softly when you press him. I have had him in the orange velvet Victorian chair that is in the flower room, and he looks perfect there; then, when the cat was frightened of him, it was irresistible to see this huge cat run away with his tail between his legs when the tiny stuffed tiger roared his tiny roar.

Monday, December 6, 1993

IT IS very early in the morning; I have just called Juliette. It is half past six here and eleven-thirty in London. The phone rang quite a long time, and then there she was, absolutely herself, saying, "Love, love, love." But she forgets everything, not remembering whether the wine I sent had arrived, not being able to tell me who is taking care of her now, although I think it is two young women, one of whom works in the daytime, but despite the frustration and the sadness, it was wonderful to hear her voice. She sounds so like herself. Of course I cried because I think we will never meet again. It has been a long love and still is, and it seems too ironic that I cannot get there, that I am so stupidly frail.

I wrote to Bill Brown this morning after I called Juliette because he knew her in Paris and has known about my feelings toward her for a long time, forty years at least. But Bill is not able to come East (he was going to see Susan in New York) because he has high blood pressure and there is the risk of a heart attack, so he has had to give up traveling at least for the time being, and this must be hard. He is ten years younger than I am and has been very well and able to travel, he and Paul together.

But I have to remember that when things are worst, there

is always something that happens that lifts the heart, as simple, perhaps, as putting a little saucer of cream on my breakfast tray for Pierrot in case he comes in. He used always to have a saucer of cream when I had my breakfast, but that lapsed at some point, I don't know why. Now I am trying to resume it because I am delighted to see him put his face way down into the cream, lapping it up. I forgot to ask Juliette about her cat. That is too bad. It was the one thing I had in mind.

It is no fun that the Christmas issue of the *New York Times* book section yesterday in their "Best Books of the Year" did not mention one of the three books I brought out this year, but I must be getting tough, tough enough to bear what I have to bear in this strained life of mine because I did not expect to find those books on the list. Still, the saddest thing was the *Collected Poems* because there was a very short list of books of poems, but they have not reviewed it, you see, and what the editors do is make their list from the books that have been reviewed. They have not reviewed any of the three, though they did review *Encore* in the daily *Times*. Well, there you are. We have not had a review of Susan's book, and it is strange, but I am hoping that within the next week or so we will. But now is the Christmas rush and all these sections on Christmas books which I am not in. We have to depend on the people who know my work.

Susan had a great success at her book signing in Riverdale and sold over eighty books, which is good since it is an expensive book. Lots of her students came, very proud.

Tuesday, December 7, 1993

RUNNING TOWARD Christmas. Every day some Christmas things appear in the mail—today delicious cookies from Peg Umberger and what looks like a wonderful book about the Iroquois for whom she does so much at the museum.

I have been trying to change my view of life here, the daily grind takes so much out of me, and when I finally get upstairs to my desk at ten o'clock, I feel so incompetent that I get depressed, whereas what I should do is look at what I have actually accomplished at eighty-one, not being well, and get a sense of triumph from that. So I am going to put down here what I had to and did do yesterday morning. I got up as usual about five because the cat wanted to be fed and that is the time when I set my breakfast tray that one of the minions will bring up to me at seven-thirty and sometimes rearrange flowers, take a look around at what needs to be done before I make a list for whoever is coming at seven-thirty. But when Nadine did come, she had bad news; she said there was a sour smell in the cellar and went down. There were two inches of water, of sludge. That means that the septic tank, which is supposed to have been completely rebuilt, in fact, a new one was to have been installed, has been making trouble again. The firm was supposed to have installed the new one last month, and of course, we have waited and waited. Well, the first thing I had to do then was call Mary-Leigh, as she is the owner of the house and always efficient. She got hold of the same kind man who had emptied it when we had trouble six weeks ago, and he was to come at noon.

My secretary was coming at nine and did come, and I had to think about what she would do as I have not been good about keeping the journal. I have not been good about it because I am depressed and have lost my impetus. Anyway, Judy came and I did something I have not done before and which I think worked quite well. I dictated a rather long letter of criticism of two short stories that had been sent to me by a good friend and a good writer, but which somehow did not work. To type this myself would have taken perhaps an hour for one paragraph; together we got two pages done in fifteen minutes; it was a tremendous help. Then Judy added up my income so I can have some idea what taxes to expect, and that was a great help. I felt she was able to see that one of my problems is the mail, which brings demands just when I want to get started on the day.

One demand in the mail yesterday was a letter from The Women's Press, who, I am glad to say, are going to republish several books of mine, including *I Knew a Phoenix*, which has not been published in England for a long time. Peter Owen did it in the late fifties, when it first came out here. The Women's Press wanted photographs of me at that time and also for *The House by the Sea*, the journal, and this is not easy because I do not know the files. It was Nancy who kept them and could find something in one second, but Judy did help me find one snapshot sitting at my desk in Nelson which The Women's Press had asked for, and I found several others that may come in handy as they do other books. It is tremendous luck that The Women's Press is bringing out my work. It means I am gradually being built up in England as never before because I have never had a publisher who has done my work, so to speak, only publishers who did one book because they liked that book, as Gollancz did *Faithful Are the Wounds,* and Hutchinson *A Shower of Summer Days*. There is now a solid group of books that is coming out in England.

That was quite a morning, but suddenly by the time I finished that and answered six notes and wrote three thank-you notes for flowers and things, I suddenly realized that it was eleven and time that I must get some fish because I could not possibly eat for a fourth time the chicken cacciatore that Sally had made for the weekend. It had been too rich and not digestible, so off I went to drive to the fish market fifteen minutes away, having first called to be sure they had flounder, which they did. All this meant I did not have my lunch until one.

But when I found myself complaining of how little I got done and how late it was and how it all had postponed my rest, I said to myself, "Rejoice that you could *do* that much. You could not have done that much six months ago, could not have possibly gone on at that rate all morning without a break." So I had a good long nap with the cat, who is in an extremely annoying mood where he will not decide to go in or out, where he asks for food and then will not eat it. I guess it is the weather as it is for all of us.

Today it almost looked like snow, and it still might, but not a heavy snow luckily. Every day my pleasure is writing the Christmas cards and thinking of the people, a continuous pleasure during December and beyond, for it takes me all of January to catch up with what has come in here.

Meanwhile, I think about Colette and enjoy Goudeket for half an hour every day. What has brought me close to Colette has been that after she became crippled, she was living in a small invented paradise which she had to create from her bed. There was the famous collection of paperweights of every kind, the *fanal bleu,* the light with the blue shade which one of her books is called, and her wonderfully relaxed and happy relationship with Goudeket, who perfectly understood that she did not want to talk literature at all but loved to talk about food, about plants, about animals, about her friends, and not at all about her work, about which she was quite secretive, although he did read everything as she wrote it and presumably made suggestions when he wanted to. He emphasizes the strictness of her discipline as far as work went, how she reworked a sentence over and over again, how she was never satisfied so that he was afraid ever to show any reservation about it because she would then say, "Oh, it is no good. I am going to do it all over again," and throw it away. But just as she was disciplined and careful, tremendously careful about writing, she was undisciplined and spontaneous about everything else like selling a house or buying a plant—everything except her animals. One of the saddest things in this book is when the two animals they cared about most, a cat and a small bulldog, both died in the same month, both had to be put to sleep. Colette did not noticeably grieve, but was tremendously silent for a long time, and then much later on, months later, occasionally she would pat the side of her couch where the cat used to come and sit when she was working and say, "Oh, that cat, that cat."

There is a wonderful description of the first of May, going to the forest of Rambouillet, as I have done when all of Paris goes to pick lily of the valley. I am now roughly translating Goudeket:

One day when I was walking rather far from Colette, behind her, I saw her with an imperious gesture push away the bull terrier, Souci, who immediately began to limp as she did every time she had a wicked thought. When I finally reached Colette, I found her on her knees giving me a sign not to go near her or only without making a sound. Among the green leaves of the lily of the valley right on the ground there was a nest occupied by a pheasant sitting on her eggs. In front of this dog, whom she had seen approach, in front of her worst enemy, man, kneeling above her, controlling her panic fear, not allowing her instinct to flee, she stayed immobile and rather than abandon her eggs waited heroically for death, her delicate head held high. You could see her jabot palpitating with anguish. Her hands sheltering her, Colette talked to her very softly, a sort of cooing language that for all we know was perhaps her own, and like the bird, Colette trembled. When sometimes they ask me whether Colette had no metaphysical anguish or anxiety about the ends of man, whether she had not looked for God beyond the creature nor ever found refuge in prayer, I would like my only answer to show her in a scene like this or another of the same sort shaking with pity, fervor, one with all that lives and breathes.

But one must not confuse the ardor of Colette to discover the world, her passionate sensitivity to the being and the object with I don't know what, blind *joie de vivre*. I do not believe that to probe always further than nature and one's own machine, one acquires very much optimism. Across her temperament [or explosions] Colette was grave; there is no respect without gravity. She was capable God knows of childishness but not frivolous; frivolity belongs to man, the vital mystery he has not lived it in his being but to make part of everything that is born, grows, prospers, and declines and can only do so at the price of crime and leads one to pose, to place innocence in principle. What to do then with the distribution of pains and recompenses proposed in the name of a morality that everything one observes contradicts! How to persuade oneself that one must devote one's days to the search for an unknowable abstraction since there is so much else to know, to find out—everything which lives in the grass at your feet, in the trunks, in the bark of even dead trunks, everything which grows and throws itself along to exist! What is this saving of your soul which they demand you to think about? As long as one must help, what are these vain ecstasies? Of what can one repent! And finally, what remains of the grandeur of man if one takes away his solitude, the sentiment of his ephemeral condition, the gratuitousness of his effort?

I go forward here with the greatest precaution. I don't deny that it is hazardous, perhaps hardly honest however well one has known someone, to interpret in this way the most intimate part of her belief. I add that I have not been the master of the meditative hours of Colette when she was embroidering her tapestry, but we respected long and confiding silences between us and that we did not believe that the first causes are a subject of conversation.

Whenever I am translating like this from French, I realize how terribly restricted my vocabulary has become and how many words I have to look up, which is why there have been pauses.

I went down after my nap at half past three and there was a magnificent white cyclamen from Deborah Pease. It is a real mystery because it was the one thing I wanted and craved. I dropped into the florist this afternoon, Foster's, to try to get some bowls to put paper-white narcissus in to give to people, and I was able to get two, but I did not see any large white cyclamen there. It makes the whole house seem festive and beautiful again. The flowers had become rather dismal.

Altogether it has been a good day because I had it to myself and I did do some shopping at eleven. My new pattern seems to be to work from nine to eleven and then to shop. I was able to finish the cassette for Judy, who comes tomorrow, and it has overlapped a little on this one now because of the translating. Now I must do some more cards.

Friday, December 10, 1993

IT IS a day of mourning because the weather is so bad that Susan cannot possibly get here for the weekend and it makes me feel abandoned. There is a wild, warring wind and rain, and it is probably going to rain all night and then possibly begin to snow Saturday night and into Sunday, so one cannot really make plans to do anything. Meanwhile, I had a very good time with Edythe, we had a good lunch together, and after that I have been writing cards.

Today I did one for Roger Sweet and Ann, who used to come here with their five children on their way to camp in Maine and would stay for a brief half hour so we could all catch up. It is a wonderful family. Roger is a doctor who was at Massachusetts General and now retired. They are living in Sullivan right next door to Nelson and they are meeting all the things you meet when you start to live year-round in an old house. At the moment I think Roger is having to dig a new septic tank, and that is going to be going on here very soon, I hope, because once more the cellar was flooded. A nice man came and found that there was some kind of obstacle and got rid of it, so now it is all right for a while.

One is still shocked, in a state of cold shock, at this murderous man who enters a train on Long Island at the rush hour out of hatred of the rich and white and shoots people. Five or six are dead, I do not know how many wounded.

. . . and that was interrupted by Deborah Pease, bless her heart, who called up because she was moved by the Christmas poem and I believe that I did something that I wanted to do in that poem, and depressed as I am, it is thrilling to see that it is making its way into people's hearts. . . .

I do not know what else is to be said. We live with terror.

Saturday, December 11, 1993

I THINK this must be one of the most miserable days that has ever been at Wild Knoll. It is steady rain, it is warm, which sounds good but is not good at this season; the garden has been covered with salt hay, and now everything is unfrozen. Susan was to have come this weekend and oh, I looked forward so much to seeing her, but of course, the weather is impossible. It is supposed to start snowing tomorrow afternoon, and she would have come in this pouring rain and driven home in snow, two dangerous drives for her and too exhausting.

In some ways a very frustrating day so far. Now it is half past four and perhaps I shall get something done at my desk. Last night I finished with real regret a best-selling novel called *Colony* by Anne Rivers Siddons, who I gather has written quite a few novels and has a high reputation. I was fascinated by it. It is laid in Maine in a kind of colony which might be Camden, or a little smaller than that perhaps, one of the islands like North Haven, that is what it made me think of. It is concerned with a group of rich people who have been coming there for fifty years or more dominated by the old women. When they die off, a new set of old women come to sit on the porch of the club. The book is not literature. I kept asking myself, "Why isn't it?" It isn't because Anne Rivers Siddons overplots, there is never any rest; in every chapter somebody drowns, somebody is nearly murdered, somebody tries to rape a young girl. There is always drama, and it is interesting because she writes well. When, for about maybe two pages, she describes the sun setting over the bay, she does it beautifully, and the characters are all quite convincing and in depth, but it is this constant explosion of action, of drama which both makes you read it very avidly and also know that you will never read it again.

How little plotting there is in my novels! In fact, I used to tell my students situation and character are life to a short story and plot kills. Plot kills something, there is no doubt, and in the kind of writer that Katherine Mansfield was, plot is not the point. It is something else. The same thing with Virginia Woolf. You might say that in *To the Lighthouse* very little happens except inwardly, in the characters, but people go back to reread books where not much may be happening but a great deal of life is being created.

The great event today was Dean Frieze coming as he did last year to help me put up the tree, and I got down two of the former stands to set the tree in. Dean tried first the bigger one, but he could not seem to get the tree to stand up and not fall over sideways. Unfortunately it is a fat tree, wide, and not very high. In fact, it is about as high as I am, and this may explain why it does not stand up easily, it leans over from one side to the other. Finally Dean thought he had it, we had tried a smaller, newer stand, and then it did fall over, and he said, "Well, we have to go back to the other."

This man is so patient and so dear about things like this. He will go on for an hour as he had to do, as he did, fussing with something and never swear and be as calm and gentle and interested as can be. It was a lesson to me because I was amazed that he never swore. Finally he went back to the first stand, the bigger one, and set it up, and I hope that this has done the trick. But then at noon he knocked on the door again and came back with a new much bigger and better stand and wanted to put that on, and I said, "No, Dean, let's take a chance and then we have this in reserve if by any chance it falls over. I don't think it will. It seems quite straight."

Meanwhile, while I was having my hair done, Margaret Whalen brought her manuscript. Margaret retired from teaching fourth grade for God knows how many years and began to write a book about her experiences, about all she was thinking about, and I am dying to read it. It is there on my bed, and I shall start it tonight. With it she left a new pen because yesterday, when she came to get me to sign something, I could not find a pen. She brought a beautiful pen. It is a wonderful gift. I am overwhelmed by the kindness of everyone.

Monday, December 13, 1993

I CANNOT believe it is almost halfway through December and very close to Christmas; at last I begin to feel the Christmas spirit. I managed yesterday to put the little lights on the tree, and this is quite a job, which Edythe always did, and I did not think I could do. It shows that when you have to do something, you can do it, sometimes anyway. I was weary but triumphant. I realized then that it is not one spectacular job like that which you summon yourself to do—and the adrenaline helps—but it is the hundred little things, like being sure

there is toilet paper in the downstairs bathroom or soap somewhere or towels out for a guest, and all that means going up
and down stairs in this house and walking long distances,
which takes its toll.

It was a difficult weekend in which I think for the first
time I faced the fact that the way I am living now is not really
possible. I do not have the energy to do it and also to carry on
a professional life which is quite successful, but that success
means constant business letters. Now The Women's Press is
considering another book of poems, and there is correspondence about that which came in today. I did write seven
cards. I must have written more than a hundred.

As for what I receive, there is a dearth this year of really
beautiful cards. I did get an amusing one from Doris Grumbach; it was good to laugh as I opened the mail.

The whole business of how to handle my life here is quite
troubling. Luckily Susan will have half a year off from school
in which she is going to be working very hard on my *Selected
Letters*, but I think she will be able to come here a little more
often or at least not in quite such a traumatic way because if
she is not teaching on Monday and the weather is bad, she can
wait for another day, and that is what has made her coming
for weekends exhausting, driving a long distance in the rain
Friday night, getting in at eleven, and having to leave again at
eleven on Sunday and perhaps again driving in bad weather.
This must not happen because she has too much on her plate,
but she looks well. Troubles aside, I still love Christmas and
look forward to Judy Matlack's nephew and his wife, Timmy
and Phyllis, the closest thing to family that I have on earth
now, coming at two and to get the *Collected Poems* I am
giving them.

On Saturday, which was the worst day, the day that it
rained continuously and I cried a great deal and realized I was
going to have to change my way of life in some way, get more

help, that evening I finally started Margaret Whalen's book, which she has been writing for a year now and revising, having learned to use a computer to do it. This is a very interesting book. In fact, it gave me back a sense of life when I was feeling quite desparate. Saturday night; it galvanized me and made me realize among other things what an extraordinary woman Margaret is, but that is no news to me.

The book is fascinating because it combines several books which do not altogether merge, and this is what will make it difficult to sell, I fear. Perhaps it should be published by a Maine publisher who would be interested in the fact that this is a woman, a Maine woman, who lives in Maine, who writes beautifully about what she sees from her windows every day, for instance, the weather. I loved coming to this every day, whether the sun was rising or not. Some people have complained that there was too much weather in my journals, but I do not think so when I read this which describes weather practically every day and I delight in it.

But there is a great deal about teaching, and about teaching thirty children in the first grade up to the fourth, and I am amazed at how progressive Margaret and all the teachers in that school were, a public school in Exeter, New Hampshire. She was so inventive. She soon stopped using any kind of reader and got the children to go to sources, to learn to use dictionaries and encyclopedias, and to study things right there before their eyes. She never had any problems with discipline because the children were so interested, and I was amused at how clever she was just before the holidays, when there is always restlessness. She allowed each child to do whatever he wanted to, so some were reading, some were making drawings, some were writing, and they were all so concentrated because they had *chosen* to do this, whatever it was, that there was no problem with agitation or restlessness.

And then, of course, there is the immense compassion

which is in her and everything she does. Her insistence that we must take children as they are and not try to change them too fast, let them go; in fact, the motif of her book might be "let them go," so that even a child who has great difficulty reading, as incidentally, I did, can be prevented from feeling inferior if the teacher is good enough. Loss of self-esteem is the hardest thing for a child, Margaret insists over and over again, and you simply must not beat a child down, verbally say, "That's no good," because it can have such a deleterious effect and last a lifetime. I am sure that nobody in her classes ever felt that they were anything less than special and that her attention to them was complete and not condescending. Some people condescend to children, and I think children feel it immediately, feel left out. The only problem about Margaret's book for the average reader is that a great deal of the part about education, fascinating as it is, is abstract, so it comes alive when she describes a single child doing something or not doing something, but when we come to the abstractions, the generalities, then some readers may get lost or not be completely satisfied. I am not quite sure what she can do about this.

It is a compendium of a book which gives us the many sides of a many-sided person because Margaret is a great cook. She thinks nothing of inviting twenty people for dinner, twenty old colleagues of hers, and they love to come as anybody would to her remarkable house right on the sea at Cape Neddick, where Susan and I have been several times for wonderful dinners and talk. The talk is always good. I consider the arrival of Margaret and Barbara into my life as one of the real blessed events of the last two or three years. As far as people who have become real friends, Dean and Sylvia Frieze and Margaret and Barbara are the outstanding examples, and I am enormously grateful for their being here. Sylvia made some brownies when she heard how depressed I was, and they are such a treat I can hardly wait to go down and get my lunch and have one.

It is a grief to have finished *Près de Colette,* which has meant so much to me in these last days. What an astonishing person she was! One of the most moving things is when she dies, Her coffin was raised up in the courtyard of the Palais Royal, where she lived and guarded by the Garde Républicaine. For three days an uninterrupted flow of people came to pay their respects, the whole of Paris one would have said, every kind of person from the simplest workman to the aristocracy itself. She was so loved by so many different kinds of people, and at the end, in the last years when she was so badly crippled, I think that her marvelous courage and indomitable need to go on creating, whatever happened, captured the imagination of the French after World War II in a way that nobody else could. So her funeral was one of the great funerals of the twentieth century, in any country because very, very rarely, for one thing, does a writer have such a wide appeal as she had. Also, the wild success and glory that she came into at the end of her life, in her eighties, when she was totally crippled, never changed her in any way. She was still wholly herself, absolutely natural, brushing praise aside always, and so interested in other people's lives. Everybody who worked for her became like a member of the family. I felt the loss when I read of her dying exactly as if I had known her personally and as if this had happened the day before. Ah, Colette, I now know you better than I thought I could due to this wonderful book and I feel I have lost a friend.

It is now half past four, the same day, and I have had a little rest after a wonderful hour with Judy Matlack's nephew Timothy Matlack Warren, and Phyllis, his wife, my family now. Phyllis made cookies; she makes the best, the traditional Christmas cookie. I do not know why they are so good. They are thin and taste very buttery. Naturally we remembered things about Judy. A wonderful find has taken place at Tim's business office. They found two hundred copies of my little book about Judy, *Honey in the Hive,* and this is good news as I think I only have one copy left except the bound copy in the library.

Tim delighted me by being pleased with what I wore. I got out a very heavy old sweater, but it has a nice scarf at the throat, and my dark blue Ultrasuede jacket. It did look handsome together. Also a pair of lovely purple socks knitted for me by an English friend, and Timmy remarked on them.

The time went very fast. I read them the Christmas poem and gave them the *Collected Poems,* which I think is what they really wanted; it was good and comforting to read the Christmas poem and feel they liked it. Phyllis said, "It's less personal. Your Christmas poems lately have been very personal." That's true and I think this is personal too, but of course, it's the way it is stated; it is "we" instead of "I," so to speak, and that makes a big difference right away.

It is still an absolutely dismal day, and it seems as if it might snow. The tree is beautiful, and every now and then I put on another shining ball so that there will not be an awful lot for Edythe to do tomorrow, but we shall enjoy doing it. This tree has such wide branches that it needs a great deal of decorating.

TAPE FOR December 13 to December 21 was empty; we think it was the other recorder.

Tuesday, December 21, 1993

An incredibly wild rainstorm is going on, and I went out to take the rubbish out at half past six this morning; the cat came with me and took refuge in the garage, which was open because of the rubbish going, and now he is still there and will not come home. In a little while I must put on some rubber boots and see if I can get him. It does not feel right without him.

Mostly I want to get back to Jamey and her friend Cindy, who were coming at noon when Maggie was here on Saturday; they always bring an enormous amount of life into the house. This time they had had an adventure making a present for Cindy's mother and for me, a video of how they live, showing the house and all the things they have done to it. It was a simple little house, but they have worked hard and one can sense how full of life it is because of what they have built there, their skills, their interests, and wonderful animals—Cindy has snakes, tropical fish, a police dog puppy. Jamey has a very old dog and a very old cat, and there is another cat. But the main reason I think they were so anxious for us to see the photos was the ferrets. They have four ferrets. Unfortunately both Maggie and I have the same reaction to ferrets, which is almost nausea. They seem so elusive. But these are pets, and they are tranquil and affectionate, very little trouble and do not eat a great deal like a dog or a cat. They seem to be perfect pets for Jamey and Cindy, so it was good to see the photos.

They came at noon and I did not give them lunch, but we had some coffee cake and some of Susan's sparkling nonalcoholic cider which was absolutely perfect; I am grateful to her because she keeps a case of it in the cellar and has told me that I can always use it if I need it.

That night Maggie and I had dinner with Margaret and Barbara at Clay Hill Farms, a restaurant in a pastoral setting. Barbara still teaches, and of course, I was full of things that I wanted to talk with Margaret about from reading her book. One of them was the marvelous, inventive thing she does with the fourth grade, sometimes using van Gogh. All over the room she hangs reproductions of the van Gogh paintings, *The Chair, Starry Night*, and so on. She does not say anything about them, they are just there for the whole semester and only at the end of the semester does she tell the children about van Gogh and by then they know these paintings almost by heart and they are fascinated, of course, to find out about the artist and his life. "Fascinated by his cutting off his ear," she says, and they end by each painting a copy of the painting they like the best. I can see that this works because in some ways the paintings are very simple. The children then take their versions home after they have hung in the hall for a little while.

It was hard to see Maggie go yesterday. Although the sun was out, the house felt terribly empty when she had gone. It takes awhile to remake what the house and I are alone. Right now it is very bad that the cat is out when I need him most, so I think I am going to see if I can get him.

Wednesday, December 22, 1993

AFTER THE most incredible wind and rain yesterday, which would have meant two or three feet of snow had it been snow, today is windy and sunny, a beautiful day. A great relief. But today was strangely depressing. I could not open the door because the wind was so high; the cat simply did not come out of the cellar until four, which was very worrying to me, but thank goodness today he came out when I called after my lunch so we had a nice snooze and rest although the men who seem to come every day at one about the septic tank and make noises outside just when I am resting are there again, but I closed two doors and it was not too bad.

Everything is piling up. Flowers come every day, which, of course, is wonderful but also tires me out trying to arrange them. There was a great red and white bunch from Phyllis Chiemingo, and they are beautiful by the tree. Then the most lovely ones arrived this afternoon from Mary Ann Parnell, white tulips and six magnificent anemones, purple and lavender and red and almost white, and the combination with the white tulips is staggeringly beautiful. I cannot wait to go down and look at them.

A lot of Christmas cards this year have angels in them so I think I must make a show on the mantelpiece, take out what I have there and make a show of angels. But underneath this hurly-burly of Christmas all is a static depression, which I think is going to be there now forever, because it is based on the fact that I recognize at long last that I will never make it as a writer in the canon. I do have readers—and God bless them—but I do not have any place in the literary world, and this is a fact. I must admit that I see a little bit why it is. I came just too late; if I had been born ten years earlier and been a contemporary of Amy Lowell and Louise Bogan, I would have fit in. As it was, I came at a time when people were turning against form. I get a lot of this from Adrienne Rich's book, which got fantastic reviews. I believe she is a great moralist. Whatever she says comes from some kind of sibyl as far as the critical attention she gets. One cannot help admiring her, however, and I am glad that I knew her when she was young; at that time I felt that we were real friends. That was before her divorce and before she became a lesbian.

Christmas Eve, 1993

AND AGAIN a beautiful day. I had an extraordinary night, something which happens to me almost never, which was that I had three separate erotic dreams, two of them with people whom I know and would never think of in that way and one with a total stranger. It was unpleasant. I was quite aware of what I was doing and enjoying it, but when I woke up, I did not like it at all. I was upset. I have also twice dreamed that Juliette was dying, and this frightens me. But it was wonderful today to get a dear card from her just saying "Dearest May" which I could barely read and then the message and signature. I hope I will remember and try to get her tomorrow morning.

What was wonderful yesterday was Susan; it is so good having her here and everything being so ordered. At the very last minute, before I got up from my rest, a dozen red roses came—there have been so many flowers this time, there are a dozen white roses in my bedroom, also beautiful, from Pat Chasse, and downstairs some tulips and anemones, just glorious. Altogether the house is amazingly festive. The tree is lovely; Susan says it is very European, I do not know why, but it is charming. It is a small tree, not higher than I am.

Now it is exciting to know that *Among the Usual Days* may be going into a second printing and my *Encore* already has and that the Japanese are buying *Plant Dreaming Deep* for a generous advance. This will help next year, when I am not going to be producing much.

It is a peaceful day and a relief that nothing much is happening. Now I am trying to correct proof, as there are some mistakes and typos in *Among the Usual Days*.

Saturday, December 25, 1993, Christmas Day

IT SEEMED like magic to wake up to a gradual flaky snow, large flakes, that have left less than an inch, but at least with the frost and the snow it was a magical sight early this morning, and peaceful having Susan here, but I have a strong feeling that this is the last Christmas. There is something of a farewell now in everything I do—writing Christmas cards, will I ever be able to do it another year? I cannot imagine it. It has been an incredible effort this year, and the disorder that it leaves behind with all the people I still should write to and the cards giving out. I do not know. It seems to me I have come to the end, and when you come to the end, then you die.

It was fun being with Margaret and Barbara, who came at

CREDIT: SUSAN SHERMAN

The field in snow, a lovely landscape.

agreed we would not do that this year, so we had nothing for them, but we have given them the three books. Also, I have not been as generous as usual this Christmas because I simply could not pack presents. So what I did was done by mail, by catalog or something like that.

Susan and I had decided not to exchange gifts, but then she gave me—not for Christmas, she said—a magnificently bound copy of *Among the Usual Days*, and this is a once-in-a-lifetime present because there will never be another book like hers. I have never seen such a beautiful binding; it is overwhelming. That has made it a great Christmas in itself.

And I have had many calls from friends. It will be in some ways a relief when there is not quite so much mail, but it has been very exciting getting all the letters and the cards and the photographs, and I shall miss that excitement.

There is a slight nervousness about Martha Wheelock coming on Tuesday to start shooting a film she wants to make about old age. She will use me as an example, I suppose.

A peaceful Christmas. What could be better than that?

Sunday, December 26, 1993

THERE WAS more snow, so it is a lovely landscape now; we have not had this view for a long time. I suppose that the day after Christmas is always a letdown. My desk is a sea of letters and cards, and considering how many I have written it is appalling that there is still such a pile; that depresses me. I am in a quandary as to how much to say about the depression I am in because it is not right to lay this on my reader, and yet there is a shadow over everything, a chronic depression because I cannot shake the belief that my work has missed the boat.

What I should do at these times is remember Hilaire Belloc, who said of his own work: "His sins were scarlet, but his books were read."

I should remember that I have been lucky from the beginning in the quality of the response to my work as people of all ages and from all of the states write me letters. Even now they come, a few every week, to assure me that what I have written works toward greater understanding. Maybe that response is as meaningful, more so, than recognition by the critical canon.

I still have joys, and one of them was watching my cat

wash his paw this morning. He does it with zest; he loves to wash his paw. He draws out the claws so he can wash them carefully, he nibbles at the soles with extreme intensity, and then he stretches out his back paws and rests. This is a great sight.

Monday, December 27, 1993

WELL, THIS is what it is like to live in Maine in the winter. At seven Joan, one of my minions, called to say her car would not start. Luckily Susan is here so she was able to bring my breakfast, but a little later Susan announced that her toilet was not flushing so there must be something wrong; so I got Fabrizio, Ralph Fabrizio, who is such a dependable man, and he was able to come, but unfortunately, since he was actually working in York, he had not brought what he needs to defreeze the frozen pipe, so he had to go back to Portsmouth to get it. He thinks that this has not happened in that particular place for five or six years, and it is just a fluke; the wind must have been at a certain crack, just bad luck, and he thinks it may not happen again.

Meanwhile, Martha Wheelock is coming to make the film about old age, and here we are with the risk of no water, and the people installing the new septic tank are on the last days of that and there is terrible noise although they promised not to start till nine-thirty or ten. It is so cold, the wind chill twenty below zero today, that I am hoping they may not come at all. It is pretty harsh weather to work outdoors.

Friday, December 31, 1993

IT IS New Year's Eve, and we have powdery white snow and brilliant sunshine. It is a magnificent winter day here, but we have been having all the problems of Maine in the winter. In addition to Susan's frozen pipe, the people who are supposed to be putting in the new septic tank have not been here all week because it has been too windy or too cold, and then it snowed.

Last night we went out to the Friezes for drinks. Their house is gracious and elegant, and going there is a party in itself. Someone had told Dean about a toy parrot which talks, and he was able to find one, which is on batteries and which, when you say, "How are you?" says, "How are you?" Whatever you say, he says back. It is terribly funny. I have not laughed for a long time as I laughed yesterday afternoon; we had a lovely time. We were there an hour, but when we came back, the heat was off and the temperature in the house had dropped to sixty; it felt terribly cold, so I called Goodwin Oil. Their line was busy; I guess there were lots of people in trouble last night, but pretty soon I got through, and they were helpful. Within half an hour a man came and thought he had found the answer when a nozzle was somehow not allowing oil to flow, so he fixed that, and we went to bed in the cold, but with our electric blankets and with the idea that everything would be fine the next day. In fact, we left the heat on at seventy for the night at his suggestion, but when I got up at five and went down to feed the cat, it was freezing cold and the furnace had gone off again in the night. So at five I called

Goodwin Oil again, and they said they would be there within an hour, which is wonderful at five in the morning at God knows how much below zero. So the same genial man came, after he worked at three other places, and decided it was the transformer that needed changing and then the motor itself. I had to tell Mary-Leigh, who has had so much trouble with this house, everything is wearing out because it is an old house. She was, as always, extremely kind about it. He will be back later today with still something else to be brought.

So there we are, and Susan leaves tomorrow for New York. Luckily it looks as though there will not be a snowstorm though perhaps on Monday there will be. I am dreading her going because all this trouble would have been much worse if she had not been here and together we could laugh about it. Now it will be lonely and I am dreading having to cope, but that is life and it is better for me to have to cope sometimes than to be completely dependent.

I did most of the quarterly Social Security for Eleanor Perkins. It is always such a trauma, I do not know why, but it is hard for me to do these things.

I did manage to write a letter to Betty Voelker, who every Christmas makes a real stocking (only it is in a box) of a whole group of darling little presents. The main thing about them is the way they are wrapped so that the whole series when I put it under the tree is a feast for the eyes, and I never want to open these presents because they look so beautiful.

Yesterday Susan helped me put away the four bottles of Piper Heidsieck champagne which Mary-Leigh and Beverly so kindly gave me. By next year I should not have any presents at all. Forget about Christmas. But the tree has been a joy this year.

Saturday, New Year's Day

I CALLED all over the place because I was feeling so lonely and everyone was having a hard time. But then at half past one, dear Fred Rogers called. It was a lifesaving call, and I think this is typical of that wonderful man. If ever a human being carried out E. M. Forster's saying "Only connect," it is Fred because I told him I was awfully depressed. I also said, "I am eighty-one, you know," and he laughed and said, "Everyone all over the world knows you're eighty-one." And then he told me that I must remember how people know and love the work but in such a gentle and believable way that it did me a great deal of good. He called from Florida, where he and his wife are staying with their son.

Sunday, January 2, 1994

AGAIN IT was gray, but now it is brilliant again although we are warned that there may be a real blizzard on the way Tuesday and Wednesday, so I wonder whether Anne and Barbara will be able to get here for our New Year lobsters. I hate holidays. All the routine things are not there. No mail yesterday, New Year's Day. But Susan and I had a good day in spite of the furnace, which did not work the day before. Susan left yesterday, leaving the house feeling terribly empty and strange. But I am little by little recapturing my solitude; it always takes time as solitude seems to be a shy deer these days.

The problem right now in the immediate surroundings of my life is that I have no wonderful book to look forward to at night when I get into bed having done the dishes and feeling that I need a reward. What I need is a marvelous biography like Marguerite Yourcenar's, but that is not around, and I think what I must do is find something, perhaps start rereading. I have been thinking lately about Elizabeth Bowen's *The Little Girls,* thinking about my own childhood and how exclusive little girls are. Barbara Runkle and I and Mary Atkins had a secret place where we hid cookies and things in the lilac bushes and were very upset when we thought somebody had found it.

On that subject in a roundabout way, I was interested in the *Times* yesterday where there was an article on some people in California who are trying to reach the neo-Nazis when they have only just joined these hate groups, when they have perhaps only been a month in the group and therefore might still be willing to look at the truth. I think they had two days of showing films of concentration camps, of people talking to them from various races, and at least two of the men or boys said that they did not want anything to do with the skinheads anymore, but others were on the defensive and said that people were against them and did not try to understand them and so on. It is an extremely good idea, it seems to me, to try to reach people before it is too late.

I HAVE been scrounging around on my desk, answered a letter written last September from a woman who sent me some children's poems which were really quite interesting that I had never gotten around to answering. I still have not thanked

Charles for his wonderful black and gold scarf that he sent me for Christmas, and I meant to do that. Maybe I will this afternoon. Edythe is coming for lunch; it is lovely to see her, a whiff of joy in the day.

The cat, I am sorry to say, is spraying in different places now, and I have to keep screaming at him not to do it. He does know that he should not do it because he stops and rushes out before I scream.

Tuesday, January 4, 1994

WE ARE in the middle of a horrible blizzard, horrible because it has every hazard in it. It started with snow, fine wet snow all night, but actually only four or five inches. But now it is blowing hard and raining and freezing; by this afternoon it is supposed to be snowing again. We are in for seven hours more apparently. Inland they may get twenty-five inches; it is a huge storm, and the danger is the freezing. I cannot get out. They did plow once, but obviously the real plowing will happen tonight. They did not shovel my path, and David Leavitt has said that he will come tomorrow morning, so I hope by morning I will be able to get out.

Meanwhile, everything piles up. A Providence television station is coming on Friday to interview me. It really is not what I need right now, but I cannot say no. It is to help Susan's book, *Among the Usual Days*, and we do want that to get a break.

I did receive a moving letter yesterday dated the twenty-eighth of December. It took awhile to reach me. This is from a sixty-two-year-old woman, and she says:

I have just finished reading *Encore*, which you say may be the last of your journals. I shall miss them. They and your poetry have given me sustenance, a calming, and strength at times when the world was all too much with me. I thank you for that sharing of yourself at a level that was at once intimate and global. So many times responsive chords were struck in me, and in them I find a renewed sense of delight and wonder at my own life.

That made me happy, and I must say that it is not unlike a great many letters that I receive, maybe two or three a week, so I should not mind so much about the critics. I realize that. If I can give somebody a sense of her own life again, that is the best thing you can be told. I am thrilled as I think about it.

But it is a strange feeling being marooned here. The cat is asleep with the stuffed tiger cub that I gave myself for Christmas, having missed the one I gave Heather; he has taken a liking to it. For a while it was a panda that he loved, a big one that is in the hall, and he used to sleep with his head on its knee very sweetly. I must not forget that he did, after all, have five brothers and was taken from that happy family to a solitary life with me.

Wednesday, January 5, 1993

IT SEEMS extraordinary that already a week of January is nearly gone. Somehow or other having a whole day dropped out because of the storm Tuesday has altered everything. I feel in a terrible rush as if I had missed the bus. It was frustrating not to be able to get out yesterday at all. This morning they did shovel my path, so ever since 4:00 A.M. I have been trying to get myself up and dressed in some warm clothes over my pajamas to go out and bring the rubbish out from the garage. They had promised yesterday that they would come and get it because I had not been able to take it out in the storm. It was slippery out there, but I did see the beginning of the sunrise and that is always exciting in the snow. Pierrot went out with me but was anxious to come back indoors as soon as I did.

I am learning to say no. I decided to tell the people from Providence who wanted to come and do a video interview on Friday that I simply could not do it. There is supposed to be another storm Thursday night, and then I will again be trapped here, unable to get my hair done and unable to pull myself together.

It is somehow disorganized, the life here. But today I did manage to get some food in, and I think I can carry things a little better than I used to be able to, even six months ago, so that is a good sign. I carried quite a heavy package in today, and I got a lot of stamps, so I am well supplied for anywhere from Tokyo to Canada.

I am reading a fascinating book by an English writer whose name at the moment escapes me. He has written two or three novels. I have ordered Sean O'Faolain's autobiography, *Vive Moi!* He boasts of having been Elizabeth Bowen's lover as well as two or three other famous women, and it will be interesting to see what he has to say about them. He broke Edith Kennedy's heart in the twenties, and I can never forgive him for that. It was done in a dastardly way, and of course, these things disappear and nobody knows, but I do not think of him with anything approaching love.

In the book I am beginning it says that it is easier to remember bad things than happy ones, that happiness is the hardest thing to describe, and I believe this. When I want to think about happiness, I think about Ogunquit when I was a child, about playing in the sand in the dunes because then, at four, I was allowed to take off my bathing suit and enjoy the sun and the wind. In one photograph I am seen with my arms outstretched and apparently was saying, "I am gathering the wind." I think about those days and how happy my childhood was in spite of realizing my mother was not always happy and not knowing why, but I was a free child, free to do what I wanted, and I always had lots that I wanted to do. But I also sometimes hear my whining child voice saying, "What shall I do now, Mummy?"

I felt a little bit like that yesterday when I could not get out of here and was too tired to invent something. I could have gotten started on the book about Pierrot, but this eludes me at the moment. It will have to wait. But I think the time of year is a very low one for me as far as creativity goes.

So I am learning how to say no. Not only did I refuse to let the people from Providence come, but I canceled an appointment with Dr. Petrovich which is simply a checkup and not essential. The idea that I would have to wait over an hour there, it never is less, and become exhausted by waiting, when there is little he can do for me except listen to my heart and say that it is just the same, made me feel I could cancel the appointment.

Today it was wonderful to have mail after no mail yesterday. There were lots of magazines, a poignant leading article in *Newsweek* about how frightened children are. They are told all the time, "Don't speak to anybody, don't answer if somebody tried to make friends with you," and they are aware that other children have been kidnapped and even killed. It seems terrible to have darkness and fear now around childhood, the time when one almost took for granted that there would not be much anxiety, that one would be free of the anxieties that come later, though that was not altogether true.

LONG GAP on tape.

IN TODAY's mail a sheaf of my mother's letters and photographs, family photographs, came from Janet Mann as part of her settling her mother's estate. There is a remarkable photograph of my mother which I do not think I have and the best photograph of my grandmother Elwes I have seen. Mother's handwriting makes me cry to see it, that beautiful hand, and what marvelous letters she wrote. Opening this package and looking at it when I should be doing other things has made me suddenly realize why perhaps I feel so queer and unreal these days, and I do. I tried to explain it to Edythe at lunch and, although I could not, kept saying, "I don't feel real." I think it is because I am poised on the past as well as the present and what little there may be of the future. The past is obsessive. I realize I ought to be making lists of where I am to leave things; I am very aware of the fact that things are going to end here because I am going to die after all, and there is no family. I have to plan and try to plan well. This is partly because of my being reminded by Polly Starr very rightly that her marvelous portrait of me at twenty-six which is in the front hall here goes to the Fogg Museum at my death, and I have now written letters to all the people, including Timothy Warren, my executor, to explain that this must be done. There are endless details. I never get through the woods anymore.

As I continually say, perhaps out of self-protection, I want to live in the present. I want to enjoy what is here, now. Something not enjoyable, another storm, is expected tomorrow. I was hoping Karen could take me to Portsmouth as we planned, but it looks as if it will be snowing hard at nine tomorrow and perhaps most of the day, we do not know yet. Everything feels difficult.

I did have a little talk with Carol Houck Smith, my editor at Norton for the poems, and she told me one piece of not very good news. The *Collected Poems* have sold only forty-five hundred, which is not much, but it is still very early, and she tried to cheer me up by telling me that I had no idea how many *The Fur Person* had sold over the years, and that is a hundred thousand since the reissue of 1983. So that was cheering.

Then Eric called about Duffy's book of her photographs and my work, which he feared would be competitive with Susan's, but I really do not think so; it will not come out for a long time and is not really anything like Susan's. It is all from work that is already available; there is nothing new.

This morning Judy came and did some typing of the journal, but we found to my chagrin that I had recorded a whole cassette which apparently had not taken. It is empty, an entire week lost, the week before Christmas when all the preparations for Christmas were absorbing. I was sending out endless Christmas poems; Edythe and I decked the tree as we always do. I am sorry to have lost it all.

We did not have snow until much later than expected. Now it seems we are really in for a terrible winter, and I cannot say that I am ready. Quite the opposite. I am not ready, and I want to be a hibernating animal more than anything in the world.

Sunday, January 9, 1994

I LOOK out at four o'clock on an enormous white field and beyond it an immense dark ocean divided from a faint yellow sky changing to blue as it rises. So this storm is over, and David came and even shoveled the roof. The flat roof of the cozy room where I eat which occasionally leaks; in order to prevent that, he did it for me. Maggie is here and made us a cheese soufflé for lunch, a great success.

I have put some Vaseline on Pierrot's paws because I think he needs a laxative and maybe this will do it. I got terribly anxious about him yesterday and could not sleep from four this morning on because I foolishly decided that he must be quite ill and that he may be, which was a dangerous idea, had no saliva because his coat is so rough, but Edythe told me this afternoon when we talked that this has to do with the weather; something happens to the fur. Apparently even her dear little shelty looks a little, what shall we say, shabby is not the right word . . . I had the word a few moments ago.

It has been a dull day, as yesterday also was, in spite of Maggie's beneficent presence and the facts that we always laugh a lot and that she does accomplish incredible things. Today she cleaned out the bird feeder that she gave me which shuts squirrels out automatically because their weight forces the door down, and it apparently had become not exactly blocked but needed cleaning out, and this she did. Now the birds can eat in peace. I noticed that something was wrong but did not have the courage to go out in this bitter cold. The wind chill is twenty below.

I should be tackling the book on Pierrot, but right now I have no zest, no impulse to work. I feel a stupid old woman, but that is very wrong of me and so I turned to a wonderful poem of Ruth Pitter's. Of course, this is old-fashioned diction, but it does not matter to me because I think it is a pure poem.

The Difference

There in the field hear the voice of the lark daylong
That leaps up loud with his love into the clear grey:
But if the nest were harried
And the mate that he married
Were fled from the place, he must cease from the song:
But you must sing ever in spite of all wrong,
Whatever is lost, strayed, or stolen away.

There by the water behold the beautiful face
Of the flower that looks up into the smile of the day:
But if the spring were failing,
Or the cold wind were wailing,
She would sink, would fall down there, would die in her
  grace:
But you must bloom still in the desolate place,
Whatever is frozen or withered away.

I am very aware of the whole concept of language, but the whole avant-garde is out to get at the language, which certainly leaves me out somewhere in the cold. The deconstruction of language. Who wants it?

Monday, January 10, 1994

THINGS ARE at last somewhat in order after the battle with the elements. I look out on a magnificent white field and then that blue, that extraordinary winter blue of the ocean, and feel that somehow the house is blessed and the New Year started as it should be with a sense of order and of being in control which I have not had for a long time. The fact that I have it now is because Maggie has been here for the weekend. She imagines all kinds of things that need doing and does them. I have no friend who has this kind of imagination and also competence, and this time she even installed a light on the dangerously dark cellar stairs and insulated the cat door to make it narrower, so there will not be quite such a draft into the cellar—we discovered Susan's pipe froze because of the angle of the wind coming in through the cat door. Maggie also perceived that Pierrot was not feeling well, and I, too, was worried about him. She decided to shovel a corridor for him near his cat door so he could go in and out and have somewhere to go other than soft snow into which he might disappear.

What else did she do? The great thing was to remove the orchids from the chest in the library where they have been all fall. There are too many and are a little ragged so that the beauty of the few objects I keep there was destroyed and a kind of disorder had taken its place. Now Maggie has moved those, and Joan this morning took them up to the second floor, where I think they will be happy. Meanwhile, Maggie rubbed the top of that big chest so it glows; it was dry because of the central heating, which is ruinous to furniture of any value.

She cooked lovely meals in addition to the cheese soufflé, and made an apple pie which she does not often do. We had it three times. That is my idea of a real holiday, to have apple pie three times for dessert.

But glad as I am always to be with Maggie because we have good talks and laughter, I felt all the time not like myself because I am so depressed. It is so strange; I do not feel real, and I suppose it will be like this until I begin to work seriously. So I have now this morning written one page of the cat book, but I do not know if I will ever be able to do it. It seems there is hardly enough to say to fill sixty pages, which is what Norton wants.

There was an overwhelming amount of mail today because we had not been able to get out on Friday; that was the storm.

Tuesday, January 11, 1994

AGAIN A very cold but happy day as Anne and Barbara finally made it. They were to have come last week, but that was the day of the big storm and so it was put off until today. They came promptly at half past eleven, bringing the lobsters, and Barbara a salad, the lettuce grown by herself in the attic. I cannot believe this, the most delicious little leaves of two different kinds of lettuce made it all very special. It was wonderful to see Anne and Barbara. I realized when we had been talking for a while that there are very few people now whom I can talk to in the way I talk with them, artists who have known me a long time and feel exactly as I do about politics. We talked about how dreadful the business in Bosnia is, how they think about it all the time just as I do, and we talked about Clinton, whom they admire just as I do.

Pierrot, who had been out of sight the whole time, suddenly appeared when we had almost finished the lobsters. Luckily I still had a little bit of lobster tail that I could let him have. I was about to eat it, so he came at the right moment and devoured it as always and then as always asked to go out. But very soon we heard him trundling up the cellar stairs so he had found his cat door in the cellar and came back, perhaps hoping for more lobster, but by then it was gone. We had delicious chocolate cake, the last of it that Jamey and Cindy had brought at Christmas and some black raspberry ice cream.

Wednesday, January 12, 1994

HERE WE are preparing for another storm. It is almost unbelievable, but this time I feel ready. There is food in the house, Karen took me shopping this morning and I got a sole fillet, and Maggie always leaves food, so there is lots now, and I have vegetables as well, and fruit. I am going to start on the income tax, which is something I enjoy because it makes me see what I have been spending money on and gives me an idea of what my life is about. So I thought I would sit at the desk in the guest room, which is now really Susan's desk, and begin to sort it out. What I do is divide up the checks into subjects and then add them up and see what I have.

The great news is that I have somehow broken out of the

extreme depression that I have been in, the kind of depression which makes it hard to do anything, and I am working on the little book about Pierrot although I dictated three pages to Judy this morning and when she had done it, she said, "I think you will be revising this for quite a while," so I gather that it is not a great masterpiece yet. But I think it may grow. It is exhilarating to be thinking about it because there is quite a lot to be said, partly about him and what he thinks about and what his life is to himself, and partly what it is for anyone, and especially an old woman living alone, to have an animal as companion. I could not imagine life without him.

There was almost no mail today, and that is something of a relief because there was so much over the holidays. There are still piles and piles of snow everywhere. Nadine, who was able to get here on Tuesday—all last week she was not able to—saw a bald eagle in a big tree in the swamp on her way here. That really is astonishing. I have told everyone, but no one has seen it. Of course, she comes very early, quarter past seven, and probably later in the day he is not as visible. But there were a lot of redstarts, a whole flock of them, at the feeder when Maggie was here. Unfortunately the squirrels who seem to be hibernating in the bitter cold have come out now that it is warmer and are eating me out of house and home.

Thursday, January 13, 1994

IT IS Carol Heilbrun's birthday and I must call her. I expect they are having a celebration. Maybe I should call her right now, I don't know. It is half past four, and I have been busy in the kitchen getting my supper ready and looking out on the snow and the early-evening light, which is so beautiful. In

Glass ornaments.

winter with snow behind them, the little glass ornaments that are hanging on the kitchen window look very charming. I remembered that I had said something about the sacramentalization of the ordinary, and as I sliced up the beans and found various things in the Frigidaire that I was going to need for my supper, and set the table, I had a sense of the meaning of all this and that it was not just housework. In some gentle way it was like a prayer, but the trouble is it takes time and it took me a little over half an hour, in fact, nearly an hour. So it is now half past four, and what I was going to do at my desk I will not be able to.

I spent most of the morning organizing the income tax; the first thing I do is sort the checks out, and I was both amused and rather dismayed at how much money I have given away partly out of absentmindedness; two or three times I have sent money to CARE, but never mind, it is all to good causes and I am glad I can do it. That is the satisfaction, to be able to send a check instead of feeling as I used to, until I began to make money a few years ago, that it was terribly painful because I could not give what I wanted to.

I did go out and get some wine to take to Barbara and Margaret tomorrow night, and this time I was able to get the Beaujolais Nouveau. In Dave's, the IGA store where everybody knows me and are my friends, where I had seen they had the Beaujolais Nouveau, I said to Mary I could not find it and asked if she would find it for me. Mary burst into laughter and said, "Say that again. I can't understand a word of it." Finally I had to write it out, and we kept laughing. She doesn't drink and confessed she knows nothing about wines.

Saturday, January 15, 1994

THE EXTREME cold has come, but fortunately it is powdery snow, about two inches that have not been plowed. I managed to get out. Triumph! And after three weeks when it was always snowing on Saturday and I could not get there, I finally had my hair done. It is a great relief because my head felt so dry, and now it is all right and especially good because I am going out for dinner with Margaret and Barbara, so I look presentable at last.

It is now a wind chill again of twenty below. Driving to the hairdresser, however, which is a short drive, perhaps four miles, I looked at all the whiteness and the complete change of landscape that this kind of winter weather is and thought what a wonderful thing to live in a place where it is almost as if one traveled long distances because the difference between summer and winter is so enormous, or between autumn and spring, for that matter. Each season has its pleasures and its deprivations, but the snow does look beautiful and the shadows on the snow are dramatic.

As usual there are tracks of all kinds of animals all over the lawn. I keep wondering who they are and wish I could see them; they are silent at night. I have not even heard a deer huff; I guess they are too cold and have given up on the apples now.

Sunday, January 16, 1994

IT HAS been an extraordinary day. In the first place it is the coldest one in ten years, simply incredible, but I got the ultimate Christmas present, which was given me by Ronnie Carpenter-Healy, who wrote at Christmas and said, "My Christmas present to you is to do whatever you need done in the house." For instance, she suggested sewing on buttons; she suggested a whole lot of things, like shopping with me. I, in my immense hope and also feeling it was a great deal to ask, suggested the other day that she might—and she had said that her husband could help her and they have a truck—come and help me clear out the attic. This has been a nightmare of a place. It makes me think of the joke in *The New Yorker* that amused me most this year, which is a woman surrounded by disorder who says, "I run a loose ship." Well, the attic was run by a very loose captain and has been for twenty-one years. It was not helped by the fact that at one time red squirrels decided to inhabit it and at that time it also had to be insulated and they loved the insulation, they nested in it and tore it up and strewed it about, so there was all this pink fluffy stuff on the floor as well as everything else and, of course, just plain dirt. There I keep the ornaments for the tree and a whole lot of other things. I had to stand there with Ronnie and Jim and decide what could be thrown away. They could not have possibly decided. We threw away a huge number of things, but I hope nothing that I am going to regret.

The relief is tremendous. I went in there and could not believe it, this airy, clean, immaculate space after years of disorder and chaos. It really is the best Christmas present I ever imagined, as I told Ronnie, and she blushed, which touched me. They did a superb job in two hours. However, that is not the end of what they had to do because they now have a truck full of stuff that has to be gotten rid of, but apparently they are willing, they are incredibly willing, especially considering that one of their two sons is still home for the holidays. I thought he had already left.

WELL, A day of great achievement, but of course, I did nothing. I got up late on purpose; I knew the attic was going to be tiring. On Sundays I have to get my breakfast, carry it up, make the bed, and today I felt particularly shaky. I was afraid I would not be able to get the tray down. I could get it up, but when it came to taking it down, I wondered how I would do it, but I did it. So it has been a triumphant day.

The only thing that has not happened is any work at my desk, and now I want very much to write to Tom Barnes, whose father died just before Christmas. It was a tremendous loss to him. And I think of Harry Green, who, in his eighties, when I was forty-five and my father died, wrote me a letter to say, "Now you are an orphan, too." I have never forgotten it.

So in the bitter cold a lot of life has been going on in this house, and I have managed to keep it warm by, I am afraid, putting the thermostat up to eighty. It is a little under seventy now in the house.

Monday, January 17, 1994

AND HERE we are, again overwhelmed by the weather. It is terribly cold, I think it was about nine above zero this morning, and there is going to be a big snow beginning this afternoon, but thank goodness Joan was able to come and was able to go, though it was snowing hard, and get me some milk, which I needed badly because I could not make my coffee without it. Then I turned on, as usual while waiting for her, the "Today" show, and about half past seven it came through that there has been a devastating earthquake around Los Angeles, the San Fernando Valley. It is a 6.7 I think they said, which is very serious. It was four-thirty in the morning there, so in total darkness the lights went out in most places and there began to be gas fires because of gas mains broken. Now it is light, it is half past eleven here, so it is half past eight there, and the damage is beginning to be seen.

It is terrible inside houses. One man said, for instance, everything fell out of the medicine cabinet. Pictures have fallen, there is broken glass everywhere, books out of bookcases, everything fallen on the floor and broken. The aftershocks have been very bad, as much as 6 on the Richter scale, and there is the faint possibility, a one-in-twenty chance, that this 6.8 earthquake was only the precursor of a much worse one. In any case there will be aftershocks for quite a while, many of them today and this week; everybody must be extremely nervous. Several of the freeways have collapsed and cannot be used. It is absolutely nightmarish. I can imagine trying to clear up when everything breakable in your house is broken. Chaos with the fires and the fire trucks and emergency vehicles and one really not knowing what to do and how to manage. So it is grim. Here we are on the East Coast wrapped in freezing cold and with a snowstorm coming, and there they are with an earthquake. I must say I would rather have snow than an earthquake.

I did manage to write a letter and to look at my desk at least. I am going to try to write to Solange Sarton to thank her for a cat book which she sent me for my birthday. It is very late for me to answer that.

Meanwhile, the great thing is that at least the lights have not gone off, so I am warm. During all these storms we have had in the last ten days my fear has been ice, and this might happen tonight, ice which wreaks havoc in the electrical system and the lights go out. Let us hope.

Tuesday, January 18, 1994

EVERYTHING THAT was foretold happened. In the middle of the night, when it was extremely warm, suddenly there were floods and floods of rain for about three hours. Then it began to freeze and snow, so on top of that ice which formed because the ground was so cold more ice fell, but finally there was a little bit of snow on top of it. I realized at once that nobody was going to get in and I probably would not get out, but I was assured that the road would be plowed and I was determined to get the mail because after the holiday for Martin Luther King there was bound to be a lot. I decided to wait and hoped that it would be plowed in time.

Meanwhile, I went back to the income tax and spent two very concentrated hours finding out what I had spent on stamps last year, which turns out to be $1,300. There were three new books of mine published this year, and I suppose I must have sent more than one hundred, most of them costing $2.90, so it is not surprising, but it is a formidable amount on top of everything else. I am learning how much I spend these days to live, and it is frightening. But fortunately I can deduct not only the stamps but also books and magazines, and that is a considerable sum and gives me a sense of freedom in ordering.

It was quite a day because at quarter to twelve I went down and saw that somehow they had plowed and shoveled my path out, but I had not heard them I was concentrated so hard on my figuring. So I thought, "Well, I am going to go now," though it looked very scary because there was no snow cover where they had plowed and none where they had shoveled, so I ventured out onto glare ice and the whole world was white. It is an extraordinary day from the point of view of its beauty because every single branch and twig is covered with an inch or two of snow. All the tops of the trees are white. As I drove out to the village, I saw that this white world lasted right into the village. I have never seen anything like it and I really wish I had had a camera. But the minute I got out onto the road here I knew it was a mistake. It was extremely dangerous, but by going slowly, I managed to get the mail, though not the *Times*.

But I got English muffins because I had an idea that I would have English muffins and Welsh rarebit for my lunch. I was looking forward to this hot lunch when I got back finally at half past twelve but found that the lights had gone out, no electric power, so I could not make the Welsh rarebit, could not have a hot lunch, and had no light. I felt I must prepare for the worst, so I found the fluorescent lamps that Maggie had given me which will last for as long as four hours and I have two of them, one for by my bed and one for the kitchen. Huldah a long time ago gave me an alcohol stove, so I found that in the kitchen cupboard and brought it down and found the wood alcohol which is put into it. I did not put it in because I thought that if the lights came on soon, it would be a nuisance to have to deal with that, but I got it all ready. Then I made myself a sad peanut butter sandwich and drank a little glass of sherry and then went to bed under two covers.

The cat, who was asleep on a straight chair and did not want to come to my bed, finally did come, so he offered some warmth for me as I was beginning to feel rather cold and lonely.

Thursday, January 20, 1994

STILL THE extreme cold. Mary-Leigh and Beverly came with two men to look at the roof that was leaking, the flat roof over the room where I sit and look at television and have my meals. It has leaked before. This time Mary-Leigh decided that something had to be done about it, so they are going to work at it next week. But that hour took all the energy of my morning from me, so I did very little.

I did write a little blurb for Christopher De Vinck's new book because I admire his style and think I found a good thing to say about him, which is that he resembles Charles Lamb; he has some of that delightful humor and gentleness, and it is lovely to see that because it is rare in any age.

The cat has been a little bit nicer to me today. Yesterday he was so detached that I wondered if he would ever come back to me or whether he really was through with his old mother, but he came and rested with me this afternoon, a great pleasure. He seems to be all right because in the morning he did actually eat most of what was there. He has not been eating, which naturally makes me anxious.

The horrors of what has happened in California go on. Maggie Vaughan's daughter, who lives in Santa Barbara, had every dish in the house broken. All the books fell from the bookcases. It is terrifying. But I have gotten this wrong, of course. Maggie's daughter has not suffered serious damage, though there was a lot of crockery broken, but she was absolutely terrified and this is a very sane and well-balanced and efficient woman. She was alone in the house and was hysterical when she called her mother. I don't wonder. It must be terribly frightening, and it goes on. That is what one cannot handle. The trauma that is there all the time. No wonder a great many people are wanting to sleep out rather than in a house, especially now in houses where there is so much damage.

It made me think of my poem about Frank Lloyd Wright's hotel in Japan. Many people have forgotten that, but Wright, the American architect who designed the Imperial Hotel, was sure that it would withstand earthquakes, and when the terrible earthquake came, they thought everything really had gone, but then a news cable came to say, "The Imperial Hotel still stands." I used the image of Wright's hotel in a poem called "Humpty Dumpty," page 155 in the *Collected Poems*.

Humpty Dumpty

Pain can make a whole winter bright,
Like fever, force us to live deep and hard,
Betrayal focus in a peculiar light
All we have ever dreamed or known or heard,
And from great shocks we do recover.
Like Wright's hotel we have been fashioned
To take earthquake and stand upright still.
Alive among the wreckage, we discover
Death or ruin is not less impassioned
Than we ourselves, and not less terrible,
Since we nicely absorb and can use them all.

It is the small shock, hardly noticed
At the time, the slight increase of gloom,
Daily attrition loosening the fist,
The empty mailbox in the afternoon,
The loss of memory, the gradual weakening
Of fiery will, defiant to exist,
That slowly undermines the solid walls,

Until the building that withstood an earthquake
Falls clumsily among the usual days.
Our last courage has been subtly shaken:
When the cat dies, we are overtaken.

Saturday, January 22, 1994

I AM about to go and have a blood test and my hair done, but
luckily it is a little warmer so I do not have to wear long johns
today. I wanted to put something on the cassette right now
because I feel it is a great mistake that I do not do what I used
to do when I was young, which was to keep a list of the books
I am reading. Often I forget the name of the author, and I
would like to be able to go back and remember.

Somebody sent me a delightful little book that she had
written, her name is Evelyn Copeland, and it is the story of
her retiring to southern Florida and gradually becoming an
aficionado of birds; the wildlife where she lives is unbelievable. It is near Lake City and therefore on a lake, not the
ocean, but a crocodile comes every day, the raccoons come for
marshmallows, of all things, and wash them in the birdbath
before they eat them. It is an endless stream of delightful
observations of the nature all around her, and I found that I
wanted to take it little by little so it would last longer. I have
been reading a few pages every night before I go to sleep and
I managed this morning to write Evelyn Copeland a note to
thank her.

We saw four deer in the dusk coming to get the yew on the
terrace; they came right up to the terrace, exquisite. Thank

goodness they do not look too thin, they look quite plump. What beautiful faces and their thin, delicate legs and all of this with the incredible snow all around! The reason they can get the yew is that the branches are covered in snow and weighted down. A marvelous sight, and I am so glad Maggie was here to see it with me.

She came about three and is now roasting our lamb for supper. We are having a very good time, as always.

Monday, January 24, 1994

I WAS so anxious to get started with Judy today, I have so much to do with her about income tax, about the preface for the poems, letters to dictate, and so on, as well as the journal, which now needs some typing on it. So it was particularly disappointing to have her call this morning and say that she has family business which will keep her from coming today but promises to come tomorrow. Everything gets put off one way or another. The weather, the season, I am frustrated right now. I think what I must do is get back to the income tax and see if I can straighten it out, maybe do a few personal letters which have piled up.

One of the imaginative things that Maggie did this time was to bring an outdoor thermometer because mine had disintegrated. It was wonderful to be able to read the temperature today, which was nine above when I went down at six but is now twenty above, which is encouraging. It is practically warm.

But the garage door is stuck and I have called the man who has come before to do something about it and he did not

CREDIT: SUSAN SHERMAN

May's desk piling up.

answer so I put it on his machine and asked him to call. I do not know what will happen, but maybe Dean Frieze will be able to fix it and when he comes home Sylvia will tell him.

I was touched this morning to get several letters thanking me for having answered a formal letter with a postcard of Pierrot. People are so touched by this that it touches me.

Wednesday, January 26, 1994

TODAY IT was four above zero when I went down, and a lot of snow had fallen in the night so I was afraid that Joan would not get here. In fact, I had gone down to get my breakfast and waited for a few minutes, and there was her truck. Oh, how glad I was to see it! Somehow she got through. They have not plowed. We have two inches of snow, but it is terribly cold. And yesterday too was a day of frustrations.

In the first place the garage door opener was still not working, and I called the Henry Door Service. He is very nice, this man, and said he would be here yesterday in the middle of the afternoon. So at three I got up and decided that I would mince the lamb that Maggie had brought. I did not dare go up to my study because I was afraid of missing Henry. Not only am I on the third floor when I am working, but I cannot see the road, so I cannot see whether anyone is there or not. I waited and waited and waited. Luckily it was a day that magazines come, so there was *Newsweek* and *Time* to look at and the new *New Yorker*. But I began to get pretty cross. Finally at five and pitch-dark I called them at Henry's Door Service, and he said, "Well, I just didn't make it. You know with these jobs you never know how long they are going to take." I then did say, "I work on the third floor and my time is worth money to me and I resent having waited that long. You might have telephoned me."

Then he promised to come today at three and I was dreading that because I knew he would not be on time, so this morning I decided I had better call him and put him off because Joan did make it, I could not believe my eyes when I saw her truck drive up, and she informed me that the door was working again and she wondered if she should close it or leave it open. I said to close it, for a big snow is expected on the weekend, and the squirrels get into the birdseed if the door is not closed.

I now think I hear the faint sound of a snowplow, so maybe they are going to plow just a little and make this road less slippery.

The bitter cold is continual worry and anxiety. Today the wind chill is again twenty below, as it is only five above.

With the good news of Joan's coming and the garage door working, I should feel a burst of energy, but what I feel is exhaustion.

Chris De Vinck has been copying out for me parts of Julian Green's journal, which I have always loved, which I have in French and not in English somewhere here. One thing that struck me that he says is, and he quotes from 1934, "The child dictates and the man writes." That is interesting to me because I believe it is true of this journal, that the child dictates, and it is also in a way true of my life. I am sure that some people wonder when they see how many stuffed animals there are here—now there is the new Bengal tiger cub, whom I look at almost as if he were a real animal—why it is. It is not that I cuddle them; I like looking at them, and this is childish of me. But it is the childish things that keep me as comforted and happy as I am in this not very easy situation this winter with so much bad weather and Susan unable to get here for weekends.

Today in the mail I had the distressing news that Eda

LeShan has to have another angioplasty, and that means she will be in the hospital probably until April, or at least she will not be able to get back to the Cape until then. And I wonder what is happening to her beloved pussycat meanwhile, but I imagine her daughter can take the cat.

Saturday, January 29, 1994

I HAD hoped to be able to get out today, having been a prisoner yesterday, rain on top of ice, nothing could be much worse. This January is turning into nothing but a report on the weather, but that is what New England does to one, and it becomes absorbing to find out how cold or hot it has been in the night and what to expect of the day.

Today I regret to say that flooding rains yesterday and last night only washed off the surface of ice, so it is lethal, as dear Dean Frieze said to me yesterday when he answered my cry for help and came over. He is more than six feet tall, I think he is eighty, and he has blue eyes and white hair and stands tall, and he is the most wonderful friend, he and Sylvia, his wife. I do not know how often they call me, maybe once a week, to say, "Is there anything you need? You know we're here and don't hesitate to ask."

So yesterday at three in the afternoon, after I had hoped that the plow would come or sanding or something, I did call Dean but told him to be awfully careful because I had tried to fill the bird feeder and realized that I was falling with the first two steps I took. I did have a small bag of Kitty Litter I suppose weighing at most five pounds, maybe ten, but the trouble is I cannot lift that much, so I was only able to sprinkle a tiny bit on the front of the steps and warned Dean to bring some with him. Instead he brought a heavy shovel and shoveled the ice. I do not know how he did it. He managed to fill the bird feeder. One of the reasons why I felt I must ask for help was that the birdseed had been devoured by the squirrels all day, so the birds never got a chance at that feeder. I felt it must be filled because I was pretty sure I would not get out all day today and then for tomorrow another storm predicted.

I want to talk a little about York, the village, the town, because when I first came here from Nelson, a small village of three hundred, to this town of ten thousand or more, for a while it did not feel like home. I loved the house and the place, but I did not feel part of the town. This is perhaps because I do not own land, I do not have children, so there is not much reason to go to the town meetings, and I have not done that. Lately I have realized that I am recognized in York and people are extremely kind, and this has touched me very much. In the parking area at the post office they never do anything about the ice or the slush, and these days it has been nearly impossible to get from my car to the post office, which is only a few feet, and I have been touched by how many men, especially old men, have offered to help me. The other day a woman saw me; she was sitting in her car and got out and said, "Let me help you," and held me up as it was very slippery and I think I would have fallen. I was extremely grateful and said so, then was in the post office quite a while because I had things to send, and when I came out, she was still there. She had waited for me so that she could help me back. I said, "You are a good Samaritan."

WHEN I go to Dave's IGA, all the girls there know me, have known me over the years, and they want to know how things are going out here.

Another thing that made a great difference in my attitude

to the town was on my eightieth birthday, when the public library had a display of all my books and lots of people came and signed the guest book. And I remember the beautiful flowers. So I now feel as though people know me and recognize me and that I am a member of the community, which I really have not felt until now.

This morning I feel especially lucky as Mary-Leigh has called and said that they would sand the road, and maybe I will be able to get out. That would be wonderful.

Later, Saturday, January 29, 1994

A WASTED day. As usual, when I cannot get out of here, I panic, feel trapped, and nothing seems possible, so I have done very little. I did not go on with Pierrot, the book. I did not have it in me to summon that kind of energy though I have written a few letters.

I had three very interesting calls this morning, one from Martha Wheelock, who lived nine miles from the epicenter of the earthquake luckily in an old house which withstood the shock, but almost everything else fell on the floor or was broken, including most of the tools for her job, which is making videos and moving pictures, and of all things, her little poodle puppy was almost buried when everything fell all around him in his corner. They did manage to rescue him; he is all right, but what a terrible moment. The other big dog, a chow, was apparently all right. Martha actually took them on a walk the day of the earthquake, and she said they did not know themselves how serious it had been. Last night there was an aftershock, a five, which is pretty bad, and I expect there will be

May's books displayed at the York Public Library in honor of her eightieth birthday.

more news of the damage done by that on the news tonight.

It was wonderful to hear Martha sounding so vividly alive and herself. She said that the material on the video that they made of me in an interview here two days after Christmas was wonderful, that my voice sounds very good, but of course, they had no time to work on it. She is teaching already, not the first week, but by the second week she was back at school, having had to help clean the school up, which has also been damaged. The aftereffects sound difficult.

On the strength of the call from Martha, I called Diane Amiel, who I suspected was also rather near the center, and she had a sad tale to tell. She lost most of her work, she is a court reporter, and she lost various mechanical things. She said that in her case FEMA, the United States organization that helps people in disaster areas, worked; she had not had to stand in line, everything was done by telephone. But her friend Marie, who was here with Diane at Christmastime, had gone to her cottage up in the mountains, a primitive little cabin. While she was away, the earthquake took place and a big tank of tropical fish in her home was thrown to the ground, the wires short-circuited, and her entire house burned down. Nothing is left. Clothes, books, everything is gone. It is tragic. So I heard all that and felt, "Why worry about not being able to get out because of the ice? It will melt."

Sunday, January 30, 1994

I was not able to get out yesterday, and I would not have gone out today, I think. Judy, my secretary, said she would come today because she had not been able to get down Friday. She helped me. She fixed up the income tax, the 1090s keep coming in, and she finished up the last cassette, so there is nothing that has to be typed right now. Meanwhile, I managed one page of Pierrot, but I have terrible doubts about it. I do not think there is enough in it.

I woke up pretty low in my mind this morning. It is partly the bird feeder. The squirrels hang on it, and I do not know whether I would be able to fill it myself, and I hate to bother neighbors, so it is a problem. Maybe I will call and see if by any chance Ronnie and her husband could come and fill the bird feeder. It would certainly help.

Monday, January 31, 1994

It is wonderful to think that we are almost through with horrible January; it has been the hardest month, I guess, that I have ever known here. Yesterday I lost my nerve. I have never done that before, and it was scary because I felt so helpless. The reason was that Nadine could not get in on Friday, so nobody has been here to help me.

Eleanor, who cleans the house on Thursday, does not bring my breakfast or make the bed, so I have had to do that, added to the constant anxiety about whether the furnace will stay on, whether in an ice storm the lights will go out, whether people could get in, and I could not get out. There was no doubt that I could not get out because if I opened the door and put one foot out, I stood on sheer ice. Finally, at three o'clock, having been awake since four worrying about what to do, not wanting to ask Dean again because he had done such a heroic job in the middle of the rain on Friday, I decided to call on Ronnie and her husband, those angels who had cleaned out the attic for me two weeks ago. I thought that after that I would not ask them for anything ever again, but Ronnie said they would come and they did. There they were, he with an adz, a special sort of pickax for dealing with ice, and pretty soon I saw him hacking away at the ice. It was two inches thick, so the little attempts to throw Kitty Litter or anything else on it had been futile. It had been totally impossible to get to the bird feeder, which was empty because the squirrels had been hanging there all day eating it up, and there is nothing I can do about that.

I think I lost my nerve because I am so frustrated by my impotence and weakness. I cannot afford to go out and fall because if I did, nobody would know and I would very soon die of the cold. It is hard always to ask for help, but there has never been a winter like this, and let us hope there never will be one again and that for once February will be kinder. At least this week we are not going to get any big snow until Thursday, so I am hoping that Edythe will be able to come and have lunch with me tomorrow. It is about time we caught up.

I have been wanting, ever since I started reading it about a week ago, to talk more about Patricia MacLachlan. I have been reading one of her books called *Journey*. It won the

Newbery Medal, or another one of her books did, *Sarah, Plain and Tall. Journey* is a remarkable story of children abandoned by their mother with the car but no money and how they manage to get miles and miles from where they live in Maine to Connecticut, where they have a grandmother whom they know almost nothing about, but it is their one chance. The children are one really remarkable girl named Dicey, who is thirteen years old, her brother James, and her two little siblings, Sammy and May Beth. These four children have to find a place to sleep every night and something to eat. Once in a while they are able to fish, and once in a while they are able to dig clams; more often they learn how to buy day-old bread or things that are on sale—once it is chicken wings and they manage to cook them over a fire. The book is a fascinating adventure and at the same time enormously human. They are very strong characters, these four children, very different from each other, and the people they meet are also characters. Finally it all comes out all right, but one has been through a stirring experience meanwhile.

It is a contrast to the best seller that I am now reading, which is a roaring good story in that you cannot wait to turn the page, *Peachtree Road* by Anne Rivers Siddons. In fact, there is a great temptation always in this kind of book to skip. Siddons is the woman who wrote a novel laid in Maine called *Colony,* which also irritated me because it was wonderfully described and the characters were real, but something tremendous happens in every chapter so you never get a breather. Finally you feel starved in a curious way, and I am already feeling starved about sixty pages into the one I am reading now, which is named for an old southern house called Fox's Earth. Apparently fox's earth is where the fox goes to hide, his safety. The Patricia MacLachlan book was so nourishing I hated to finish it.

Now I realize that I must write down the titles of what I

am reading because I want to talk about the books and rarely have all the information up here.

Yesterday several people did manage to get through, not only the dear ones who helped me with the ice, but also my secretary, Judy, did not plan to come today because there was supposed to be a storm (thank goodness we did not get it), so she offered to come on Sunday and she finished up the income tax for me except for my agent, who is always slow on the 1090. This is hard on me because everything is ready to send to Mark Meizler, my man of business, to do the income tax, and I am anxious to know what I have to pay this year, I cannot pay it now because of the income from royalties tax form not coming.

Judy came and worked, then in the afternoon Ronnie and her husband came to deice me, and at four Pat, who is a visiting nurse, came and brought with her her friend who is a Sister of Mercy, and I was by then rather tired because of all the stress of this weather, of being anxious, of not knowing what to do. Anyway, we did have a good talk about everything under the sun; they are so intelligent, both of them, so caring. So it was a good hour that we had together, but then I was really exhausted. I did not know how to get my supper, but I finally did it as I always do. One manages; that is what one does.

Tuesday, February 1, 1994

IT HAS been a hard day, at least in its beginning, this February 1. It began as usual with the mail. Nadine was able to get through the ice, thank goodness, and when she brought the mail, there was a letter from Ann Crooker's sister to tell me that Ann had died on January 16 peacefully in her sleep. I was very moved by this, actually in tears, although I have never met Ann Crooker. She wrote me because of my work, as so many people do, and I enjoyed her letters. They were not many, but every one that she wrote had meaning for me, and I think it meant something to her that I answered so that we carried on something like a correspondence. About two weeks ago she called me on the telephone. We had a long talk, and I thought, "This is a person after my own heart," and I was so delighted to think that she was really planning to come and see me in the spring. So it is strange that she suddenly is not there, just as we were on the brink of a kind of intimacy and certainly a real friendship she had felt for at least a year.

She was a remarkable woman. She lived on Long Island, had grown-up children who adored her, and after we had corresponded maybe once or twice, she told me that she had just been diagnosed with cancer and it was obvious that they did not expect her to live very long. She was on chemotherapy as well as radiation possibly. What was so marvelous about her was that she immediately began making plans, knowing that she had perhaps a year at most to live, to do everything that she had wanted to do and had not done. So she went to England to see a son of hers. I do not know all the different things that she did, but it seemed to me so brave and so imaginative not to lock herself away to die, but to try to take in all the life she could.

It is a kind of miracle that she had such a peaceful death. On Sunday I was reading a review of that new book about death by a doctor which is very gloomy because he says among other things that everybody dreams of a peaceful death and the myth is that most deaths are peaceful and that people have resolved their lives, but actually a death such as Ann had, a peaceful death in sleep, is quite rare and death is often quite painful, to say the least, and he makes no bones about it. So the juxtaposition of that review of that book and then the letter about Ann was interesting. I do miss her and wish I had known her.

After taking that in, I really had a good morning, almost the first one in maybe two months, at my desk. I first worked on Pierrot's book, which has been a block in my mind because I could not get the right tone. I did not like what I had done, but now today I enjoyed it for the first time and began to have all kinds of ideas about it, so it was a wonderful morning. I think I wrote two pages, which is about as much as I ever do these days.

After that I read over the book of poems, *Coming into Eighty,* which I wrote in my seventy-ninth and eightieth years and which Norton brings out this fall. I had to be sure they have everything right and read the final typescript before it goes into proof. I was pleasantly surprised. I think it is a distinguished book, and I am pleased with it. But there were several curious things that happened. Two stanzas were left out of two rather important poems, and as Norton has been complaining that there are not enough pages, at least this means two pages more, so I was delighted to find them.

Pierrot.

Wednesday, February 2, 1994

IT WAS twelve below zero this morning, and I must say I wondered if I would ever feel warm again. But now I have taken off a sweater over another sweater because I was too warm.

I was thinking yesterday while I was resting that having a two-hour rest seems in some ways rather self-indulgent except that most of the time I am not resting but thinking, thinking especially about what I want to do for the rest of the day, for the rest of the week, and perhaps even for the next year. It is a time when my mind is at rest and I feel clear and able to think things out. Yesterday I planned to get gas for my car and some dry gas put in because Edythe is coming for lunch today and will drive me; I will not be taking the car out tomorrow, and the tank was nearly empty. Also, there is the anxiety about the garage door, which now freezes up and then unfreezes, and I never know whether I can get in or out, so I decided that it being two o'clock and the temperature just under thirty, the chances of my getting out of the garage were good, and I was right. I had to take in the cart and the bin that we put things that can be recycled into, so I got them safely lodged in the garage again and set out, at the odd time for me of half past two, and got gas and felt triumphant when I got home because it was only then a little before three, so I had most of the day still before me.

I called Carol Houck Smith and had a good talk. She is delighted with the preface I wrote and thought the tone was just right, and this pleased me because I think at last that yesterday I may have got the tone right for the book about Pierrot, so that which seemed impossible may turn out to be possible.

Planning is half the battle for me now, simply clearheadedly planning, for instance, what I am going to have for supper. Last night I remembered there was one more white turnip that I had not used the other day and that it would be good with my supper, chicken thighs that I had cooked yesterday, sautéed with a little bit of consommé and some wine, and they turned out to be very good. So I decided that. I often think about what I am going to have for dinner because if I know ahead, it is much easier to do it; I am tired when I go down at five after working a couple of hours at my desk.

Monday, February 7, 1994

I SPENT a half an hour this morning trying to get this recorder to work, and now I have come up from my rest at four o'clock and thought I would give it a try and it seems to be working. That is good news because I was about to write by hand. I have not dictated for quite a while, partly because Maggie was here for the weekend. That always means fun, especially as this time she had brought a videocassette and we saw D. H. Lawrence's *Women in Love,* which was, as I remember, very much praised when it first came out as a movie. I did not like it, although there were some wonderful things in it, one a fight between two men who are rivals in a way but like each other. They take off all their clothes and in an amateurish way battle and throw each other to the ground in front of a big fireplace in an old English house. This was a wonderful scene. There is a great deal of physical lovemaking, and I do not really like it. I did not feel at all like it yesterday; I do not know why. I was upset by it. Of course, Lawrence is upsetting and means to be upsetting. Much of the language I did not like. And also I had thought that there would be a portrait of Lady Ottoline Morrell, who appears in *Women in Love,* but I have never read the book. I would have been thrilled to see her played by a good actress.

My preoccupation in the last week has been a remarkable book given me by the author called *Dead Men Walking: An Eyewitness Account of the Death Penalty in the United States,* by Helen Prejean, CSJ. As a sister she got involved in being the spiritual adviser of a murderer who had been condemned to death. For some months she saw him every week and at the end every day, and was with him at the very end. She tells about this and the extraordinary brutality that killing a man by the state is. It is more brutal than a usual murder. Usually the person murdered does not know that he is about to be murdered; at least he does not know it for months, having been told it is going to be on such and such a day at such and such a time, and then that date is put off and another date given. The murder involved was brutal, of young people, a young couple, and there was also rape of the girl. The prisoner does feel remorse, although he is much more concerned with the principle of the death penalty and of trying to get a pardon for himself than he is about anything else.

One of the reasons why the book is so moving is that Helen Prejean is so honest. For instance, it is only near the end of his life that she realizes how strange it is that she never thought of visiting the parents of the two young people who were murdered, and if it ever happens again, she certainly will do so.

She is able to communicate with the parents when she finally sees them, to some extent at least, but of course, they resent her because they have suffered terrible pain and loss and are mostly concerned with the murderer being killed. They are waiting for that, and it absorbs months of their time and preoccupation. This is one reason why the death penalty is so bad. It is a strange, abnormal thing that the state should murder. I liked the book because Sister Prejean was so honest about not having thought of something. You expect nuns to think of everything, don't you? And she admits that this was a new experience for her.

One of the things which I am sure is true for anybody who enters prison life as an observer is that it is so terribly brutal because of the confinement. The death cell is something like eight by twelve with a toilet at the back and some sort of hard bed. The man is allowed one collect call a week or something like that, perhaps near the end of a day. Letters have to be censored. He is taken out to get exercise one hour a day. Otherwise he is caught there. He does have a television in the last day and for the last hours.

It never confronted me in the way that it has here, that the electric chair is not a quick death. In this case, the first case she discusses took four minutes. You only have to imagine one minute of extreme pain. The flesh is burned, but the body is strapped so that nothing can move, no hand can move. She watches his hand bent over backwards by the force of the shock when it comes, and afterward she throws up.

Then there is all the intricate legal stuff to try to get pardons for people and to try to persuade a governor to pardon a man even when, as quite often happens, it looks as if he is not guilty of the crime. In this case he was and admitted that he was. I think Sister Prejean did not imagine that she would ever have this experience again but then was asked by somebody who had been helpful with her first case whether she would take a young man who had committed a terrible murder of two young people, a boy and a girl in their teens, and she agreed to do so.

This was quite different from the first experience because this young man had almost no remorse, did not show any, wanted simply to be tough. "They won't get to me. They won't break me," was his stance. He was contemptuous of the parents. What the author met was nothing but a desire for revenge and waiting for him to be killed. So it is a hard book to read; I do not think I have ever read one harder because it is a mixture of our seeing these two men, getting to know them in a way, and then everything that is involved in the death penalty in the United States and how terribly wrong it is. A lot of it is legal, explaining the infinite ramifications that go on as people try to get pardoned.

This afternoon I tried to get valentines, and it was a nightmare. They are so ugly, and if they are not ugly, the thing that irritates me most is they are all designed for "my goddaughter, my wife, my cousin, my father, my husband," but never just for a friend. The relationship has to be defined. I did buy at vast expense about six, but none of them seemed worthy of the people for whom they were purchased.

What I want to do is make one for Maggie at least about all that she does, the extraordinary things she does. This time she did hack out a space next to where I would park the car so that I can get out of it and not slip. This was a difficult job; the ice is two inches thick at least and as hard as iron. It was an act of pure love, and I was touched by it.

It has been a day of frustrations because the light over my bed is gone and an electrician has to come and do something about it. I called Bruce Wood, who has often come here before and who is so kind, and he will, I hope, be able to come tomorrow. As it is, I have moved another lamp that is not a good light, but it will have to do. But that was frustrating after spending half the morning trying to get this cassette working.

Wednesday, February 9, 1994

WE HAVE had enough of winter. It is simply depressing, not exhilarating at all. We were supposed to have a lot of snow. Luckily we did not. I was relieved to get up this morning to see that there was perhaps four inches when they had thought there might be a foot. But nobody came to plow, and it felt isolated and mournful here. The cat does not like the weather and is unrelated to me these days; that does not help. The house feels so big, and I am so lonely. I have never been as lonely as I am now here because never has Susan not been able to come since she started coming, and for the whole month of January I have not seen her. She feels just as I do. We both feel sad that we cannot meet, but she cannot possibly drive from New York and back on a weekend when the weather is threatening.

Margaret just called and agreed that it was the worst winter that she ever remembered. I rushed into the post office at one-thirty after they finally came and shoveled me out and did the road, and I said to Tony, my friend at the post office, "I'm through, Tony, I'm ready to go. I just want to be taken out of here." I just want to die; I did not say that, but that is what I meant, and everybody laughed, everybody feels the same. It is a long struggle.

Only I wish I could do something creative. At the moment I am stuck on Pierrot because now what I have to do is describe the time when he was apparently chased by some wild animal and we saw him in a state of stark terror, something I have never seen before, and I am going to describe it in the book, so I am not going to describe it here.

Somebody sent me Arnold Kenseth's poems; I used to know him. They are pure lyrics and beautiful, some of them.

Thursday, February 10, 1994

IT WAS a cold day today, but extremely beautiful because right now I am looking out—it is about half past four—on a miraculously blue sea. It is a soft, pale blue. The field is absolutely white with shadows now because of it being late afternoon.

Mary-Leigh Smart's and Beverly Hallam's house, which I see from my window, looks stunning. It is a modern house which faces the sea, so what I see is the back of it; sometimes it looks a little stark, but this evening it is taking the light beautifully, the white snow on the roof glamorizes everything.

It has been a curious day, a frustrating day because there were too many things that I had to remember to do—one of them to call the York rubbish department because they had not got the bin, which they take every two weeks with the things to recycle, and that is out there now and they have not come yet. But the man did promise me that they would come today, so maybe they still will. Then I was not sure that Eleanor, my house cleaner, would be able to come because her car was totaled last week. But she did come, and it was wonderful to have the house cleaned. Then dear Joan, who works for me, had called last night and said that she would get the mail and get the newspaper for me. She had not been able to come yesterday. It was dear of her and very like her to do this and walk through the new snow that is now about three inches on top of ice and on top of what was left of the old snow; the roads in here are all white. In some ways it looks very Victorian. Usually there has been salt put down or something has happened so that you see the macadam through, but now the road out of here for about two miles is white. It is very beautiful now.

The good thing about the day was that at last Sylvia Frieze and I have managed to have lunch. We have been trying to do this for a month at least, but every time there was snow or she had to go to see a doctor in Boston or her granddaughter was born. Anyway, at last we did have a wonderful talk, and it made the day, but I felt tired the whole time. This is what is irritating. Sylvia seems to think it strange that I am so shaky and cannot walk. Maybe I should try to find out. Maybe one of the drugs I am taking is making me lose my balance as I do.

Maybe I should not accept all this but try to fight it.

The day was also not as happy as it could have been because Pierrot did not come up, and as I cannot lift him up the stairs, it is hard for me when he is there, downstairs, and I call him and he does not come. He is put off by the bad weather; all cats are. Apparently Maggie's cat is impossible these days.

Here we go again! It appears that there will be snow over this weekend. It is hard to believe, but so we are told. I do not think there is much else to say about this day. I have got two artichokes ready to cook for my supper. I am going to have frozen cheese ravioli and an artichoke, which seems to me a very good meal indeed, and maybe, who knows, a half a grapefruit. Food is important to the old; at least it is important to me, and I have to try to generalize here. It is one of the sensual pleasures which remain. A lot of them do not remain, but the sense of smell does. That is one reason why flowers are so precious to me. Just now I cut off some paper-white narcissus which had fallen down and took them up to my bedroom, and oh, the scent as I carried them upstairs was intoxicating!

And so I end this day as I have so many others lately, with gratitude for living in this beautiful place and for still being able to function alone here. I am lucky.

Friday, February 11, 1994

AND HERE we are in another storm which will go on all night, it seems. A gray, grim world. It is getting to everybody now. It is an unnatural and terrifying winter.

Karen came and took me out for a big shopping because

she is going to be away for a week on holiday with her husband, so we got some heavy things like the pineapple juice I take, the V-8, which I sometimes take as a pickup, and I got two Cornish hens so I have some food for the weekend. I have not had a Cornish hen for a long time.

I was hoping today to write a page or two about the walks that Pierrot and I used to take. Of course, now I cannot walk, but for a few years I was able to walk with him. He came when I called, came immediately, and walked ahead of me, his tail straight in the air, or sometimes behind me but usually ahead of me, and we always made the same walk, which was a full circle around the driveway here and back up around the Firths' driveway and then home through the woods. At the beginning of these walks he, for quite some time, used to disappear into the wood and begin to meow very desperately as if he were lost. Whether he really was lost or frightened, I do not know, but it was strange. I called and called him, and then finally he came out, happy to see me and his tail went up, and he walked with me. When we got quite near the house, he always ran a blue streak; it was wonderful to see him run so fast and leap over the terrace wall, about four feet high. I miss those walks. I wish I could do them again, but that was three or four years ago.

Otherwise nothing has happened. I called Anne and Barbara; they say it has been more than ten below zero, seventeen below zero every night there. Cold has been the thing. They have not had the ice, I am glad to say. The ice is the terrible thing here. It is incredible. When Karen and I were driving, we once met a truck, which was absolutely terrifying—to see this huge thing bearing down on us on the one-way street—but the driver managed to pull over into a driveway. Then one of the girls who works for the Ramseys, the horse farm here, came much too fast right towards us when we were on our way, but luckily Karen was able to back into a driveway there.

Nadine did manage to get here this morning, and it was so wonderful to have my breakfast brought up and not have to make the bed, but then as Karen was coming early because it was snowing already, I did not do much at my desk, almost nothing, even to sending the Puckerbrush Press book, *A Celebration of May Sarton*, about the conference for my eightieth birthday. It is wonderful to have that to send to people, but again it means packing them up and spending $2.90 in stamps because I like to send them by priority mail.

But then it was satisfactory to get the income tax off, and that Judy helped me do because she did come today and typed last week's cassette and got it finished. She was here all morning and will come back next week. I am going to get her to help me tidy the files here. For instance, the file that says "Insurance," where the insurance goes back for ten years maybe, is ridiculous. A lot of it can be thrown out, and that will be a tremendous satisfaction. Little by little things will get done, are getting done.

Meanwhile, Pierrot is detached, miserable, meows at me to be let out, sees what it is like out and comes back, then half an hour later has forgotten and tries again. He is disgruntled, and I do not blame him.

Monday, Valentine's Day

VALENTINE'S IS my favorite celebration of the year because nobody has to send a valentine, nobody need feel that they ought to, whereas on birthdays, at Christmas one has to give some presents and send some cards out of a sense of duty and it all piles up and there is more and more, whereas Valentine's still remains spontaneous. So I am a delighted old Valentine who got twenty-three this year. Isn't that wonderful? One of them is a single red rose that Janice brought yesterday and which really seemed like the essence of what a valentine should be. I woke this morning with this extraordinary fragrance around me, and it was the rose; I had forgotten it was there. I am surprised that the cat does not go to smell it because I saw a film about cats two nights ago, and it was pointed out that they have an extremely strong sense of smell, but Pierrot does not seem to be interested in this rose at all. I am, and it is beautiful.

I am recording this in my bedroom, where I have had a rest because I feel tired. There is an icy wind blowing now, howling around the house. Yesterday was a dismal, absolutely dismal day except for the fact that a bunch of flowers and a beautiful pink cyclamen came for me. So now I have tulips and iris here in my bedroom from Phyllis Chiemingo, faithful friend, and there are beautiful yellow lilies and chrysanthemums and white tulips downstairs from Norma, who also sent me a charming painting that she had done as a valentine and some medicine. She is a doctor and she knows what I take, the immense sums of money that I have to spend for medicines, and occasionally supplies some, which she has just done.

I used to send valentines I made myself, buying the materials, the lacy hearts that you could then paste on a red heart and then find some kind of landscape in a magazine or somewhere, or even a photograph of myself. Some of these were quite charming. The worst Valentine Day for me was a day when I had taken a great deal of trouble to make what I thought was a clever valentine for Miss Putnam, who was the science teacher at Shady Hill, a great teacher whom I adored in a distant way as she was quite a distant person. What I did was to copy out from an atlas the world formed into a heart. It was charming, but at that time you were not supposed to tell who had sent a valentine. It was a secret, so I did not ever dare admit that I had made it. Miss Putnam loved it and kept hinting that she would like to know who sent it, but I felt that it was wrong, unethical to say anything, yet I wanted her to know. That was one valentine. Valentine's Day was competitive at Shady Hill, and I think it probably is at most schools as to how many you got. It is satisfactory at eighty-two to get twenty-three. A spoiled old Valentine, I am.

The awful weather goes on; however, we are promised that there will not be a big snow this week. I do not think we could stand it. What has happened now is a few flurries, it is warmer, and now the road is really horrible because it is frozen into ruts and you do not skid exactly, but bump along. It is tiring. I did go to town today to cash a check and also to mail some things, *A Celebration of May Sarton* on the conference at Westbrook, which I got off to two people, and a contract to London for The Women's Press, which is going to bring out *Journal of a Solitude* and *I Knew a Phoenix*.

Pierrot is not well and I should put Vaseline on his paws, but he hates it and I hate it because everything gets so sticky. He did not eat anything last night. He eats at night, and usually when I go down, everything has been eaten, every crumb. So it was disturbing this morning to find that nothing had been eaten though he demanded something, and I opened a fresh can and put it down and gave him cream, but neither of them did he eat. Just a tiny bit of dry food.

Tuesday, February 15, 1994

IT IS ten above zero today and it feels terribly cold, but valentines go on and on. Foster's called me last evening and said they had flowers but would be grateful if they could deliver them today instead of then in the dark. And the road is practically impassable, so I said I was only too glad. When I went down to take rubbish out about half past ten, there were flowers on the table. These were all purples and lavenders and another little bunch that I took to my room separately which was purple anemones and a flower whose name I cannot remember, it grows in California and is a bulb actually, white ones, beautiful, and two or three small roses. So that is by my bed now, and there is a big bunch of lavender chrysanthemums and heather and purple iris that looks very stunning under my mother's embroidery there in the room where the chaise is.

Even better than the flowers was the note from Michael Sirmons and his friend Craig with a quote from Shelley. "My spirit like a charmed bark doth swim upon the liquid waves of thy sweet singing." So I guess they have been reading the *Collected Poems*, isn't that dear?

I am in a bad way about the Pierrot book. I think it is all craziness, but now Judy will help me because she is going to come on Thursday and we are going to type it out, try to correct it, and make it a little better. Maybe I shall write one page this afternoon, but I am beginning to be stuck for what to say even though it is about me, an old woman living with a cat, more than *The Fur Person*, which was really about the cat and nothing else.

The poor cat himself is miserable, keeps trying to go out, and then, seeing how cold it is, really wants to play. What he needs is a wonderful toy, and if I could be that, I would.

I am now reading a novel by Pam Conrad, who has written very successful children's books and, I think, a couple of novels. This is the third. She is a very good writer. She is also a sailor, and when she writes about sailing, then she is super. I have a thing against sex, the sexual act described in novels. I simply do not like it, and when I try to think why I don't like it, it is that it seems to me that cold sex, which is, after all, what it is on the page, does not work. It is repulsive rather than anything else and the same thing with active sex on film, as we found the other night with D. H. Lawrence's *Women in Love*. I did not like the sexual scenes; they were repulsive. Pam does this well, but it does not work for me. I hope I can do a satisfactory blurb for her book because I am fond of her, and she is a good writer, even though this is not, perhaps, her best.

At least this is the day when all the magazines come and the science section of the *New York Times*, so I am now going downstairs to have an orgy of reading, and maybe this afternoon I can do some work on *Pierrot* and also, oh, dear, write some notes.

Thursday, February 17, 1994

A BEAUTIFUL day and a little warmer, but for some reason both Edythe Haddaway and I were feeling tired and even ill when she came to go out to lunch with me, so it was not a very successful day. I am troubled because I do not believe the book about Pierrot is going to work, and today Judy was here typing it and, I could feel, is not wholly convinced either.

I have been answering a couple of letters. One, a charming letter from somebody from Palo Alto who has had a stroke as I did and has been reading me since then. She says something that delighted me, which was; "I realized as I read I didn't see you living your life as much as I thought I was living it and I looked out the window and saw the records in the snow of the night visitors. I stroked Pierrot and saw the leaping sparks. I felt the overwhelming burden of all the to-do's. I felt the anxiety. Is the fibrillation back? I'm glad it wasn't. . . ." . . . and so on. She says that she is now going to read the poems, and that pleases me very much.

I do feel extremely tired in the winter; I do not even like looking out at the snowy field, though of course, it is beautiful. It seems as if the snow would never go and we would never be released. We are in the grip of something we cannot do anything about. I also did something today that I guess is one of the reasons that I did not feel well because it was such an effort, and that was to write to a writer friend of mine that I could not blurb her book which I have been reading, and the reason is that it just did not convince me. Yet it makes me feel so badly not to do it. But I learned a long time ago when

Elizabeth Bowen was at the height of her fame and was blurbing every other book, so the *New York Times Book Review* on Sunday was simply filled with "Marvelous," Elizabeth Bowen; "Wonderful book," Elizabeth Bowen. So finally her praise became devalued, and I swore then that I would never blurb a book unless I thought it was remarkable.

Maybe that should be something that I stop doing, eliminate that. But then what would be left of my life? It is so little now anyway that I suppose the books that are sent me in proof make a kind of excitement, always a new book, to see it before it comes out, to have a chance to praise it and help a writer along. This is valuable.

Now I am going to go down and get my supper and pray that tonight the cat will eat the sole. I bought some expensive sole, really more for him than for myself, and last night he would not come down when it was hot. I called him and he did not come, and when he did come, it was cold and he did not eat it.

Monday, February 21, 1994

THIS IS a holiday weekend, which I never enjoy, and I realize that I was too depressed to be alone for the three days, so I invited Chris and Judy Burrowes to come, and we all had lunch together. Judy kindly took us to lunch and made it a festive occasion. We laughed and laughed and had a wonderful time. I was so grateful to her.

But depression which is very bad cannot go away fast. Something that has made my depressed state a great deal worse is a mean *ad hominem* double review of *Encore* with Doris Grumbach's second memoir, *Extra Innings*, in the

Women's Review of Books. Everybody who saw it was dismayed. I have never had a review quite like it.

Three years ago it was an impulsive decision to accept Margot Peters's wish to write my biography, but I had not imagined, could not imagine what it would be like to be asked to delve into the past, that rich compost accumulated over eighty years. I felt honored by her request to be my biographer, and pleased to read her excellent biography of Charlotte Brontë, lucid and unsentimental. I was pleased, but wholly unprepared.

Waiting for a letter from her, I have to remember that she is living, as she begins to write not with me as I am now but with me as a child. So in a way my presence and the memories I am forced to dig out may stop the flow of what she is creating. She has made it clear that a dispassionate contemplation is what she must hold herself to. I like her very much and am a little surprised that we cannot be friends. When she is interviewing me, it is a passionately interesting conversation and I find her stimulating, but then there is no real relationship involved, and that dismays me since I am used to being open myself and expect my friends to be open with me. Margot is on the defensive; after all, she is dealing with a living subject, and that is a first for her, as it is for me.

We share the same sense of humor. It is a comfort. But what troubles me, I think, is that I have no idea of what her point of view is about either my work or my life. She has said, "The work is going very well," but has never told me anything about it. She has talked with a great many of my friends, and with a few former lovers, but has not confided what the atmosphere of those talks may have been.

What did they say about me? What is she writing following on what they said? How does she know they are telling the truth? Margot is very secretive about these interviews, and I am in the dark. She seems to be a prisoner of her own theory.

Tuesday, February 22, 1994

THERE IS a high wind, and now our little time of relief from the cold is ending and it is supposed to snow tomorrow night and perhaps as much as six inches. Let us hope not. But it has been a wonderful relief to be able to go out without trembling with the cold, and I have had quite a good day because I wrote one page of the Pierrot book, which is beginning to take shape in my mind. I think it is a series of vignettes and should be divided not into chapters but just marked with dots or something that show that it is a new beginning. It is really not good enough, but at least I have done what I said I would, which is write twenty pages, and if Judy gets here tomorrow, she will be able to give it to me so that I can mail it off to Norton. Then I will have a little rest and catch up on correspondence.

I have been writing some letters, but I spent a half hour in a perfect trance of pleasure at the pamphlet which the New York Public Library has printed to accompany a marvelous show of Virginia Woolf and her friends. The photographs are so moving that I found myself sitting and looking for five minutes at one of them, one where both Toby and Virginia Woolf's younger brother are shown, as well as Vanessa, and this is when they were quite young, and suddenly they all looked happy, which one never thinks of them as being. Leslie Stephen is also there in the foreground. That was great—to sit and look and think about Virginia Woolf. There is a wonderful photograph of Vita Sackville-West, looking very Oriental.

Then I was looking at, so it has been a day of looking at things with great pleasure, a wonderful card of a Vermeer that is in Amsterdam called *The Love Letter*. The floor is black and white squares, and the woman has a yellow brocade dress on and is apparently playing some kind of mandolin with the letter in her hand. It is like music the way things are shaped, the whites particularly in this painting which make it seem luminous.

I have written a few notes of thanks for flowers; I am touched by a few of my readers who realize that the winter here has been particularly bad and so have sent me flowers. It is wonderful to have flowers in the house, and I have now some marvelous red tulips, and today I went to Foster's and chose a bunch from a reader of mine who lives in Atlanta, Georgia, and sends flowers every now and then. This time I was allowed to choose and to choose only half the wonderful amount that I can spend eventually, so I will have another bunch later on. This time I chose yellow lilies, marvelously brilliant yellow lilies with some stock, white and purple, and some dark purple chrysanthemums, single like daisies, you know, and some lavender ones, and two of those Japanese Fuji chrysanthemums, white; so it is all white, yellow, and purple and is very beautiful, but I think I have it in the wrong vase, and I must go down and find something with a slightly wider mouth so they do not look crowded as they do now.

Pierrot came up all by himself without my carrying him part of the way, and we had a loving time and I went to sleep for about half an hour.

Before that I came up here and struggled with some letters that have been much on my mind. One to Diane Amiel, who lives in Sherman Oaks and therefore was at the center of the earthquake. Her description of the sounds was staggering in her letter. It was a roar, she felt that a train was coming which was going to run into her house, this tremendous roar. Several other people have mentioned this. She sent me photographs in which everything was strewn on the floor, every book, everything on her desk, fallen on the floor in complete chaos. It made me tired to look at it and to think of what getting it into order will mean.

Now I have a better sense about what my friends have been through because Joan Palevsky also wrote me and described the sound—the sound must have been absolutely terrifying—and told me that in her house too, although the house stood more or less fast, everything fell on the floor. And they keep getting the aftershocks, which must be traumatic to anybody who went through the earthquake itself. Heavens, how peaceful it seems here! There isn't a sound.

The only excitement here today was that I saw a fox, a beautiful slender fox with a bushy tail out in the field. He was against the light, so I could not see his color or whether he had a red tail or a red coat or just buff or what. The strange thing was that he was crossing in front of the biggest bush which is there on the wall and then disappeared. He did not go down the field; he did not go across the field; I do not know where he could have gone. It is a mystery. I wondered for a minute whether he might have a burrow there somewhere and had disappeared into it. I have to watch for him.

Wednesday, February 23, 1994

I KEEP forgetting to speak of a real tragedy that has taken place in York. The other day, driving to do some errands, I came upon what looked like the scene of a terrible war on the street that runs right past the shopping center. The left hand was always beautiful because of a line of very old maples towering high up in the air; there must have been twenty of them, in the autumn absolutely glorious. As I drove by the other day, I saw suddenly nothing but their bodies. They had been cut down. It seemed incredible, it was such a shock. Every time I have gone by since, I have not been able to believe it, although now the great bodies have been cut up and carted away. There has been a great deal of misery about this in York. I have been making notes for a poem which I hope I can do. It is really the first time that something has moved me in the way that makes for poems.

Thursday, February 24, 1994

WELL, THEY told us there would be a big storm, and it is incredible although we are not going to get eight or ten inches of snow. It looks like about three, but it is now raining and sleeting, and this is the danger. I got up at five because I was so afraid that the lights would go out and I had better get everything I could done like getting the house warm. I put up the heat. It is not very cold, it is under freezing, but the house felt chilly, and it was windy all night and I think that is why. I put the dishwasher on to do a load of dishes so that I would not have dirty dishes all day if the lights go out.

Now it is near ten, I cannot believe it, and I have made my bed. I did not want to get up at all, and I am about to wash the dishes and then go up to my desk.

Yesterday was a strange day. It was a gloomy day and yet some good things happened. I had two important things in the mail. One was that The Women's Press in London is going to do an edition of *Kinds of Love*, and that is my favorite of my novels, so I am pleased by that and also they pay a thousand pounds for the rights to redo it, so that adds a little to my account in London and makes me feel quite rich.

The other letter that I opened was from a German man with a good address although in a town that I did not recognize, but then I do not know Germany. His first sentence said that he lived alone and that, therefore, he thought a great deal about the past and also about the future after he was dead. The second sentence said, "I hope you will accept that I would like to make you my heir, and it is a considerable fortune." The third sentence talked about how much he owed me for my work and that this was one way of thanking me. There was a postscript saying, "If you'd like to do something for me, would you copy out something from *Shadow of a Man* and sign it and dedicate it?" Well, I was absolutely astonished, but it did not seem totally impossible. In fact, I must confess that this is a fantasy that I had when I was beginning to write in my twenties, that somebody would leave me money someday. So I wrote him a short note and felt quite gleeful about this.

But I felt also rather depressed all day. I do not know why, but I do know why. It is everything that is on my back at the moment, and I had been really terrified, thinking that I was going to have a stroke at night the night before because I had all the symptoms that I had had in London when I did have a small stroke, symptoms such as violent nausea and diarrhea and my head ice cold and sweating so my hair was soaking wet. This fright went on most of the night, so I did not sleep and I got agitated because although I had my Life Line there by the bed, the door was locked downstairs and I was afraid I would fall if I went down to unlock it; I was extremely shaky, so shaky that I could barely get to the bathroom, which is about four yards from my bed.

Anyway, the letter from the German man was an event and sort of interesting, and I called a friend that night, Betty

Lockwood, and told her this as a piece of interesting news, and she said right away, "Oh, I remember reading something somewhere in the *Washington Post* that this is a new scam and that it is happening in Germany and was very successful when one man did it and now a second man has actually borrowed the letter that the first man sent." There is nothing terribly wrong about this; it is just always annoying to be had, and I suppose that he can make a little money, very little certainly, on my signature and the page that I copied for him. So that is that.

Friday, February 25, 1994

THERE WAS a little more snow last night and I am praying Nadine can get here. I think it may be very slippery. But the great news is that Maggie will be able to come tomorrow for the weekend. Susan and I had hoped so dearly that at last we would have a weekend together; it has been now seven weeks or more, almost two months, and there is so much to catch up on, but there is going to be more snow and she simply cannot risk it. It is too dangerous.

Carol Ebbs, as a valentine, sent me several wonderful things, one a photograph of an engraving on glass by Rex Whistler of a mystical kind quoting the famous statement of Julian, "and all shall be well and all manner of things shall be well when the tongues of flame are enfolded in the crowned knot of fire and the fire and the rose are one." Julian . . . the first three sentences, and then T. S. Eliot borrowed them. I have always resented this, the quotes that fill "The Waste Land" and then are quoted as coming from Eliot. Carol also sent me that rarest of things, a perfect small lyric which was written in the ninth century as a requiem for the Abbess of Grandestine, who died young. Here it is:

> Thou hast come safe to port,
> I still at sea
> The light is on thy head,
> darkness in me
> Pluck thou in Heaven's field,
> violet and rose
> While I strew flowers
> that will thy vigil keep
> Where thou dost sleep,
> love, in thy last repose.

The first four lines are magic.

Saturday, February 26, 1994

THE EXPECTED storm is turning out to be mild, about two inches, and it has stopped snowing. I have asked Ronnie to get the mail for me. We are promised a big snow on Wednesday. I think that is why I felt too frail to go and get it this morning, and she did say when she came that the roads were very slippery. This winter does not end.

I have been thinking about how low I am and how frustrated clumsiness and incapacity make me feel. Tonight I saw that I guessed right with the title for this journal. It is a time of radical transition into old age, but I have been refusing to accept it. It is not strange that I am no longer interested very much in things; buying even writing paper irritates me. I do not want anything coming into the house, anything that has to be disposed of in any way. I am even bored by my hundreds of books and by the books that constantly stream in here and used to be of great interest and satisfaction. I think a great deal about breaking up this house, which will happen, of course, when I die, planning what objects or pieces of furniture should be listed and with addresses of the possible recipient. My most creative time is when I rest in the afternoon and I have long thoughts about life and death.

It has come to me that my lack of balance shows I limp slightly on the right side, as Nadine told me without surprise. She recognized it as a result of a small stroke, the one in March in London. It is since then, I see today, that I have entered a new phase and am approaching my death. If I can accept this, not as a struggle to keep going at my former pace but as a time of meditation when I need ask nothing of myself, will nothing except to live as well as possible as aware as possible, then I could feel I am preparing for a last great adventure as happily as I can.

Most of the time I am happy, learning a new kind of happiness for me which has nothing to do with achievement or even with creation. Each day I plan something I can look forward to. Today it may be ordering bulbs. I think of a letter I want to write today, perhaps to Norma, who sent me a charming valentine she had painted, blue and purple and truly romantic. And I will make out the March checks; I greatly enjoy making out checks and spending money in every possible way. This is not only true of my old age; it has always been true.

Monday, February 28, 1994

IT HAS been a ruinous day, and I am ashamed because yesterday I put such wise things on this cassette and had about decided that I could live not trying so hard and not feeling guilty and be a wise old woman enjoying every day for what it would bring. Then today there was a series of shocks, one after another.

One was a letter from Heather Frederick, who has been editing ten books of mine, mostly the journals and autobiographical work which will be put on records and sold by her Audio Books. She wanted a whole lot of photographs, including a photograph of my grandfather, of me with my father and my mother, of me as a child, of me as an adolescent. Finding all this is a lot of work, and there were all the photographs for Susan's book; they have all come back now, but they have not been arranged; some of the photographs that Margot chose for her biography have come back and have not been arranged. So there is this awful chaos, and going back over old photographs brings back so much; it is the pain always of going back into the past.

Then, and this is more or less humorous, but nonetheless it made the day perfectly awful for me. I decided to have canned ravioli, which I sometimes have for lunch, because I did not want to have to take any trouble. I had cried; the woman who is doing the recording had called me back to say she was sorry to have upset me. You see, I had meanwhile taken the entire morning to do what she asked me to do and so I had to talk to her and then after that there was another phone call. Anyway, I could not get the can open. I have an electric can opener which is completely maddening, and I think I must get another. You try and try, and finally there is this humming sound, but you don't know why it did not happen before. I got nowhere, and I had to open it with a regular can opener, a manual can opener of a simple kind that takes tremendous strength, and about a third of the way through it simply gave up and would not cut into the metal, it had gone too far over into the side of the can. I thought, "I do not know what I am going to do because here it is, it will spoil." The phone rang fortunately, and when I came back, I had a spurt of energy and managed to get it open. That had taken me twenty-five minutes of trying, so I was exhausted anyway and by then at the end of my tether.

Then I had a glass of beer and tried to look at the news and Nancy Kerrigan came on again. I am tired of her, and I think a lot of other people are. So it was that on the news and nothing else. I had hoped to hear a little bit more about bombing in Bosnia; maybe tonight there will be something on the news.

It has certainly been a difficult day. The cat did not want to come and be with me until five minutes ago, when he suddenly decided this was the moment, and I did give him a little brushing, which he needs. His fur looks very miserable. I think it is because of the cold, I am not quite sure.

Today there is still an icy wind, and it is impossible to tell how depressed I feel. I have cried and screamed today and exhausted myself. For what? It is not a life right now.

Wednesday, March 2, 1994

EVERYTHING IS in suspense before what may be one of the biggest storms for many years, although I somehow have to believe that it will probably go out to sea and we will not get the two feet of snow that may fall tomorrow the whole day. When it snows the whole day, it is very dismal and a little frightening. So we have been getting ready. Karen, whom I have not seen for two and a half weeks, she has been away, is the kind friend who takes me shopping and carries the heavy packages in; it was a godsend when she called yesterday and said that she could come this morning, and she came before ten and we went to DeMoulas, the Market Basket, it is called, a great big store in Portsmouth with everything, and got in a whole lot of items that are heavy to carry like the pineapple juice that I take every night with Colon Clenz and tissues and vegetables and a Danish ham, so we are all right.

As we were leaving and I was jubilant, a Federal Express truck drove up and handed me an envelope. I took it and opened it in the car while we drove to Portsmouth, and there was a letter from Cecil Lyon to say that Norton is making a new paperback edition on better paper and with a new cover and so on of *I Knew a Phoenix*. This is good news but also pressure. She is asking for all the photographs again; this book was written thirty years ago, and there is a folder in the file that says "Photographs for I Knew a Phoenix." but the point is there have been other books since, things have been taken out for them and for Susan's book, and to try to do what Cecil asks is next to impossible. I felt terribly ill because I knew all the time we were shopping that when I came home, I would have

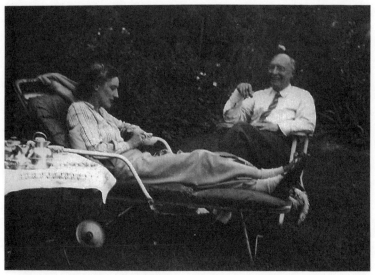

May and her father, George Sarton.

this ordeal before me. I have found everything except one photograph which I cannot bear to have lost, a photograph of S. S. Koteliansky and Juliette Huxley at Huxley's apartment over the zoo, where I saw them so often in the forties. It is a precious photograph for me. It is in the book, of course, but I cannot find the photograph itself, and I have looked everywhere now. When I do this, what I do is find all kinds of other photographs that I had forgotten, some really good ones of me as a younger woman, then I begin to feel terribly old because I do not look like that now. It is a fairly depressing thing, on the whole. I did find a photograph of Wondelgem, the house that we had to leave in 1914 that is so dear, and that is a lovely photograph. So I did find a few things that will help, but not the one I wanted most.

Monday, March 7, 1994

FOR ONCE a rainy day, a gray day. It is restful, but it has been one of those days when it seems as if everything went wrong for me. I got up at six because the cat wanted me to get up then as usual and went down. Before I got down the stairs, I heard that there was water running somewhere, and I thought I must have left a tap on. It turned out to be a leak in the ceiling of the porch where I sit and look at television and have my meals. It has a flat roof, and we have had a great deal of trouble with it. The problem here was not that it was just a drip, but that it seemed to be torrential. In an hour I felt that the pail would be full and I would not have the strength to lift it, so it was quite a problem.

Meanwhile, something has been overturning the garbage pail under the sink every night and strewing whatever is in it on the kitchen floor, which is not the happiest thing to happen on any day.

Never mind. What happened best today was that I suddenly realized that the top shelf of the cupboard I had built here to keep papers and so on in has been a mess of ragged Christmas wrapping for a long time, and now I asked Judy to empty it and find a place for it all so I would have a whole lot of space amongst other things to keep the boxes of the checks from 1993. That was a good happening.

Then I managed to write one letter immediately to somebody who had written me in today's mail. I have learned that if I do not answer a letter the day it comes, then it may never be answered, as indeed is true. This afternoon, feeling rather dim-witted, I started going over some of the boxes of letters that are here around my feet, and I find myself in a box of letters that had come for my birthday in 1993. So there you are. There is all that that must be eventually ordered, God knows when, because I still live on top of a swamp of depression for which I do not foresee any solution unless I can somehow start creating something, in all the clutter here wrest out some small poem.

I did write a poem because the murder of the number of maples in York moved me more than anything has in a long time. I was driving along Long Sands Road and suddenly realized that a whole magnificent line of very tall maples had been cut down and their huge bodies, some four or five feet thick, lay strewn about. The first time I went by and saw this mass murder it seemed quite unbelievable. That magnificent line of trees was among the treasures of this town. The great bodies lay along the road in a brutal desolation. Who committed this crime? Central Maine Power, who had them cut by eminent domain . . . and who permitted them to do so? The selectmen. I did manage under this blow to write a little poem which the York paper published in the letter column of the *York Weekly*.

Murder

Not people
People do not live and grow
For two hundred years—
Trees!
Their massive trunks broken to pieces
and thrown down,
Their burrowing roots
Torn from the earth,
Their bodies
All along the road.

> The old maples
> Have been murdered.
> How can we bear it?
> Never to see again
> Their splendor,
> Their autumnal
> Crimson and gold.
> They are gone forever,
> All along the road.
> How could we do it?

I needed to write a poem, but it is not good enough, only a small sign of hope.

So up till noon anyway it was rather a dismal day, just the one event of clearing up a shelf as a positive thing, until Judy Burrowes came to pick me up for lunch. I took her to Stage Neck Inn, where she has not been, she told me, and for once the bar where I always sit was closed, so we were forced to go into the very formal dining room. I was disconcerted by this, I did not feel properly dressed, but Judy looked charming. We had a nice table looking out at the sea and had a really delicious lunch as well as a drink. It was an intimate and at the same time formal lunch, and it had a certain charm; I think Judy enjoyed it as much as I did. I managed to mail six or seven letters, mostly bills that I had paid in the morning, so I did not have to ask her to do any errands with me.

I came back and almost immediately went to sleep; I felt tired. I feel tired all the time, and I guess a great many people do because of this prolonged gloomy weather, which really eats into one's soul. For me the extreme lack of energy remains a problem that does not seem to be solvable except by giving up even more than I have already given up.

Tuesday, March 8, 1994

A GRAY day again but warm, and I am excited at the idea that I am going to go out and find a book to read, although one has come from HarperCollins that they want a blurb for, so I have something to read at least. I have nearly finished the Belgian novel that I have been enjoying a great deal. It is laid in Brussels, and it is called *La Plage d'Ostende*. It has been fun to hear references to the things that I remember so well about Brussels, but when that book is finished, which will be tonight, I was going to be suddenly without reading matter, and this is always terrifying. It is like being without food, only perhaps even worse.

And then I have had Lee Blair's birthday on my mind that I wanted to celebrate in some way. But I am afraid because I am so depressed; it does not lift, and there is little I seem able to do to change it although I am certainly trying. I will explain some of the things I do, some of the things I try to invent to feel better. One is making a little order here, and this I am going to do every day.

Right now I have been browsing through a huge box of birthday messages last year; I was too ill even to open some of them. It is disturbing when you open a letter that was full of love and worry and you have not even read it. Eventually that box will be thrown out completely, and that will be one thing less at my feet.

I discovered a good box to put photographs in. The photographs were falling out of a gold Godiva box because there are so many. People send me photographs of their pets, and there are many photographs of me from when people have come here. It is a mess, and I still want to make another billboard with some newer photographs of friends, although I do not know quite where to hang it.

But what do I do to get out of despair? This morning I decided I was going to change my clothes radically. I have been wearing the same lavender waistcoat and gray pants and purple cashmere sweater for days, so I changed the color scheme completely. Now I have on an orange shirt, a big shirt, and a brown tweed jacket in which I have been much photographed, and I actually found brown socks. So this is a total change and should be making me feel better, and maybe it will.

Today at least there is nobody coming, and that is in some ways a relief. I have time, I do not have to hurry, I'll go out about eleven, and I think I will get some flowers because there are almost no flowers in the house now. That is a bad thing. But what else do I do? Mostly it is tidying things up to feel better.

Last night, and this is typical of the kind of frustration I have to deal with, I was tired, and when I came up to get undressed, I got caught in my shirt. I cannot button things, so I try always not to unbutton a shirt but put it on and off over my head. In pulling it over my head, one sleeve got mixed up in the rest of it, and I could not find the button to undo it. This was humorous, but at the same time it was frightening because I could not get my arm out, I could not have telephoned, I really did not know what to do. Finally I found the button, but it seemed impossible to get it opened. Finally I did, and by then I was very tired and simply wanted to go to bed and to sleep. But I know that these things which are part of old age can be taken care of, are taken care of sooner or later as one moves from one humorously clumsy thing to another. The day before, I had knocked over a bottle of red wine on the table just when I was in the middle of my dinner, and that is typical.

And of course, there are two flights of stairs here, and I am always trying to remember what I should have when I go down, to be sure to take it so I do not have to go back up again to get it. This is often my glasses as I wear different glasses for working up here at my desk and for looking at television.

What I still do to try to conquer depression is quick meals. I felt rather desperate about not knowing what to have because the fish stores are all closed in the winter, and I have not been able to have any fish, and that really leaves very little that I want. I have been eating some of the Danish ham that I managed to get undone with a little slice of pineapple; it really wasn't bad last night, with some fake mashed potatoes, the kind that come in a box, and those little peas that come in a can but which I then fix up with lettuce and a little bit of onion and butter as the French do, and they are good.

Probably I am not clinically depressed if I can still manage to do these things and do not simply say I cannot do anything, I am going to lie down. There is part of me that only wants to do that, that wants to lie down, if possible with the cat, and if possible go to sleep, for sleep is the way out of depression. I do have extraordinary dreams, often nightmares, often funnily enough, since I cannot travel, about trying to get a suitcase packed and of being unable to do so. In a letter that I wrote today to a woman who is concerned about my not eating the right things, I told her—she is ninety—that I do not want to live to be ninety, and I am damned if I am not going to have a piece of chocolate every day and some things that I like which probably are not the best things for me. I do not want to be here at ninety. I ended the letter to her, I think, "but my head has been invaded by a second stroke, and I am not myself." Where is my self? God knows.

I have been going through a box of the letters that came for my birthday last year. It has been moving, I must say, to see how many people wrote and what dear letters there are. In one today, somebody from Wichita, Kansas, quotes Madame de Staël to me in a wonderful quotation which is: "Life appears like a long shipwreck of which the debris are friendship, glory and love, the shores of existence are strewn with them." It is a persuasive image and particularly suits my mood.

Today I did several things that I hoped would help me, and perhaps they did. I have done some clearing up at my desk and written a few notes since I had a nap. I went to the bookstore, and it was difficult to find anything there I wanted to read, really a disaster. But I finally left with three paperbacks by best-selling women writers, and we will see what makes a best seller. At any rate I know they will be readable, and that is what I need.

I also got flowers, because there were no fresh flowers in the house, and that is very rare—none in my bedroom, so now there is a lovely bunch that I created, and they are right there, some yellow daisy chrysanthemums and some lavender ones, one purplish one, and some darling small asters which are like something that you might pick in your garden.

Saturday, March 12, 1994

THE DAY before yesterday I really was so low that I did not know what to do, and I tried a few things. One was to order some anemones and tulips, and they are a kind of wizardry because looking at them, I think they swell up with joy, with delight, and seeing them open with their dark purple hearts is such a magic thing.

It has been an extraordinary morning. Susan called and I think really has flu, which is not surprising because she has been working so terribly hard and stays up sometimes till three in the morning. I think this is dangerous when you teach, as she does, and have eighty students and all those papers to read, and besides that she is working on her books of letters from me, which she has been sleuthing out all over the country, and they will eventually be books, which is exciting, but I do not think she should be doing it now. Luckily she does have some time off next year, and I think she will see what a lot she can get done when she has, at last, that free time which she needs so badly.

Then it has been an extraordinary morning because early this morning after Susan's call, Polly Starr called, and I had told her how depressed I am yesterday. She called to say, "I have two houses. Come and live with me." She has a house on Beacon Street amongst other things. That I even consider moving out of these two offices, the six or eight gigantic files, the whole business that is done here is just tremendous. I could not possibly do it, but it was generous of her to think of that. Then, much to my delight, Doris Grumbach, who has been in Mexico, called and said that she and Sybil had an absolutely wonderful restful time. They had been in a small accident which damaged their car considerably, a skid, about two weeks before they left, and they were still getting over bruises. Doris said it was a perfect time and they did nothing but lie in the sun and walk and swim and I guess they must come back restored, but she had a hard time getting there because it was one of those weekends of storms when the flights were all canceled. She finally took a bus from Bangor to Boston and then from Boston to New York by train. Somehow or other she got there, but it took hours and hours, was exhausting, but she is as pleased as I am by the fact that people read her journals and read mine and see that we know each other and think of us in a way as together, which is nice. It was a lift to hear her voice because she has been gone for some time and I have missed her.

I should say more about how every single day in this house I see things that Maggie has done for me, imaginative things like rubbing the old mahogany chest in the guest room so it is gleaming. She always brings manna for the birds—by that I mean suet wrapped up and hung—and every bird around waits for that and thanks Maggie, I hope. Everywhere there are little things. She cleans silver when she sees it needs it; she sees what needs to be done and does it. I have never known anybody like her. In the first place, most people do not dare enter somebody else's house and see something that needs to be done and do it. It takes a lot of gumption and especially a lot of love, which is what she puts into it, I know.

So here I am, in many ways a lucky woman but still depressed. It is as if there were a pane of glass between me and almost everything. The only thing that a pane of glass does not separate me from is Pierrot.

Now I am about to go and get the mail because Char is here and I am taking her out to lunch, and I must get some things done before that. I have, perhaps, not said enough about that absorbing novel called *La Plage d'Ostende* by Jacqueline Harpman. This is a very readable book; it is a strange book in which the plot is a child who falls in love with a man when she is eleven and he is thirty and determines that she is going to marry him and finally does after he has been married to a rich woman. He is a painter. All her life she lives this great love, and this is the story of it; it is moving, but written with a little bit too much melodrama in the actual words. However, it is lovely for me to be reading French. I looked forward every night to being in the language and had some dreams in French, which I have never done before. I must write to this dear woman in Belgium and thank her.

Monday, March 14, 1994

ALMOST HALF the month is over, so we are moving toward the
spring and every day is a little lighter—it is now quarter to
five and quite light still. I have been deciding to make it fun to
go over all these boxes and bundles of letters that go back.
This afternoon I went back to sort out last Christmas's letters,
and it is very touching to find all these friends, now six months
later, writing such messages. Especially, I had two or three
letters from the Japanese people who were here to celebrate
my eightieth birthday and who are mentioned in *Encore*,
which apparently they have all read with great delight. So
that was one lovely thing, and luckily I did not find anything
that was upsetting, that I felt badly not to have answered. A
great deal can be thrown away.

ANOTHER SET of letters I discovered today had to do with my
radio appearance on "All Things Considered" on National
Public Radio which was in October and apparently had quite
an effect on people because they got a lot of letters and I got
quite a few. This was satisfying, and I now have a file that
says "All Things Considered," and the letters are not scattered about among other things. How it will ever all be ordered, I do not know, and the depression does not lift for a
single morning; I wake every morning dreading having to
make the effort of the day, dreading having to get up. It is
much easier, of course, when Joan or Nadine is here. Today
Joan was here, and it was wonderful to lie in bed and have my

breakfast brought after four days in which I had to do that and also make my bed myself.

Little by little I get something done, certainly not a great deal. But some of the most important other things do not get done. I must write to Angeliki, my adopted Greek daughter. Our relationship goes back forty years at least, because I started to help support her through one of those charitable organizations where you pay twenty dollars a month. But then I got to know her because I was in Greece and managed to get in touch with her, which you are not supposed to do, and we became friends. She is a lovely person, who has two grown-up daughters now, one married, the other a great teacher, and a wonderful husband, whom she adores. So I do not have to worry about her anymore. In fact, she worries about me and wants me to go and live with them. Since I do not speak a word of Greek and also could not be parted from my files and from this whole office floor of the house, I do not know how I could ever move.

But spring will come. Yesterday when I went down at six because Pierrot had determined that he was going to get up at that time, when I opened the door to let him out, there was a bunch of daffodils from Penny, who does occasionally a Japanese massage for me. She is English. It was six in the morning. When were those daffodils delivered? I simply cannot imagine. There was a note saying she was on her way to England, where her parents live, for the spring holiday, but we shall surely meet after the various things that are going to happen now.

Soon the long desolation and loneliness of this winter will be over. Susan, if she is well enough—she has flu at the moment—will be coming this weekend on her spring holiday and be here for a week. And then Margot, who will be staying with Margaret, not with me. I do not entertain guests here anymore. She will be coming for a week, so there will be interviews. One of the good things about her coming is that I have been reading Carol Heilbrun's letters to me from the beginning. We have known each other now about forty years, certainly twenty. She came to Nelson, the first critic ever to be interested in my work, and she has done an enormous amount for me since then, and we have become friends, good friends. The beauty of reading those letters was in seeing how a friendship grows, and now it has become most nourishing and adorable, and I am extremely grateful for Carol, who signs her letters "With love and admiration," and I love that. She is so distinguished herself, that she can admire me is very satisfactory and unexpected.

I have not found a great poem for a while to publish here, and I wish I could; that and if I could play music again would really do something for me. It has to happen if I am ever to start writing again. It is hard to handle this strange limbo when nothing happens inside me. Things happen, they always do, like those daffodils arriving, which is a sort of a miracle, but I am not there in the way that I could be if I were well, well in spirit as well as physically.

Tuesday, March 15, 1994

I CALLED Deborah Pease because she has not called for quite a while, and the winter has been just as bad, if not worse, in New York, so I wanted to be sure she was all right. As always we had a good talk, and I think she understands pretty well why it is that I am so depressed. She has written two poems, and it always gives me enormous pleasure when Margaret

Whalen sent me a poem today which had come out of her reading the *Celebration for May Sarton* book and my own book *Writings on Writing*. It is a remarkably good poem, a really dense, thick (and by "thick" I mean "meditative") poem.

Now dismal fog has come in. I am glad I went out as I did before lunch to get scotch and some sherry for Erika, who is coming on Thursday, so at least that is done. Meanwhile, how is it that everything disappears so fast? I bought paper napkins the other day, I think the other day, and they have all gone. I noticed at the time that the package seemed to be much thinner than it used to be, and that is the answer. The firms charge the same amount and give you less.

I read *Newsweek* and the paper. *Newsweek* was pretty depressing. I have been meaning to talk for days about how horrified I was that Diane Sawyer opened a new program that she is the anchor for which is about transition. What she did was to revive the Manson case, that most awful murder under the cult of Manson, who is now in jail for life. She even interviewed two of the people who had been among the killers; one of them described murdering one of the people with a fork, simply driving a fork into them. The terrible thing is that in *Newsweek* it implied that what people want is that kind of thing; they want to hear about murders and torture and everything grisly like that, and the media gives them what they want.

I had a fascinating letter from a Japanese woman in the Middle West who has been teaching at a small college in Illinois, I think, or maybe Ohio, teaching Japanese. She has lived in America for twenty-six years. She is anxious to translate me into Japanese and to find a Japanese publisher for me, of course not realizing that I already have one who has done four books and will do, I believe, another two, and who made *Journal of a Solitude*, the first one they did, into a best seller.

The kind of thing that keeps me from doing anything creative is, however, a letter like this which is flattering. She feels deeply about my work obviously, but it meant looking out addresses, the address of Kyoko, because Kyoko has just given a speech about my poetry in Tokyo and I thought might share it with this woman and might help her with general ideas about what she wants to do about me, and the address of Mrs. Naoko Takeda, who was the translator for *Journal of a Solitude* and *As We Are Now* and who, I have heard, is on her way to Japan, where they are going to discuss what to do next, what she would translate next. So they are really committed to bringing me before the Japanese public, and this is thrilling. But writing that letter—I was also shaky and finding it hard to type—took me nearly an hour, and it is not any good and full of mistakes. I have said so often that if I do not answer that day, it probably is going to get lost in the pile.

I have been spending these last days going over the Christmas mail from last Christmas and have found some things which I feel I must answer. One is a delightful card from a woman who reads my poetry to her little girl, whose name is Brittany. The little girl is only eight months old, and her mother writes on the back of this delightful photograph of the little girl with her tongue out looking very excited, "Brittany Alexandra says I love the sound of you, Miss Sarton, I just love the sound of you." It made me remember that my mother always read poetry to me just before I went to sleep from the time I was quite small. Now I must try to do a little bit more than throw things away; I must be a little bit more creative and write to Brittany's mother.

Wednesday, March 16, 1994

I HAVE been reading these days a best seller called *A Thousand Acres* by Jane Smiley. It is about big farms out in Nebraska, and it is well written, a good novel. But I thought suddenly that what makes a best seller seems to be, at least in the ones that I have read recently, and I have read quite a few, is sex, there has to be explicit sex, there have to be sexual scenes; this is what readers must have. Whereas I have never had an explicit sex scene in a book of mine because I do not like reading them. I think cold sex is boring. But I am proud of the fact that without sex my novels have a big audience, and people cannot put them down. This is a small triumph which I am happy to record today.

Sunday, March 20, 1994

THE FIRST day of spring. Susan and I woke up to snow. Luckily it stopped in about an hour and the sun is out now and it is very windy, there are still two feet of snow everywhere, so it certainly is not spring and heaven knows when we will see the daffodils. Today I am expecting Raymond, who is coming at four with an amaryllis for me that he has been growing, and I think that he was pleased that I talked about him in the short piece I wrote for *Yankee* when I talked about grace in Maine

and how extraordinarily gracious people are, workmen especially, and told a few stories about them and Raymond, who
was one of the most truly kind and polite men I have ever
known and, of course, a great gardener.

So right now, as I am ordering seeds, I am nostalgic about
my garden as it used to be. I have a gardener now, and Susan
thinks she does extremely well, but nobody will ever be able
to prune the bushes the way he did so that the ones right in
front of the house were as flat as a table. Nobody can do this
but Raymond.

Susan is here, which makes everything seem possible
again. She arrived at about five yesterday, wonderfully early
so that she was not too tired to be able to enjoy her dinner,
and I enjoyed getting it, a simple one, very much like what I
have almost every night, of broiled sole and fresh beans with
parsley and those little pink potatoes that are so good and an
excellent ice-cream dessert with brownies made by Sylvia,
lucky woman that I am.

I wish more birds would come to the feeders. The gold-
finches are beginning to turn, one of the great signs of spring.
The other one is the birdsong; there is some birdsong in the
morning, and that is exciting, a lot more exciting than the
endless cawing of the crows. I have never been as aware as I
am this winter of the crows. They are everywhere, and especially early in the morning their cawing is incessant.

The other day a friend of Erica's lent me a mystery story
laid at the Friends Meeting House in Cambridge which so
many people I know have belonged to, including Polly Starr.
So it is amusing to visualize it all and to be back in Cambridge,
a treat for me, and a break from a book that I am not very
persuaded about which they want a blurb. HarperCollins in
San Francisco sent it, and it is about a brother watching his
brother die of AIDS, which certainly could be an important
and moving subject, but I think the problem is that it was a

Heaven knows when we will see spring flowers.

short story originally and it is not quite a novel. It should have been shorter, perhaps a novella. Who knows?

Susan is out walking for an hour and a half for the five miles that she wants to do as a regular thing and has been deprived of in the terrible weather in New York. But I am happy to see that she is much better. Either she is much better or is hiding from me that she is not. Her voice sounds better. I felt she had walking pneumonia when I listened to her in New York, and she was dreadfully overtired. I wish she could retire right now. She reminded me today that March 20 was the first day that she ever went to the Berg Collection to start working in the archives on the work she is doing on my work, and that was eight years ago on March 20 and has now become *Among the Usual Days* and will become at least three more books of letters. So it is exciting.

This week is Passover, and on Saturday Susan is going to prepare a Passover Seder for Nancy and me. It is going to be very moving, I think, and an experience that will make the beginning of spring seem very precious.

Monday, March 21, 1994

HERE WE are with snow on the ground and no sign of spring and no glimpse of earth. Meanwhile, the birds are eating a great deal, and the squirrels are incredible—there are three who come every day, at least one of which must go back at least ten years, and there are a couple of red squirrels too.

The great event yesterday was Raymond Philbrook coming. It was great to see him. And it is one of those miracles that he who had always been lonely, lived with his mother and sister, never married, now has a dear companion, a young woman who has fallen in love with him, and after doing a lot for him for two or three years, maybe more than that, she has now moved in. It is a blessed thing to imagine his waiting for her to come home after work, then her getting him a nice supper, and their watching television together. She is a darling person. He brought me a magnificent red amaryllis with six blossoms that he had grown for me. He does look old, and like me, he does not walk easily. I could see that he came very slowly from the car, but he still has the same twinkle in his eye and we always have a good talk. I teased him that he must write a poem for Madeleine. He used to write rhymed verses for me on my birthday and Christmas, and he worked hard on these, so for several days he would be hard at work saying, "No, it isn't ready yet," and then he would read it to me. This was a big event all those years when he worked for me. Since Raymond, I have had three gardeners, none of whom comes anywhere near to his skill. He was a brilliant gardener. So it was a tremendous pleasure to see him and Madeleine in the middle of this terrible winter when so many people are ill and everyone, including me, seems to be depressed. It was life-giving to be with them for half an hour.

After they left at about half past four or five, Susan and I as usual watched a video, this one of Piaf. This video is more about her as a singer, not as a woman, not her love affairs and so on. Absolutely fascinating. Singing all those songs that we remember so well. It was fascinating to realize how hard she worked on each song, on the gestures, for instance, and her gestures were minimal but tremendously telling. After this had been spoken about by someone on the video, you were aware every time you watched her, what chary gestures, but always so meaningful. And that marvelous face and that haunting voice which haunted me all night. Seeing it was a tremendous treat. And then, as a third treat—Raymond first, then Piaf—we had lobsters. As usual Pierrot is quite aware when there are lobsters in the house, even before they are put in the kettle, and sits waiting patiently for his claw as soon as they are brought to the table.

Yesterday was one of those dismal days, we have had one other this year, of heavy rain, and it began to leak in the study.

There seems to be no hope this winter as something keeps going wrong and there is nothing we can do. But at least it was not snow. It was a bad day because I picked up *Time* magazine, which comes on Tuesdays, and for some stupid reason opened it to the part about tigers, that tigers are now almost an extinct species, and there was this magnificent face, the golden eyes, the extraordinary majesty and fire of this animal, and then a grisly photograph of one being skinned very shortly after it was killed, and there was something about this skinned body and the eyes still there, not seeing. It was terrible, I started crying and could not stop. It seemed as if we are destroying everything, the air, and now the tigers, the whales, the elephants, the glories of God, what creation is all about. We are destroying the planet. People say this all the time, but they do not really feel it. It does not hit them, but it certainly hit me with that portrait of the tiger on the cover of *Time* and then what was inside. They are being slaughtered because the Chinese use the bones for some kind of medical reason, and of course, the poachers get a lot of money for this and probably are very poor. Everything is done for money. The elephant tusks are taken for money.

I felt woe. I guess everything piled up inside of me, but finally I stopped crying and came up here and tried to do something at my desk. I wrote, as I remember, a couple of notes and that was about it. Now at eleven o'clock, Mary Winslow will be coming to collect Polly Starr's wonderful portrait of me that is in the front hall and has been there ever since I moved here. I really should not have had it for so long as it now turns out that Paul Sachs, who was then curator of the Fogg Museum, bought it for the Fogg at a show of Polly Thayer's and then found out that it was May Sarton, the daughter of his colleague at Harvard George Sarton, so he lent it to my parents with the provision that it be given back to the Fogg after their deaths. This was never put in writing, and

I must admit that I forgot it and so took it, after my father died, to Wright Street, where Judy and I lived; then Judy had it for a while while I was at Nelson, so it is high time that it gets to the Fogg, and I am happy to have this way to do it because Polly is having a show. She is ninety now and blind, and she is having a last show, I hope with some of the wonderful landscapes she has painted in recent years. This portrait will be a key piece, also because of the date, 1938.

I finished the whodunit that was given to me. It is laid in the Cambridge Meeting House; it is called *Quaker Silence* by Irene Allen. I think it is a first whodunit by her, and the unlikely sleuth is the clerk of the Cambridge Meeting. It interested me because it brought back so many memories, the Copley-Greens lived right beside or just opposite the Meeting House, Polly Starr was a member, and so was my Judy Matlack, who I think did not want me to join because she was afraid I would talk too much—I do not think she was right about that, but she, of course, did fairly often say a few words. There is always the problem in Quaker meetings that people talk too much; I hope I would not have done so, but then there is the problem of what you do without hurting people's feelings to tell them that the silence is really the point, not what is said. This is a good book, and I am glad that I was given it.

Susan is here, and that makes an enormous difference. The house feels alive again, and Cybèle gives her little barks when someone is coming so we are warned.

Friday, March 25, 1994

PASSOVER. SUSAN has done a marvelous exciting and difficult
job of making a Seder here for Nancy Hartley and me. I shall
describe it; she has been preparing for days, brought things
from New York, then has been buying things here in town
where there are not many Jews, so that the tables in the big
food stores like Shaw's have only a small amount of the traditional food that she needed. Sylvia made a marvelous lemon
dessert. One of the traditional things is macaroons, which I
love, and it will be wonderful to see Nancy, so it is altogether
quite a celebration. And today felt like a holiday because we
went out for the mail, and I wanted to see whether the Easter
lilies had come in at Dave's yet. There they were, so I got two
lilies for the house and that was wonderful. Then I realized
that I had never taken Susan to the reservation where the
birds are, the ducks, and there used to be a black swan, which
I did not see this year, but lots of geese waddling across the
road and swimming away and honking away, ducks quacking.
It is the most delightful place imaginable, a little heaven right
in the middle of York. It is not easy to find, and we got lost
coming home but managed then to stop at the sort of semista-
tionery there is, and I was able to get the envelopes that I
need, and, in fact, in the mail which I read when we came
back was the contract from the Japanese publisher for *Plant
Dreaming Deep* so I was able to get that packed up.

A very satisfactory day altogether whereas yesterday I, let
us hope, reached the bottom of depression. I have never been
as depressed, and it has to do, I now realize, partly with the

feeling that I no longer control my life because of a biographer being invested in it, because also of Susan's doing a wonderful job on collecting letters which will be published to a great extent after my death. In other words, I do not have control anymore over my past. It is a strange feeling, and I am sure is slightly neurotic but not entirely so, and I am sure it has to do with the fact that Margot, my biographer, comes on Monday, and I have not seen her for months. Every time she comes, of course, things are dug up from the past, and I have to think about things. I dream so much now. I dream a great deal about people I have not seen for years and people who do not even interest me very much, but they are in my dreams, and I have to pay attention to them.

Meanwhile, the massive mess of Whitewater goes on. I was impressed by Clinton. I thought he did a remarkable job. We have never had a president who is quite as good on the actual information that he has to know as he is. He is amazing, the ground he can cover. It gives you an idea of what it is to be president. One certainly does not envy someone who is. But I am hoping, and I think it may well happen, that in the end the Republicans will pay for their glee at finding something they could accuse the president of because in the end it does not seem as if it were going to be very, very bad—whatever they find. We shall just have to wait and see.

Sunday, March 27, 1994

IT IS Palm Sunday, but what I am still celebrating is the Seder which we had last night and Susan had taken so much trouble to give to Nancy and me as a total experience. I felt at the end of the evening that we had made a long journey back into time and through an enormous amount of struggle and pain to a beautiful serenity and richness of life and the wish of the Jews for all people to be free. This is something I did not entirely expect. We were given, each of us, a beautiful Haggadah, the text of the service, in which there are long passages by the rabbi or whoever is officiating at the dinner which the group leads, and these are moving because even in the case of the miraculous escape of the Jews when the Red Sea was parted by God and the Jews escaped and the Egyptians were swallowed up, there is a prayer saying that they grieve for the Egyptians who could not make it, they who had enslaved them for centuries.

Susan had taken an enormous amount of trouble with the table, which was lovely with a big white cloth and candlesticks—I was happy to see my grandmother's candlesticks—and the symbolic Passover plate which must appear on the table and which contains a shank bone, bitter roots, a hardboiled egg, parsley, horseradish, and something called *haroseth*, which symbolizes the mortar the Jews used when they were slaves. These are all things that have historical references, which are metaphors in a way, so that plate was there, and a little pot of daffodils. We were three, and there is a glass for Elijah, who at any moment during the dinner might turn up at the door and is then offered a glass of wine, but there is also a chair and a set place for anyone who needs shelter and food, anyone who is not free. So the whole celebration is a celebration of freedom from slavery, years of slavery, and it is a peaceful and happy time for Jews.

We were very happy by the time we had our first glass of wine after reading quite a lot from the Haggadah. With that we had gefülte fish, which looked beautiful, two little humps of gefülte fish each with a sliced carrot on top that looked extremely pretty and were delicious. Pierrot did eat some of the pollack as a special treat later on. I should say that we had a drink beforehand with some chicken livers, the traditional Jewish chicken livers which Susan had made for us, and we had that with the matzoh because for the Seder you can use nothing which has yeast or flour in it, so there is only the matzoh instead of bread.

We started out with the reading, then had the first glass of wine with the fish, and a delicious chicken soup which had matzoh balls in it, and then, the pièce de résistance, a perfect roast chicken which Susan had cut up so it was easy to handle, with asparagus and a boiled potato. I forgot to say that at each place there is also a hard-boiled egg in a small bowl of salt water. I do not know what the reason for this is, but it is one of the traditional things. You can eat it, but we saved ours, and I am going to have a Seder egg for my lunch, I think mashed up and on some olive bread that I have.

After we had really enjoyed tremendously our chicken and our main dish came this ineffable lemon torte which Sylvia Frieze had made for us that very morning, and I must say it is one of the best things I have ever tasted. It is so light and so lemony and so sweet.

It seems hard, nearly impossible, to realize that Susan will be gone in a few hours. It is going to snow or rain or sleet, it is a dismal day, and I suppose I reached the lowest ebb of depression yesterday, but the Seder certainly did something, and I am now determined to make a new start and to pull myself up by the bootstraps and behave better altogether. This afternoon somebody comes to look at books and to buy some possibly and tomorrow Margot comes, so this is all a crush of things that make for memories and for thinking about for a long time to come, and I suppose that is to say that it is still a rich life.

Thursday, March 31, 1994

. . . AND THE sun is out, as it was yesterday, which is really magic after all the sullen, windy, rainy, stormy days that we have had for so long. Of course, everything is gray now that the snow is almost gone, although there are shoots of daffodils coming up.

But this is a tremendous day because for the first time in a year, I can hardly believe it, I am leaving York, and for the first time in a year I am going to be away from home for a whole day. Margot is driving me to see Anne and Barbara in North Parsonsfield. I am excited because I shall have a rest after lunch, and I am told that their owl, their small owl with a broken wing which they saved, will be sitting on the top of the door in the bedroom where I shall have my nap, and I wonder how it will be. He is a darling little owl, and I will remember his name when I see him. Altogether it will be wonderful, and I am going to enjoy the drive as well though everything is still wintry, but I shall see what has been happening. I know every house on the road there, and I think Margot is relieved that I am going to drive with her because I know the way and she got lost last time. It is easy to do.

Otherwise, having her here and the hour and a half every day that we talk is exhausting. It brings everything up, of course, and extraordinary things come out that I had not expected because Margot knows things about me that I had totally forgotten. She is always telling me things that I have simply forgotten, and this is fascinating, but it leads to all kinds of thoughts and sometimes miseries. She was surprised that I forgave Rosalind Greene entirely after she had prevented my theater company from getting a job with Radcliffe College because she had felt that she had to go to Ada Comstock and tell her there were lesbians in the company. It was a real betrayal, and at the time it was hard to take. But oddly enough, I more or less forgot it, and it occurred to me, and I said to Margot yesterday, that I think the things that are terribly painful that you cannot forget are the things you did that you wish you had not done, and not so much the things that people have done to you. At least in the case of Rosalind, I totally forgave her and wrote her many letters which are in Susan's book.

Lovely Easter cards come these days. I am hoping to write a poem for Bill Ewert for my birthday, but that will have to be next week; anything else will be much too late.

Friday, April 1, 1994

SOMEONE SENT me an Easter card that has really made Easter, and so I must read it. Her name is Linda Lyon, and she is not somebody I know well at all. It is a poem by Carl Sandburg.

> If I should pass the tomb of Jonah
> I think I would stop there and sit for a while
> Because I was swallowed once deep in the dark
> And came out alive after all.

Of course I felt that was written for me this year and perhaps for a great many other people who have been through this winter and have been depressed. All the Easter cards are dear to me. Though I now remember the people to whom I always used to send cards, I simply have not had time this week with Margot here. My desk is unbelievable, and God knows when I shall get at it because I must write a poem for my birthday, to be printed for my eighty-second birthday, and this is not done yet.

Saturday, April 2, 1994

THE WONDERFUL thing was to go yesterday to Parsonsfield, to go deep into Maine with Margot driving a Chrysler Le Baron convertible and the chance to talk in a quiet, ordinary way, not in the way when we are working.

It was wonderful too to see Anne and Barbara, and I was horrified when they told me it has been two and a half years since I have been there. I went to introduce them to Susan— two and a half years ago! It seems impossible, but of course, for most of this last year I have been too ill to go anywhere. The proof is that this was the first time in a year that I have left York.

Everything about their life, Anne's and Barbara's, the values are so incredible. You are in a kind of paradise, but you are also aware that this paradise is extremely costly because of all there is to do. Just keeping the wood cut for the fire, just shoveling the snow off the roof as well as using the snow-blower for twenty-four inches of snow falling every now and then, quite often this year. Unfortunately the birds were not at the feeders because a hawk had come, and so they were all scattered. But instead of that there was a live-in goldfinch that lives in the house and flies around as it wants, a goldfinch rescued when it was a tiny little forlorn bird that had probably been pushed out of the nest.

Margot showed great courage because she is terrified of wings flying over her head, and the bird was excited by strangers being there and flew around a lot and even landed on a cuff or a shoulder. The bird was interested in having ice cream. It was fascinating.

And then I rested for an hour with the pet owl, also, of course, a rescued animal. The only animals they have are animals that are brought them usually by people who know how phenomenal Anne's gifts of healing are. This owl's wing was so hurt that he could never fly again, so he's there and has to be fed. Anne was saying the goldfinch is the easiest bird they have ever had to feed. They had a robin called Edward for a long time who died finally, and he ate cat food, wet cat food, and it was always so messy, and of course he made messes all over the house. But this is a seed-eating bird, the goldfinch, so it is easy to feed and inexpensive. It does not eat very much, and it is, I must say, adorable. It was much like being in heaven, looking out, strangely enough, on rather deep snow, so that Anne was concerned because there is a whole bed of crocuses in front of the barn which should be in flower now and is under two feet of snow.

Afterword, April 2

As I came to Easter Day in reading the journal to correct here and there, I was astonished to discover that I had not mentioned that I suffered a stroke the Saturday before, when I was alone here. I slipped off the chaise longue and could not get up. Fortunately a young man came to deliver flowers, saw my plight, and gallantly pulled me up from the floor. I felt very queer and ill but was determined to arrange the flowers, which I managed to do. Meanwhile, the young man was disturbed by my abnormal behavior. I thought it was a TIA, and perhaps my speech was strange. Anyway, the young man went to Mary-Leigh Smart's across the way, and she and Beverly called an ambulance right away and then phoned me to tell me they had done so. I was not pleased, because a TIA is over in an hour or so. But they were right, as it turned out to be a stroke after all. While I waited for the ambulance, I managed to pack my suitcase for the hospital, as I have done many times before. I called Maggie. She realized that it was not a TIA, that my voice sounded strange and made the decision to drive down at once from Hallowell, a two-hour drive. Meanwhile, the ambulance came, and the medical assistant as usual took my blood pressure, temperature, et cetera and asked me a lot of questions about my health. It is terribly irritating, but one is helpless. I was hitched up to oxygen. The emergency room at York Hospital is very familiar to me, and luckily Dr. Gilroy was in the hospital at four o'clock and could see me. Maggie found a note on my door to say where I was and got to me just after four. What a savior! They took some X rays and had a heart monitor going. The problem was that there was no hospital room ready. I finally got one around ten o'clock P.M., glad to go to sleep and that Maggie could go home and get something to eat. The long wait in emergency had been exhausting.

On Sunday Margot Peters came to the hospital for a good-bye. We were to have had dinner that night.

On Monday they did a CAT scan, and on Tuesday I was allowed to go home. The whole thing was a nightmare because I felt queer and ill though not crippled, only a little shakier than usual and more off-balance. I did not need another stroke, the second in a few months. The first had been in London in April '93.

Monday, April 11, 1994

. . . AND IT certainly doesn't feel like spring, temperature is forty, but at least the sun is out and Maggie is still here and will not be leaving until Wednesday, which is a great blessing because she can take me to the doctor tomorrow, and I look forward to telling him how really awful I feel. My head is not itself, so I am not myself. Everything, the smallest thing I have to do, is a tremendous ordeal.

Tuesday, April 12, 1994

MAGGIE DROVE me to the hospital to see Dr. Gilroy this morning at nine, and I was impressed by the quality of his listening and the way he responded; he answered everything I asked so honestly, but was unable to give me a date when I might begin to feel better, so it is a matter of plodding along and thinking that eventually my head will begin to feel more like that of a human being and less like that of a Stone Age person who perhaps does not even know that there is such a thing as a wheel.

I do find it more interesting to read now, and I am greatly enjoying the book about the two black women who lived to be one hundred one and one hundred two. They have been much in the news, and they are amusing and warm and give a great deal. The whole book is based on interviews with them, so all the words that are said are their own words. It is great to have a book that I look forward to reading. Tonight I'll finish it.

With Maggie's help, we are making my lentil and sausage dish with onions, which with sour cream is one of my favorite meals.

No interesting mail today. *The New Yorker* didn't come, which made me mad, and I read the whole of *Time* waiting for the doctor and found almost nothing of interest. Everything is depressing, every single thing, not least the terrible massacres in Rwanda.

Pussycat has been very good and very comforting to me. I do not know what I would do without him.

April 13, 1994

AN ABSOLUTELY dreary day, a strong pouring rain, and it is supposed to go on all night. It does not really matter what it does because I am not going to feel any better, whether the sun is out or it is pouring rain, and I began to think this afternoon, well, if it had been at the end of a drought, this would have been an absolutely wonderful day, everybody rejoicing in so much water falling at last. So one has to take things as they come.

Chris De Vinck sent me a terribly idealistic speech written, I think, for his students in which he begged them to think of beauty when they use offensive language and, therefore, to censor the ugly words that permeate the language of students today. He is rather an optimist to believe this would have the slightest effect, but perhaps it will. At least he will be a wonderful role model for his students, and perhaps some of his purity and gentleness will rub off on them.

Thursday, April 14, 1994

THE SUN is out after an abysmal day yesterday. I woke up this morning wondering how I can be more intelligent about the depression which is what I wake up to every day, wondering how I am going to get up, how I am going to do what has to be done, which today was making the bed as well as getting my breakfast, which I have done and carried it up, which was terrifying because I was so shaky but I got there all right. So I decided that in order to deal with the depression this morning, I was going to think about all the things I can do instead of all the frustrating things I cannot do.

For instance, I can write checks. Suddenly I realize what a frustration it would be if I could not and somebody had to do that for me. The only trouble is simple mathematics, eight and six, seven minus two, sometimes I am stopped for several seconds, trying to do simple arithmetic. And as for dealing with 6 percent, which is the Maine tax on everything, this is next to impossible for me.

The fact that I *can* make my bed, that I *can* carry a tray upstairs and downstairs is good. I can water the plants, though I am not good at it and do not like to do it. Everything is such a mess. I did write four little notes yesterday, and that is difficult to do. I am very slowed down when it comes to writing, not so much slowed down, although I make a lot of mistakes, simply the tremendous effort. I guess it is the effort of getting my head together to say anything. Now I have certain formulas, one of them is "thanks for the lift" for the kind people who write me about life and my work, and I must say that ill as I am now, these letters are of paramount importance, and I am extremely grateful to anyone who takes the trouble to write. It is not always restful to have a ten-page, single-spaced letter all about the life of someone I do not even know. Sometimes even these self-engrossed letters are interesting because they come from all over the country, for one thing, and they come from such different people, from such different walks of life, from so many states. So there is the excitement at least of the mail when it is Monday after the weekend without mail.

At any moment there will be daffodils out along the woods, they are the first ones that come, and I am so excited that I think I may try to walk down there with a cane, possibly early this afternoon. I am having lunch with Edythe today, and that is something to look forward to.

Another trick about depression is to try always to find something to look forward to. Susan is coming this weekend. It will be so wonderful to resume all our little traditions.

Pierrot is asleep on his chair, a soft ball of fluff.

I can go up and down to the third floor; it is rather scary coming down, but I can do it. Making the bed is the hardest thing, but I can do it. I guess a hundred times a day I say to myself, "You can do it," about something. But some things I cannot do, and one of them is buttoning my shirts. So more and more I am getting turtlenecks and things that do not have to be buttoned. But I do like a nice clean shirt and miss them. I can walk out to the car. I can drive. Not right away. Dr. Gilroy suggested that I not drive for two weeks, and it is now just a little over a week since the stroke. This is Thursday, and the stroke was a week ago Saturday.

Friday, April 15, 1994

A PERFECTLY beautiful day. Yesterday was a low day; I felt
very ill, I had a long cold sweat lasting almost an hour and
then decided that I could not get up, that I was feeling too ill,
so I stayed in bed. Susan was here, which was wonderful. I
could not eat my breakfast, just slept, and did not ever get
dressed. The only thing I managed to do was go up to my desk
and write the weekly checks and one letter accepting that a
photographer come in June who had wanted to photograph
me before and apparently I said no. This time I was impressed
by the magnificent portrait of Adrienne Rich.

So yesterday was a zero day in which the big event was
Susan bringing me a little bunch of daffodils from the garden
and also some forsythia. I did look at a TV show that was
devoted in large part to Bosnia and was so depressing that it
made me feel even more ill. I never even looked at the paper
yesterday.

I tried to get Maggie. She was away, but she did come
back just as I called at about three-thirty and said she could
come right away, which is wonderful. She did, and I got supper all fixed so that she could cook it in a few minutes, and we
had a nice supper of sole which Susan had brought and little
red potatoes and some broccoli with that wonderful béarnaise
sauce that Maggie makes.

Late in the day Norma, my doctor friend in St. Peters-
burg, called and was upset that I had again had an hour's
cold sweat yesterday morning and felt so ill, and she has

persuaded me to try to get to Dr. Petrovich today or tomorrow. She thinks that the cold sweat may have a cardiac source and that I should see him, so Maggie is trying to get an appointment for me.

Monday, April 19, 1994

I was able to see Dr. Petrovich at the hospital today in Emergency. He is an immensely thorough and wise physician. He examined me carefully and did not find anything wrong. Tomorrow I will see whether Petrovich's office can supply one of those heart monitors that you wear for two weeks, which will give him an idea of what is happening when I have this cold sweat.

It is just an "up-in-the-air" feeling, not to know anything, to feel so queer in my head. I did manage to write a letter to Marianne Dubois, who had written me an extraordinary letter and sent me her book. She has become—the only thing I can say—intimately acquainted with Jesus Christ, who visits her and who answers her questions and those of other people. She has written a book called *The Joy of God*. All that she says seems wise, but what a tremendous responsibility because people turn to her now and want advice all the time, and she is, I gather, doing public performances rather than seeing individuals. That relieves her of the terrible weight it would be to see people one at a time. So something accomplished today.

April 21, 1994

PIERROT IS a great blessing. He spends the whole day on his chair and does not even come up on my bed until about half past four. It is strange.

The daffodils are now out, even in the field. If only I could walk down and see them!

I am enormously grateful to Phyllis Whitney, who writes murder mysteries and sent me one of her books called *The Ebony Swan*, which I am finding extremely interesting and just what I need at this moment.

And of course, I, with everyone else in America who has heard about it on the news, am horrified that somebody buried a poor police dog, a female who had had puppies within the last two weeks, buried her alive with just her head out having either kicked or crushed her stomach with stones so she could not get herself out and someone heard her moaning and went and saved her. But it was too late. They could not operate. And now there is naturally an uproar about trying to find out who did this.

Friday, April 29, 1994

A GRAY cold day. This minute I saw a cardinal, brilliant at the feeder, and Ronnie is coming to take me to Shaw's to do a big shopping for household things. That will give me peace of mind because I seem all the time to run out of things. I love the cartoon I have pinned up on the Frigidaire. It says, "I'm running a loose ship." The only way to make it a tighter ship is to get certain things in that need to be gotten in.

I am having trouble eating. I do not feel at all hungry. It is hard for me even to swallow a peanut butter sandwich, although ginger ale seems to help, and the medicine which I am taking for the pain in my stomach has worked. But I'm still nauseated most of the time. I mostly simply feel ill, feel "not well," feel that something serious is wrong which I cannot control and which I do not understand. The doctor seems to think I am in fine shape, and thank goodness, I heard yesterday that I can drive as soon as I feel able to. I think I'll wait till after my birthday. Then I will start driving; it will be a tremendous freedom to be able to do that.

I am reading Sean O'Faolain's autobiography, *Vive Moi*, a horrible title. The fact is that he is, although he was a real male chauvinist pig in relation to Edith Kennedy, an extremely good writer. His descriptions of the skies over Ireland, especially County Cork, are staggeringly beautiful. One had to be a very good writer to do that, and he is a very good writer. He was in love, well, one wonders if he was really in love, with Elizabeth Bowen, but he was in love with the writer Bowen and quite rightly felt that *The Last September* was a great novel, and one of the great novels, the few great novels about Ireland. Apparently he wrote a novel about the people, the revolutionaries who burned those great houses down. *The Last September* is about a house very much like Bowen's which is burned down.

One gets the feeling, and his daughter, who writes an introduction to the book, suggests that it is so, that he was not really in love with Bowen. He was apparently later very much in love with Honor Tracy.

Saturday, April 30, 1994

A GRIM, rainy day, although Susan said it was her favorite kind of day, very gentle in a way, and all the brilliant gold and white of the daffodils shines out in the rain. I am waiting for Penny Morgan to come. Her massages are wonderful, first I have had of any kind of Japanese massage that she does very quietly.

The birds are now eating me out of house and home, especially the horrible grackles, who assault the feeders. Once in a while the squirrels chase them off, and I am so glad when they do, but now the feeder is half emptied in one day.

I have been trying to decide what poems for The Women's Press. They are publishing a book of my poems next year. I am thrilled about this, and the choices Kathy Gale made were good except that she left out all political poems, and I do want "The Invocation to Kali" to be used and a couple of other things. I wonder whether a poem called "At Kent State" will mean anything in England. The list they sent me was an excellent list; only it did not include any of *A Grain* of *Mustard Seed* or *The Silence Now*, and I think there should be some of those later poems included.

Once more I have been upset by something that my biographer has perpetrated. She asked to see Carol Heilbrun's letters to me. There is a big folder of letters. I read them and was moved by the growth of this friendship and what a rich and wonderful thing it has been between us. Carol was a little dismayed that of the hundreds of letters, Margot has asked only to use one paragraph, which is, as Carol said, "negative." I am sure it is about my need for editing on the journals—Carol feels strongly about it, as does Margot. But in every letter in which Carol discusses this, she always ends on a positive note, writing of how valuable the journals are. I cannot believe they are as bad as I am told. Why do people copy out such large parts of them? Why do people carry them around with them wherever they go? Why do people sleep always with a journal of mine by their bed? Because they want to be able to refer to it in the night. Something is natural and open in these journals, and they are deeper than they look.

Sunday, May 1, 1994

I AM thinking of my parents today, perhaps since I am nearing my own birthday.

As I have written else where, my mother found out that she was illegitimate when she was engaged to my father and felt, having learned this, that she had to go to all his relatives and tell them, confess if you will, that she was a bastard. My mother almost died of this, I think. She felt betrayed by her father, whom she adored, because he had not told her, because he left her undefended before the world, to deal with the world undefended, and I think she never got over this. She never wanted to meet English people. She never went to see the rather sophisticated Elwes cousins in London, although characteristically my father did.

He humiliated her; he did not give her credit; he never once that I know of said, "I have a wonderful wife. I could not have done what I have done without her."

He never acknowledged in any way that she sometimes earned more than he did, because my mother never stopped creating. At one time she was designing the dresses for Belgart in Washington, dresses which were bought by Neiman-Marcus and Lord & Taylor in New York and Marshall Field in Chicago. For a few years, she was earning more than he did. But did he ever admit that or ever thank her? Never! She put me through school; he did not. She paid for my camp and the clothes to go to camp; he did not. He was not fatherly in the ordinary sense of the word. I think he came to enjoy me after we could talk together, but even then we used to fight. After my mother died, our relationship became better, but while she was alive, I suffered too much from what she was suffering and too much from the way he treated her.

She got four meals a day, and she was often not well and had terrible migraine headaches. Never once did he take her out to dinner. Very, very rarely, if ever. When I lived with Judith Matlack in Cambridge, we could invite them for Sunday dinner in the middle of the day. Often my mother called me that afternoon to say, "You have no idea how wonderful it was because I could write letters in the morning instead of cooking." And when we did go there for Sunday dinner, as we did sometimes, then we cleared up for her and washed the dishes, a thing, as I said, which my father never did.

The Limbosches, who were intimate friends of both my father and mother, were very much against the marriage and later wrote terrible letters when my mother became pregnant, because they knew that she might die if she did, and it was little Alfred who, instead of Mother dying, died at five days old because he had an obstruction in his intestinal tract which was operated on but could not save him.

What I remember is the charm of our single bedroom where we all three slept, which Mother had converted into a kind of heavenly bower for the baby. There were shelves made and piles of diapers and things laid out and a lovely bassinet on wheels, if I remember.

When she left the hospital, she did not come home. She went to stay with the David Smiths. He was a great mathematician, and his wife was very fond of my mother. I do not know whether she asked to go there or whether the doctor said she must be given a haven, but they took her in and loved her, and she was there for three months before she came home. I have often wondered whether she thought of not coming home, because after they were both dead, I found a letter from my father to my mother written at the Harvard Club in New York saying, "I want to welcome little Alfred into the world," and that meant, of course, that my father had simply run away and not faced being with Mother while she gave birth to this little son, and I have often wondered if she thought of leaving him at that point, as she may well have done. His not being there when the baby was born is unforgivable.

I have been generous to my father in everything that I have written about him. The poem "A Celebration for George Sarton" and the portrait of him in *A World of Light* in which he appears so charming that people who read it thought that I adored him, and of course that was not true. I suffered very great pain because of the way he treated my mother and how much she suffered and also how much anger she buried. I am convinced that she died of cancer from buried anger and that this perhaps happens more often than we know.

But now, after remembering my father's chauvinism, I have to remind myself always that my parents had a marriage of true minds. They not only loved each other deeply, but shared a great deal. How I often think of their afternoon teas in the garden, the animated talk about art, literature, music, where my father's superior knowledge was nourished by my mother's intuitive wisdom. And above all they shared in George Sarton's great dream of making the History of Science a major part of any study of the humanities. By the time he died there was a department of the History of Science in every major university and college. The five great tomes of his own *Introduction to the History of Science* were translated into Chinese, Japanese, Arabic, Turkish, Greek. He was a heroic scholar, and he had a great dream which my mother helped him attain.

Friday, May 8, 1994

AGAIN A beautiful day and it is supposed to get colder and be gray in the afternoon, but this is wonderful luck because Ann and Barbara are coming to celebrate Ann's and my joint birthday, as we do every year. Usually we have lunch with lobster and champagne or whatever we wish, but they suggested very wisely that they come just for a drink at eleven and that we would have a good chance to talk but not make all the fuss about food.

Margaret left me an outdoor phone so I do not have to run to the phone; I can take it wherever I am. This is wonderful because when she and Barbara were here two days ago, from five on the phone rang every time I put it down, and we were trying to have a drink out on the terrace. Margaret is such a generous person; she wanted to give it to me, but I could not have that, so I am paying for it.

But the trouble with my life is that it is distracted by tiny unimportant things; they are so numerous that I never get out from under. I never feel there is time opening out, it is always closing in. For instance, this is typical. In the mail today came the telephone bill, and I like to pay bills the day they come because I am so afraid of their getting lost in the chaos here, and often they do. After I had climbed the two flights of stairs and looked at the mail, intending to write a check right away, I could not find the telephone bill. I looked three or four times through the whole maybe fifteen letters that had come today, and it was not there. So what to do? The only thing to do was to go back downstairs and see if it had slipped out of the pile because as I was coming up the stairs, three times three little boxes which had birthday presents in them fell out of my arms as I was carrying the letters, and three times I had to stoop down and find the little box again. The fact that it happened three times was enervating. Well, I decided that perhaps the telephone bill had fallen out with one of the little boxes, but it had not. I found that it had, however, fallen on the floor with two letters that I wanted to keep. It might have gotten lost. Now the check is safely written, and it is ready to go.

It has been a tremendous birthday. People are so kind. And I like to think that they find joy in writing to me to tell me how much they have enjoyed my books, that this gives them pleasure. It is always moving to me the kinds of things that people say. This avalanche of letters and cards over my birthday has been a little overwhelming, but sustaining just the same. Now the whole couch in my study up here is covered with cards and envelopes—the problem is always to find the address; sometimes people do not put the address inside, only on the outside, so I have to keep the envelopes.

Eric called me yesterday to wish me a happy birthday. He has been away. And he gave me the very good news that they are still going to bind my books. This is such an extravagance, and I am spoiled that Norton has over the years bound in leather every one of my books as they came out, and as there are now three this year, it is an expensive business and I had a terrible feeling I was going to be considered retired. But Eric said, "Not at all."

Yesterday I called Carol Houck Smith about the proof on the poems, which had upset me a little; it was not very good, and she agreed and is going to do everything she can about it. But she had great news for me. She had just been to a marketing meeting, and everyone was astonished by the sales of my books. I can hardly believe it myself. I think she said *The Fur Person*, a hundred thirty thousand since 1985. I know that several were over twenty thousand, really amazing numbers. The only one that surprised me a little that had not sold a great deal yet was *Encore*, but I think it is still going strong. In the mail today someone wrote that a bookstore in New York was saving the last copy for her. Of course, there is no reason why they should not reorder, but I am afraid they often do not. And I do hear that now the big dispensers of books, the super stars, have my books, and that means that people discover them and know that they exist.

But the great event besides this business news is that a raccoon began to get in the cat door, which I first realized because the pail of birdseed had been tipped over and a lot of it eaten. Then I heard the cat's dishes being pushed around, but I did not register on it until I went down as I often do at about half past four to feed the cat and saw that there was not a thing left in his dishes, and he does not usually eat everything. Not only that, he was extremely nervous. He is like Tom Jones before him, a Quaker cat, a pacifist who does not want to fight. It is rather surprising because after all, this

invading raccoon was on Pierrot's territory. In a way I am glad
he did not fight because the raccoon could have rabies; they
are around with rabies these days. I told Maggie, and she was
very upset and immediately said that she would bring a Hava-
hart trap; she is coming tomorrow night, and we shall catch
the raccoon, and she will see that the warden gets it. So that is
solved, but for the last two nights I have simply kept the door
closed so that Pierrot cannot go in and out as he likes, but it
seems to have worked all right. I let him out at about eight
and then get him in around midnight, as I used to do when I
was writing poems.

THERE HAVE been several good events. One is that Margot
Peters called me the other day and we had a very good talk,
which has helped me because I was worried. I began to think
that she did not understand about my father, and I now realize that she does. It was a warm and friendly talk, which left
me touched and exhilarated and happy that she is doing the
biography.

THERE HAVE been tremendous amounts of flowers. It is a pity
that my birthday does not come in December, when there are
no outdoor flowers. Now there are literally thousands of daffodils, and I like them better than any florist flowers. But some
of the florist flowers have been magnificent. They are now
beginning to go, but I hear that there are two more bunches
going to come tomorrow. Unbelievable! But it is rewarding to
feel that so many people care, so many people hope I am in
good health, but there, of course, they are wrong.

A new friend who is a great fan of mine, a woman who
lived in Germany until very recently and now in Boston,
managed to get lily of the valley for me. She must have read
somewhere that it has always been my flower and that when I
was born, they brought my mother a bunch from the garden,

from her garden. More and more I realize what leaving Wondelgem must have meant to her, to her more than my father
because she had created a garden there. When they finally
knew that they could get through to Holland and from there
to England, they had to eliminate and eliminate and finally
left with only a steamer trunk, and this, of course, had to
contain some books and things of my father's. But the miracle
was that they buried his notes for his *History of Science*, I
think in a tin container of some kind which was then wrapped
in a rug. I do not know how they managed to bury it, but they
did, and when we went back in 1918, it was unburied and
intact. Without it, George Sarton probably could never have
done the first volumes of his *History of Science*, so that was a
bit of luck. It is strange that I have been thinking about this
departure from Wondelgem a great deal lately.

I am impressed by Doris Grumbach's book *Fifty Days of
Solitude*, although it seems a little bit too planned. After all, I
have lived a life of solitude for fifty years. In the short time, in
that fifty days, she learned a great deal, and so the reader
learns a great deal, and I am grateful for the book. I think it
may become a classic. It will certainly persuade a few people
to try the same experiment and see what they find inside
themselves. She quotes from many of the people I have lived
with in my solitude from Valéry and Mauriac to Yeats and the
philosopher with a Dutch name whom I cannot remember at
the moment.

From what I have said here, I realize that it has been a
rich time, but also a terribly pressured one because I had
business to do all through my birthday. I had to call London
twice, and that is always somewhat agitating, once to speak
with Kathy Gale, my editor at The Women's Press because
they are going to do quite a big book of poems, and she had
made some suggestions using Brad Daziel's book *Sarton Selected*, which has a great many poems in it. All her sugges-

tions were good, but there were some things that I feel strongly had to be in, and now she has agreed. She let me add twenty poems. One of them was the "Invocation to Kali" because all these terrible things were happening in the world, and to have no mention of them in the poems would seem strange.

I also wanted "Birthday on the Acropolis." I climbed the Acropolis on my fiftieth birthday. I had planned a trip around the world to move from the ancient civilizations back finally to Greece, which would seem the youngest, and it was a tremendous experience. Now the air is so polluted you do not see the extraordinary soft gold of the pillars, I understand. Pallas Athene was my favorite goddess when I was a child. I think she perhaps was a real Muse, so the poem has something to do with that. Kathy Gale was so kind and welcoming on the telephone and so ready to take my suggestions that it was a very happy conversation.

Then I had to call my agent in London about the contract for these poems. The Women's Press is very generous, a thousand pounds advance, for things that have all been published before. It is quite amazing.

Tuesday, May 10, 1994

WELL, I feel proud of myself. This morning Kelly, a visiting nurse, came to draw blood because of my taking Coumadin, and I was prepared to tell her it would help me if she would not write the first half hour of the time, which she usually does, but just do the few things she has to do to draw the blood, then do the writing later while I go upstairs so I will not waste an entire hour of my best creative time. Kelly was very cooperative, also dazzled by the daffodils. I told her how terribly ill I feel, and she seemed to be impressed and will get back to my doctor so perhaps something will be done.

While she was there, Nadine brought the mail, which fortunately was very dull today. And I looked at *Time* and *Newsweek* superficially and began to feel sicker and sicker and wondered how I could get upstairs and whether I could work. By about quarter to ten I thought, "I am simply too ill. I have to give up now. I cannot go on any longer." But something else in me said, "You have got to climb the stairs, those two flights of stairs, and do a little, a very little, and that will be it for the day." So I did, and then I got into the whole hash of stuff here at my desk and everything there was to do and managed finally to write five notes, one of them at least quite important to Andrea Lockett, who did an excellent interview with me that appeared in the *New York Quarterly* this last issue.

But it is an extraordinary life I am leading because it is all the time impossible. The effort is staggering. The wish to die is staggering. To give up. Not to have to make the effort any longer. But at the same time there is the marvelous joy of Mandela coming into his own. Everything that is happening in South Africa, however much of a shadow there is nevertheless, and how much doubt as to whether they can really make it, Mandela is a shining joy. Every time I see him I feel blessed.

I realized the other night that I have had a real enemy, and this took place when *Faithful Are the Wounds* came out or shortly afterwards. In 1954 I had received the Lucy Martin Donnelly Fellowship from Bryn Mawr College to write my novel *Faithful Are the Wounds*. The fellowship does not exist now, but the first one had been given to Eudora Welty, the second was given to me, and the third to Elizabeth Bowen. It required no residence, although one was expected to come for a few days to the college and then go off and work. I wrote *Faithful Are the Wounds* while I was teaching at Harvard, as a lowly instructor, of course, and I wrote it out of anger at the reaction of the faculty to the suicide of F. O. Matthiessen. It got the best review I have ever had from the Sunday *New York Times*. So I went to Bryn Mawr for a few days to celebrate, I thought, but I have never been so cold-shouldered in my life. The faculty at Bryn Mawr had been poisoned by Harry Levin, who, as a result of this novel, became an implacable enemy. He thought Ivan Goldberg, the Jewish professor in the book who was the only worthy antagonist of Cavan and by no means a caricature of anybody, was a portrait of himself. He was not Harry Levin as I wrote him. The model for this character was a man whom I had seen once at a faculty meeting, who wore thick glasses and had stiff shirt collars.

Harry was the only Jew in the English department, so he was convinced immediately that Goldberg was a caricature of himself, and he was livid. I am sure that he wrote to the committee at Bryn Mawr at once, and I know that he wrote to Marianne Moore. That letter must be extant somewhere in her letters to me because she wrote me rather a severe letter about the book. I explained to her that it was not Harry Levin and there was nothing in my intention to do him any harm, but I think over the years he probably is responsible for the fact that I have never won a prize and that I have been so neglected by the literary establishment, of which he was an important member. No doubt he had something to do with my not being a member of the Academy of Arts and Letters, for instance. For once you realize that somebody is out to get you, and he really was, you realize how subtle that poison can be. It was quite a revelation to me lying in bed sometime last week, and I spent the night thinking about this; it was disturbing to know that I had had a real enemy, because I had not taken this in. Although at the time I was upset, naturally, and felt that I was not being well treated.

One reason why I come up thinking of this now is that I got a letter from a woman who was at Radcliffe at that time the other day who spoke extremely feelingly of the book. I have not answered it yet, but what I must tell her is something about this which she evidently did not know. I wish I could find the letter. I spend half my life looking for things that I cannot find. Literally.

Thursday, May 12, 1994

DR. GILROY is now going to try Prozac, and the terrible thing about Prozac for somebody as nervous as I am is that you do not know that it is going to do you any good for two weeks or more. Meanwhile, I read the small print and realized what the dangers were, which seem to be infinite, that you may get a sudden rash, that you may become dizzy, that you may have trouble sleeping, or lose weight, which I would gladly do now that I am over 120 pounds, that you suffer from self-starvation, I have forgotten the word for that, suggested that you do not drive, that alcohol may affect you adversely, but I simply cannot pay attention to this.

Yesterday I went to get the thing that monitors the heart. You wear it for two weeks, but I did not realize that it does not work alone. You have to put it on, and then you have to telephone headquarters and put it on the headphone in some way so that they can hear it. I went back in the afternoon because I tried it and it seemed to be too difficult for me to do. I am going to ask Gilroy tomorrow whether I can give it up. The drug may be enough; let us hope it will work.

Meanwhile, I do not feel well. I am frightened. I am dreadfully lonely, and thank goodness Susan comes tomorrow night. Examples of the frustrations in my life: A woman who wrote me a good letter about *Faithful Are the Wounds.* And who had known a great many friends of mine such as Eleanor Blair and Ada Comstock, whom I admired so much, the president of Radcliffe. In the first place, I lost the letter in the vast confusion here, and I must have spent two or three hours trying to find it. Half an hour today and I did put my hand on it at last only to discover that she had not signed her name and her address was nowhere on the letter, so then I had to find the envelope. By extraordinary luck I did find it, but I did not recognize the name. She appears to live in Stanton, California, so I had to put a note on the envelope of the letter, "If this isn't the right address, please send this back." I can well understand doing such a thing myself, but it was irritating and frustrating, I must admit. Such triumph when I found the letter at last, but then such dismay when I could not find the address! However, little by little I am improving things here.

The hardest thing for me right now is that dear Kathy Gale at The Women's Press in London sent me a list of the poems they want to do and said that she would need the dates when they were written. This is nearly impossible for me because the dates are nowhere. . . . I suppose if I went over a lot of papers, I could find some of them at least, but I have to depend on what books they were in and where I was then. It has proved to be difficult. I am using three or four different books to help me. One is *Sarton Selected,* which does show which books they come from and then the date of the book; then I am using Elizabeth Evans's *May Sarton, Revisited,* which is in the Twayne series and has a good chronology; and at last I am sure about the deaths of my mother and father because I could not remember those dates or when I first went to Nelson. There is so much that I do not remember.

Today has been a gloomy day, extremely gloomy. I wonder how I am to survive this time, but I must do it. I must try, which means living from day to day, from moment to moment. Now in a few moments it is time for me to go down and make a drink and look at the news. Every time Mandela appears on the screen I am happy, but that is the only happy news.

The daffodils are still wonderful, but they have nearly gone. Now the tulips are the great thing, and so far the deer have not eaten them. Every morning I am terrified that they may.

Friday, May 13, 1994

FRIDAY, MAY 13, turned out to be a good day because I had an excellent talk with Dr. Gilroy, who has persuaded me that Prozac may be the answer to my problems. This is the fourth day I have taken it, and I have not had any serious side effects. He said that usually if there are going to be any, they show up the first or second day. Next week he is going to give me a slightly stronger dose although in the end the dose I am taking now, which is just one a day, may be the answer. He said I could drive, which was tremendously heartening because in the small print, which I read with dread about Prozac when I got the medicine, it said no driving. He said the reason it has had such a bad press is that at first it was given to extremely disturbed people, and they often had violent reactions.

Karen Kozlowski came to take me to the doctor's, which was awfully kind of her, and then we did a shopping at

Golden Harvest to get some vegetables, as I try to do when Susan is coming, and she is coming tonight, but late because she is stopping to see her parents. I am afraid it is going to be awfully cold, but it is happy news. Altogether I think four days on Prozac made me more optimistic and more able to look forward. What has been so bad about the last weeks has been that I did not look forward to anything, even to the next meal, whereas now in the middle of my nap I was thinking how nice it would be to have my drink this afternoon and look at the news, though there does not seem ever to be enough about South Africa and so much of the other news is depressing.

The other great news, and it is really wonderful, is that this morning at about quarter past eight I saw the oriole, first in the ornamental cherry right outside the window and then at the bird feeder. What a sight and oh, how it always makes my heart leap up! So now I am going to go down and see whether I can find a contraption that I used to have which I could spear a half an orange in and hang it up because they like them so much. Nadine says that the purple finches love them too, so everybody will be happy if I can manage to do this, and then I must pick some daffodils in the wind because they are going so fast now, and then get up to my desk.

Meanwhile, I discover that it is Margot Peters's birthday today, so she is a Taurus too, which I had not realized, and that is quite a bond. I am hoping that they can get flowers to her today because it is an hour difference there, so off I go.

Sunday, May 15, 1994

SUSAN CAME and went in a flash, it seemed, but it is marvelous
what she accomplishes in twenty-four hours. For instance, she
cleaned the oven, which I should have noticed needed it, and
she brought an absolutely wonderful film, a French film
called, it is not a good title for it, *All the Mornings of the
World*, which, as Susan said, is really about what music is. Its
hero is a great cellist in the seventeenth century, and the
music, at least some of it, is Couperin. This man is a genius,
the cellist. He loses his wife, whom he adored, and really
writes for her and plays for her. He has two daughters, whom
he teaches the cello, and eventually they play concerts about
once a year. The king tries to get him to the court, but he will
not do it. He is a solitary; he plays all day alone in an old cabin
and then agrees to teach a young man who comes to him,
adoring, and begs to be taken on. It is an extraordinary film.
Everything about it, the exteriors, not a château, but a rather
formal farmhouse where they live, and the way they are
dressed, and the colors of the film, which are all beige and
brown, very subdued. And the performance by Gérard
Depardieu is staggering. He has an extraordinary ability to
project thought and feeling, a man of great anger and love,
and really the film is about love, I think, more than anything.
It has tragedy and passion in it, and I was mesmerized by it. It
lasts two hours, and I must say that I was extremely tired
when it was over, and I did not even want a drink. I wanted to
go to bed and think about it, and I certainly will think about it

many times. The cello is such a marvelous instrument that to have a whole two hours in which you hear heavenly sounds only from cellos . . . I must see if I have any Couperin records. I might.

So that was what we did. Then I asked Susan to show me how to put a little cassette into the machine that she gave me for my birthday, which I am ashamed to say I have been very bad about using because I am so bad about machines, but she showed me how to put a cassette in. The cassette I put in was a requiem by John Rutter, who died of AIDS, and it was sent to me by a friend of his who sang in the same choir with him, they stood side by side. Michael Sirmons who lives in Austin, Texas, sent me this, and I have just listened to it. It is full of tenderness; of course, the Agnus Dei almost always is, but this is a particularly beautiful one. It has great melodic variety. I found it very moving and want to hear it again more than once, I think, now that I know how to put a cassette into the machine.

I do not know whether my problem right now is old age, the stroke, or the drug I am taking, Prozac, which alters the mind, and Norma Adams tells me that it really does alter the mind. It changes certain circuits if I understand it, so it is a little frightening. The first five days I took it I felt a sense of relief. I began to look forward to things for the first time in two months, and I did not have any strange feelings or side effects that I could not handle. Whereas today, possibly after being fairly exhausted by this film, I woke up not feeling well at all and have been shaky all day. Just now when I took out the cassette, I had to get on the floor to do it to see properly, and then I could not get up, which reminded me of the stroke, but I did manage to get up, onto my knees, and pull myself up. Naturally anything which you know is going to affect your mind causes anxiety, so that today I have been very anxious, partly because I am afraid it is affecting my digestive system, and that is such a problem for me always that if the drug adds to it, it will probably not be something that I want to use.

It is marvelous that John Rutter, who died from AIDS, wrote this beautiful tender requiem, for surely many people will listen to it and feel blessed, as I did.

My dream now, now that I did what I should do, which is to listen to this record, is to write four or five little notes and begin to clear the desk. It is intolerable the way it is. But first I must write to Michael to thank him.

Tuesday, May 17, 1994

I HAVE been reading my journal, in the last two months anyway—that is, March and April—and it has been a painful experience because it is a description of severe depression, and I have been wondering even if it should be published, wondering also how I have managed to live through this really awful time. I discovered as I was reading today that Margot, my biographer, had already been reading it before I did, the typed copy from the cassettes, and she made some remarks. I shall be happy to tell her that Carol Heilbrun is going to edit it for me and was warm in her agreement to do that. I am surprised that Margot would read something which I myself had not yet read. It is a difficult situation, there is no getting around it.

So even though I feel quite ill, I keep telling myself, "In a month you will feel a lot better, and won't it be wonderful if Prozac works?"

I went down to speak to Pat, the gardener, and she had

been able to get lobelia, the deep blue lobelia that I love so much, and her helper is planting it. This is wonderful for the garden. It suddenly gives me hope.

Bill Ewert has printed the poem I am sending out for my eighty-second birthday, an old poem, "Of Molluscs," one of my favorites, and so I want to get at writing a few notes to people right now to send it out tomorrow.

Wednesday, May 18, 1994

ANOTHER HORRIBLY gloomy day, but I was determined to go out and do some errands to get food in the house, for one thing, and I did that this morning and quite enjoyed it. It is fun to go out and see the world now I am allowed to drive. I made myself get up at three from my rest though I was longing to have another hour on my bed, but I made myself go down and stuff a Cornish hen for my supper.

Nanette de Muesey, who lives in North Canton, Ohio, sent me magnificent flowers, three branches of white and red lilies that smell so sweet, and a very large purple delphinium standing among them, and four-long stemmed, sweetly scented freesias—a beautiful event today. But I do not see that I am better.

Polly Starr called this afternoon. She is much worse off than I am because, in the first place, she is ninety, and in the second place, she has what so many old people have, deteriorating eyesight which nothing can be done about. She will be entirely blind in time. She says she does know if there is sunlight. I was glad to hear that, because these days of rain have been so dark, a real darkness.

Betty Lockwood is a great support. She was the librarian on Star Island and has sold a great many of my books. She knows several people who have been enormously helped by Prozac and is very supportive and sure that it is going to make a difference. I hope she is right. There is time. It is only a little over a week since I started it, so there are three weeks to go.

Apart from the flowers coming, the nicest thing that happened today was dear Joan offered to sew on a button for me. I tried to do it yesterday and simply could not. I could not get the little knot at the end to work, so it kept slipping through. It was nostalgic and beautiful to see Joan sitting in the rocking chair and sewing, there is something so familial and wonderful really about a woman whom you love sewing. I think of my mother, who made such beautiful clothes and did one lovely thing, well, she did many lovely things, but one that I remember today is that she made dresses for my dolls exactly like my own. Eleanor and Nancy were my two dolls, and I loved them dearly.

Saturday, May 21, 1994

ANOTHER BEAUTIFUL day, and I must say the world is glowing right now. This is the peak of spring, when the leaves are still fresh green and the trees are still transparent, one can see the branches. Yesterday I went to David Upton, my optometrist, who would be able to tell me whether my eyes have changed because of the stroke. I had forgotten how tiring that concentration on seeing small print and slight differences of dark and light is, but he is extremely able and kind. There was some good news, no glaucoma, but I do have cataracts beginning in both eyes. However, I am so old that it may well be that they will simply stay there or else in a year they might get bigger and need help. He says there are two good surgeons around here that he could recommend, so that is good.

Pat Stanton, a new friend who has offered to drive me now and then, drove me there, a charming woman who is head of the board of trustees of the library and about to face raising money for a new library. They are bursting at the seams, so when I went to sleep last night, I began to think about helping, what I might be able to afford, because the library is so important and it has done a wonderful job of bringing children in.

Sunday, May 22, 1994

AN ABSOLUTELY glorious day, a soft blue sea, no surf, the field very green now, so it is that green field and blue sea, and I am here on the third floor struggling with a little over two weeks to go of this ordeal by Prozac, and I understand well why some people simply will not stay the course, but I want so much to feel better. I think the incentive is great. My life is made up of small endeavors and small rewards.

Yesterday Bill Ewert brought a great fan of mine whose name is Betty Towmes, and I signed fifty pieces celebrating my eighty-second birthday. It is an old poem, "Of Molluscs," but one I am fond of, and some people will not have the *Collected Poems* and so may not know it.

There are two things that have been on my mind to record here. One of them is about Fred Hollows, whose autobiography I have been reading. Fred Hollows is a tremendously civilized man, not only a great eye doctor and eye surgeon but also a generally civilized man. He was a great climber, played chess, and in talking about climbing, he says:

> That is one sort of high, that is climbing a high mountain. It has always been important to me, the physical kind involving endurance, some nerve, and paying off with a sense of something accomplished. There is also an aesthetic high which is harder to describe and account for. I can get it from music, but mostly I get it from reading verse. I think verse is terribly important. It's to do with communication and the neopallium, that's the newest in evolutionary terms part for the cerebrum, the front and upper part of the brain which is formed by the development of new pathways for sight and hearing. Our greater development in this area distinguishes us from the other animals. Verse lyricizes human communication, or the kind of verse that I respond to does. I agree with those critics who say that verse works against the transitoriness of emotions and ideas and makes their expression universal and enduring. For me, John Keats, at his best, epitomizes lyricism in English. And lyricism contributes to that heightened form of consciousness which is what poetry is all about. It's to do with economy and rightness. The best lines of verse say things with the greatest possible concision and precision. Good surgery is the same.

I love that.

Many of the small incidents in my life now, and there are no big incidents, are full of poetry, and sometimes I am aware of it, sometimes not, as was Joan's sewing on that button for me last week.

The other small or great happening this last week has been the return of the oriole, and now Nadine has strung oranges across the wire. It is an incredible sight, that orange and black, but the strange thing is that I have not heard the oriole sing. Is he already so mated that he does not have to woo his bride? I do not know. It is such a marvelous song I have missed hearing it.

Bill Ewert has lost a great deal of weight. He used to be a teddy bear, and when he came in yesterday, I barely recognized him, this lithe six-foot-tall man, very elegant, but somehow I miss the teddy bear that he used to be. It has been a valiant and great fight because he had a serious heart attack a year or more ago, and losing a great deal of weight is part of his keeping his health now. So after I had signed the poems, we had a good talk in the library, and although I got tired, I enjoyed it. I had dreaded this event because signing fifty poems I was not quite sure I could do, and before it I had been shaky in my bed and uncomfortable and up to the very moment they arrived I wondered how I could possibly manage it. Betty, whom I had not met before, is a charming woman, one who poured faith into me and talked movingly about what my work had meant to her and laughed when I said I did not know why people like the journals so well.

The view from my windows here on that brilliant green field and heavenly blue sea beyond would transport the painter Joan Gold, who did the paintings I have on the wall here—the Sarton Quartet. I bought them because I was so thrilled by her color. Somebody wrote me recently who said they were glad I had bought paintings of hers, what a good painter she is, and that pleased me very much.

This afternoon I am going to be picked up by Margaret and taken to supper. Isn't that a great event? It really is. It will be so beautiful to look out over their their nostalgic marvelous view across to Short Sands. It is a romantic part of York where they live, and in the summer Margaret Whalen is really a seal and may swim five or six times a day. It is still too cold now.

Tuesday, May 24, 1994

IT SHOWS how ill I have been that I have not yet recorded the delightful dinner I had with Margaret looking out over their ravishing view of Short Sands and the great show of tulips already in the garden and the trees that frame their view, still intact after all the winds of this terrible winter. Margaret is such a beneficent person I am sure she must have been a tremendous figure to her first-grade students, whom she loved and some of whom turn up after thirty or forty years old and remind her of how much that first grade meant to them.

She does so much for people and seems to enjoy thinking of things for them. For instance, during this illness of mine she made an enormous half gallon Johnnie Walker Red jug of whiskey sours for me, and it is only recently that I finished it. This time she had been at Dansk for some other purpose and saw some glasses that she thought I could use for my drink at night, and so there are four glasses, and considering the numbers of glasses that I have broken by being clumsy as I am now, this is a treat. The great thing is that Margaret is so enjoying writing poetry and that the poems are remarkably good. She has a voice of her own. It is very much a painter's way of looking at things, so that she describes what she sees, but she sees far more than most people do. These poems are simple and clear, true lyrics, and that is rare indeed.

But today has been a total disaster. I felt extremely ill on Monday and had an appointment with Dr. Gilroy at the hospital this morning at nine, so I had to hurry and get up and get dressed and get off there, and I waited almost an hour and he did not come. He was paged over the public-address system but did not answer, and I do not know yet what happened. They said it was some sort of freak thing that had happened, and he is going to see me tomorrow at nine.

Also today I was to have lunch with dear Betty Lockwood, but I realized when I got back from the hospital and lay down for an hour that I simply could not go out to lunch. So when she came, I offered her to share my lunch, which is these days cereal and banana, so we shared a banana and some cereal and had a good, more than an hour's talk. She is a darling person who loves me in the most inspiring and also accurate way I think, although of course, she gives me credit where I do not altogether deserve it. But the point is she is such a civilized person, and all the talk after we got through our various ailments was such good and civilizing talk that I felt tired when she left, but happy just the same. I am happy to have her as a friend. She is eighty-six.

Thursday, May 26, 1994

I DID see Dr. Gilroy yesterday. He as always was helpful, kind, on time, apologetic about having kept me waiting so long on Monday, but he is not entirely comforting about Prozac. If it does not work, I do not know what I will do because there are other drugs like it—that is, mind-changing drugs—but they too require a month of waiting and testing to be sure they are going to work, and I do not know that I can go through another month as bad as this one is being. There are still a little less than two weeks, and then I should have some idea although Gilroy said that it sometimes took longer than a

Spring at its most beautiful.

month, and it is not a sudden transformation like a miracle. I guess you feel a little better and then pretty soon you feel much better. Let us hope.

Saturday, May 29, 1994

It is turning into a beautiful day for Susan. I am so glad. She had a terrible drive on this holiday weekend; it took her seven hours from New York, two hours longer than it should take, and she was exhausted. It was midnight by the time she got here, and I had a strange delusion because suddenly the radio in the clock by my bed came on with a strange guitar and a woman's voice singing the same rather haunting song over and over again. I must have been fast asleep because I woke up and thought that it was Susan. It was then midnight, and she had just come in, but I thought she was singing outside the door, and I could not make out how she could do it and hold the dog, and I wondered if there was a child with her. All this was completely crazy and I suppose has to do with Prozac because Susan heard that the music was coming from my radio and was able to turn it off, thank goodness.

It is about time for me to get ready to go for my hair. It is always a pleasure these days because it is so beautiful out. Yesterday I was able to pick a little bunch of flowers for Susan, a marvelous one with parrot tulips in it, a purple allium, and one iris; I also managed to pick a little apple blossom, but I could not lift the long-handled clipper. It is frightfully frustrating to be able to do nothing that you want to do of this kind. But at least the flowers are beautiful.

Sunday, May 29, 1994

WE ARE having absolutely glorious days to end May with and begin June, I hope. For once Susan is here on a weekend which is perfect for her walk. She did more than an hour's walk yesterday, and we had a supper of halibut and peas, the peas I got at Golden Harvest on Thursday, and strawberries on pound cake with a little raspberry liqueur; it was delicious.

Susan brought the much-admired movie *The Piano*, an Australian movie made in New Zealand. This is in a way a fantasy; there is a lot that is not quite believable, amongst other things, the hauling of a piano in an enormous box from a wild beach with big surf coming in through winter woods with marshland where the women went in to their knees with their long skirts wet. The story itself is strange because we never really understand a small child is pledged to marry a man when she is still a small child, a man in New Zealand, and pledged by her father. Then she marries someone else and is with him when he is hit by lightning and killed. The shock of that has left her mute, so she cannot speak and arrives as a wife unable to speak, speaking the language of the deaf to her little daughter, who can speak and who can hear, and she can hear and not speak.

It is a great drama around the piano. She plays magnificently all through the film. Meanwhile, the piano is auctioned off for land by her husband. She exhibits no affection for him, and he is quite reticent himself, although always hoping. Meanwhile, there are also Maoris, a strange group of people whom one does not really believe in. A lot of this film I did not believe in, even while I was held in its tension. It is an extremely tense and passionate film because a man not her husband falls in love with her playing and wants to play himself and finally makes a bargain that he can have the piano in exchange, if I understand, for some land.

Memorial Day, May 30, 1994

SUSAN TOOK off early this morning hoping to avoid the crush of people going home from this weekend, and she called me at about half past three to say that she was home, that it had not been bad, and that she was even able to stop for a half hour and see her parents. That is good news.

Now I have been proofreading the journal again and cutting out whatever I can. It is painful to remember the winter and how really terrible it was, but good to know that I survived.

Wednesday, June 1, 1994

A GLOOMY day, and like many of my days now, wasted. Yesterday I spent two hours waiting downstairs for the man to come to fix the cable television that went off last Saturday when Susan was here. Then at eleven Vicki Runnion came bringing a huge bunch of flowers with two magnificent peonies and a lot of other things in it. I was feeling, I think because of the long wait, extremely ill, so I did some bad things, like saying to her, "You should not bring large bunches of flowers to very ill people." She was good about arranging the flowers, and I was able to find one jar big enough for them. They are lovely, very summery, and it was extravagant of her, and I feel terrible that I did not respond better. In fact, it was a hard time because it is very queer, but I am too ill to see people, even though my doctor thinks that it is good for me.

Today also I waited from quarter past nine until half past eleven to get a message to and from Dr. Gilroy because I have been feeling so ill and have no appetite. I was hoping that he might have some answer. Mary, the nurse, is extremely kind and said she would call back by eleven-thirty, so again I waited, taking my small work time, which is an hour or an hour and a half, at my desk, to be sure that I was there for that call. She did call just before half past eleven and told me that Dr. Gilroy thought I should try to take less laxatives as I have been having trouble with diarrhea. Well, I have already tried that, and it did not work, so Prozac is having a bad effect on my digestive system, also complete loss of appetite. Can I believe that suddenly or in a little while after the twelfth of June that I will feel differently and life will be worth living again? It would be wonderful, of course, and that is what I am banking on.

Today my bad luck was that I left my wallet in Dave's, and I must say Donna was extremely helpful. She said right away, "We must call." I thought it might be in the florist, where I had got some beautiful flowers as part of an order from Norma. They were white lilies and deep blue delphinium, really magnificent, and they were for my room because there were no flowers in my room. Well, it was not there, so then the only possibility was Dave's. And at Dave's they had found it, so after Donna did my hair and told me not to worry, to pay her next time, I went to Dave's, and the nice girl at the counter there said that she had found it and this happened to people so often and that one must not feel worried about it. She could not have been nicer. And when somebody from the back brought it to me, I knew there was a hundred dollars in it, I offered her ten, that seemed to me fair. She brushed me aside, nicely but firmly, and said, "It's my job. I wouldn't think of it," or something like that. I was very touched.

I do not know what bad luck is before me tomorrow, but with Judy coming, who always has a positive effect, I hope it will be a good day.

Sunday, June 5, 1994

I SEEM to be pursued by the furies so that time is constantly taken from me that I need at my desk. I am way behind on everything. Today what happened was that at five o'clock I felt cold, it was forty outside, and I went down and realized that the furnace was not working. I waited until seven to call Goodwin Oil, called them, and a nice man said that it would take him an hour and a half to get here, that he would be here as soon as he could but he was not dressed and had not had his breakfast. I figured that he would probably not get here until ten, so I made my bed, I had my breakfast and carried the tray down in my wrapper, lay on my chaise longue to wait for him, and finally at half past nine he came.

He went down and explored in the cellar and came up with the news, which really made me furious, that there was no oil. I am under contract to Goodwin Oil to keep it filled; he was apologetic. He said, "We never mean this to happen," and he called somebody to come with oil. This man also could not get there right away, was coming from Portsmouth, I guess, so I waited. He thought it would take him about an hour and a half. It was then ten, a little after ten, I guess, so I waited, and finally an extremely nice man drove up in a huge truck, but I did not realize how long it would take first to fill the tanks, there are two, and then to prime the furnace so that it would start. It took about twenty minutes to fill the tanks, and then it took about half an hour to prime the furnace.

Then finally it worked, but it was then eleven, and I realized that I had better scurry out and get the paper so that I could listen to Brinkley, as I often do on Sundays, and this was to be a ninety-minute segment on D Day. You cannot believe what those men had to go through. They themselves cannot believe it when they remember. There is something beautiful about the gratitude at last given them in full measure, also by the French, who in this case have behaved warmly and welcomed them in every possible way.

Brinkley had interviews with German soldiers and with Americans who had been there. There was a great feeling of gratitude and of nostalgia, in a way, for the marvelous unity and communion that these soldiers felt towards each other. When men who had been there were asked why they came back, they often said because of the graves. "I come to greet my buddies underground." Very often I had tears in my eyes. If ever there was an argument against war, it is these pictures of this cruel, frightful brutality of men being shot down like rabbits trying to get up that beach.

What made it so moving is the old faces, because the men who were nineteen and twenty when they assaulted those cruel beaches are now seventy or seventy-five. The camera work was marvelous. Sometimes one saw a tear, but not often, and one got the sense that for all of these men the important thing was the dead, their buddies. They came to give homage to their buddies, and so many spoke of them and the extraordinary courage and initiative that went into the taking of these impossible objectives; the Germans had a whole division on the beach, so they were walking into fire. One of them said, "I knew that if I stood there, I'd die. I just had to go forward."

I felt that Clinton did a fine job, difficult for him because he was not in the service and had opposed the Vietnam War. It was apparent, even in the way he saluted, that he is a civilian.

I found myself weeping at the playing of the "Marseillaise" and our national anthem. In fact, I had tears in my eyes more than once. Many of these men had never talked about the experience, never even told their families; now with their families present alongside the thousands of white crosses in that peaceful green field, they were able to talk at last.

Often their officers were killed almost immediately, so they were without command. They gathered in small groups. A moving speech was given by a man who had been awarded the highest military decoration for leadership and for finding a way to avoid the million mines that had been planted. The bombers went farther inland than was planned rather than bombing the coastal fortress, which Hitler thought would withstand any onslaught, so the paratroopers found themselves in the middle of German troops and were taken prisoner.

Lloyd Bentsen, secretary of the treasury, was there, and spoke well. But when the men spoke for themselves, one sensed the relief of talking about it at last after fifty years. As the camera caught one old face after another, that is when I cried. When they cried, as the *New York Times* editorial said, it was partly for what was won and partly for what was lost, for what was lost on the beaches of Normandy was nine thousand or more Americans, Canadians, British, Polish, and Germans.

Several Germans were interviewed, one of whom was trying to explain that for some Germans who were anti-Hitler, the crack in his armor was good news. Yet one could not forget that while the beaches were being stormed, the clouds of smoke were rising over the concentration camps as thousands of Jews were burned alive. Thus the continual call for fellowship and the story of the Germans agreeing to a three-hour truce so the Americans could carry away the wounded and the dead were somewhat ironic.

If ever there was a plea against war, it is surely these photographs of the beaches of Normandy. It was intense, the television a magnet. Clinton's speech was excellent and made me proud of him. He held himself well, spoke exactly long enough but not too long, and said what had to be said with eloquence. One could not help feeling proud of this country, proud of being an American citizen today.

Wednesday, June 8, 1994

I CALLED the fish places, and only the one in York Beach had sole, so I decided I had better go out and get it and drive along Long Sands. I love to see the big waves coming in there. It was intermediate tide, which is a good time.

But I was so shaky walking out to the car that I wondered for a moment whether I could drive all that way. It's not a long drive, about twenty minutes each way. I decided I had better do it. Once I was in the car, I was able to drive all right, but I am aware of my state of weakness and illness all the time, and under everything and over everything is this fact: that I may fall at any minute or grow dizzy at any minute, and that I may simply not have the concentration to drive. It seems as if I am worse rather than better, so I can only pray that this is a final resistance to Prozac and that next week, when I have been taking it for a month, I may suddenly feel a lot better. Wouldn't it be wonderful? It is like an impossible fantasy to imagine feeling well, but perhaps I will.

Meanwhile, I wait for a letter from Margot, who does not write. I expect she is busy with her new house and the final struggle with the biography.

The cat stayed on his chair and never came to be caressed when I had a rest this afternoon. I did manage to get the fish, and by great good luck that awfully nice man at the market told me that he had frozen the last shad roe and would I like to put some in the freezer? So I bought one set of them; it is such a treat, and it comes back from freezing well.

I arranged the flowers and had my cereal and banana, which somehow or other is not entirely what I want right now. I think I have to invent some other lunches. When Susan is here, she will do that.

Today I managed to type very badly a paragraph to insert describing the holocaust of the maples on Long Sands Road, which has really been a traumatic visual experience, going by those great shattered bodies. I felt strongly that I must write a poem about it, and I did write a not very good poem, but at least it has broken the silence.

Now in the back of my mind is a Christmas poem, and I wonder what that will be, what I can say for Christmas this year. What haunts me is the end of Clinton's excellent speech in Normandy. "We are the children of their sacrifice." This will last.

When I got up from my nap at half past three, I went out into the garden to find a tiny little bunch for Maggie, and I found some English bluebells, some little white flowers that close in the shade and open in the sun, lovely they are, and

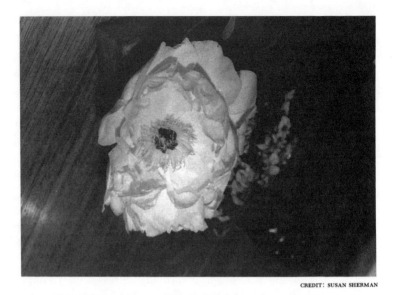

Tree peony.

one miniature orange rose, which is effective. And great glory, I found that the tree peony in the left terrace border has flowered for the first time and has two flowers, so I picked one to add to the bunch that I managed to get this morning as well as the fish. It was quite a luxurious shopping morning to combine sole with some lovely flowers, especially a little one I have never seen before that is a curious shade of pink, rather brilliant. I hope it will last, as the tree peony surely will.

Yet under all this today, I am extremely depressed. This morning, when I wondered whether I could drive, I was terrified suddenly that I may be totally dependent soon. Thank goodness Susan comes in a little over two weeks, and I hope this great weather we are having will hold so that she can take walks.

Friday, June 10, 1994

ON TOP of everything else I have lost the murder mystery that I was in the middle of; I cannot find that little book, and it seems totally mad to me that I could lose it. I have looked everywhere that it could possibly be.

I tried to walk around the garden a little to pick a bunch of flowers for Maggie, who comes tomorrow. There really was not anything to pick, but I saw the disasters that have taken place this winter. Two big rhododendrons are dying, have no leaves, bare branches because the deer ate the leaves. And there used to be a big puff of a white wild rose which had to be pruned severely every year but was quite glorious when it was in flower, and it is gone. I do not know where it is. There is a small rugosa right in front of the big rugosa. That should never have been put there and must be transplanted. I thought Pat was coming today, but it is now half past four and she is not here and everything needs watering.

Of course I do not want to die, although death seems to be the only solution to my problem at present. Let us hope that Prozac will help me, and it might even begin to happen next week. But the fact that it has not happened and that I have to take strong laxatives or I am constipated does not help; it is the worst thing possible for me. Why talk about this? But I say also, "Why not?" I seem to be totally absorbed now in my body and what it is doing, and this is miserable.

Tuesday, June 14, 1994

I AM frightened because I wonder how long I will be able to write a note with a pen. I have spent five minutes trying to find my pad which has my name on it to write to Naoko Takeda, who has translated *Journal of a Solitude* into Japanese. It is now going into a sixth printing, and the publishers, Misuzu Shobo, are going to do *The Fur Person* with new illustrations. Apparently they are going to try to do all my major works, which is wonderful.

Meanwhile, I heard that *House by the Sea* in paperback has sold altogether 79,657 over the years. That is pretty good.

Sometimes I have this crazy dream that someday I will feel well. It would be so extraordinary to feel well, and maybe it will happen. I have to keep hoping that even two weeks more and I might be out of this, I was going to say this grave, but it is rather like being dead and still just managing to make it. It is getting harder and harder for me to walk and to climb the stairs.

The paperback that I was reading and which disappeared after Eleanor was here cleaning last Thursday has never turned up. A good description of frustration is to have a book disappear when you are in the middle of it and eager to go on.

Monday, June 20, 1994

THIS IS the great day when Susan will arrive for the summer. I cannot believe it. She is leaving New York with probably a hundred degrees today, stopping in Connecticut to see her parents, so she will get here sometime late this evening.

I still have a poem in mind that I want to do, God knows whether I will get to it, but it is creeping up on me that by August I must have the Christmas poem written.

I have now taken a drastic step, which is to ask for a second opinion from my doctor because I have now had ten days of acute pain in my muscles and bones and nothing has been done. They did blood tests that showed nothing. They did a chest X ray; there was some fluid in the lung, and I have had no word about that. So I have really had it. On Friday I finally demanded a pain-killer for the weekend as I was going to be alone, and I thought after all, one doesn't have to have acute pain; there are ways out. Unfortunately this thing did not work well, and Prozac continues to elude me.

Now I am going to go on a cheerful errand to get some white sneakers.

Tuesday, June 21, 1994

MY FATHER and mother got engaged on a June 21 and went rowing on the Lys and stopped to have asparagus on the way. Belgian asparagus is white. Apparently it was a lovely day, and they remembered it happily.

Today it is cooler. Yesterday there was a little breeze and it wasn't bad. But today it is gray and cool. That is a great blessing because Judy Harrison is here and that office across from my study where she works is hot when it gets hot. I have not used my air conditioner once this year, and that is because of the sea breeze, which has been a lifesaver. While it was ninety-five or something in New York, here it did not go over eighty-six yesterday.

Yesterday at last I got an appointment with another doctor, whom I will see at the hospital. His name is Dr. Poulin, the same name as Sister Lucy at HOME, so I wonder if they are related, and I must ask him. He is an oncologist, and I myself have wondered whether my problem might not be cancer because it is so strange to have so much pain in all the muscles and bones. The lymph glands had been taken out with the mastectomy, I presume. Dr. Poulin's nurse called me to get some information, and I realized that my folder up at the hospital must be six inches thick because I have been in the hospital so much. I had my mastectomy there eight or nine years ago, and later they tried electric shocks to get the heart-beat regular. The doctor tried three times and every time it was perfect for about five minutes and then it went back to fibrillating. That was when they gave up on it.

Yesterday I went—a big event!—and bought some white sneakers, which I have wanted for a long time, and at the same time I picked up prescriptions for $139. A funny thing happened at the pharmacy because Carol said, "One thirty-nine," so I took out $2, not thinking that to get anything in a pharmacy for $1.39 was beyond belief; then I charged the $139, and that means that this month I will have spent $500 on medicines, which is a little much.

Thursday, June 23, 1994

DR. POULIN, who is an oncologist, made a good impression on me. He is forty, which is a good age for a doctor, and obviously very competent. He had various ideas but could not make an instant diagnosis. So he set me up for a CAT scan and bone scan tomorrow and hopes that he will be able to diagnose then. He thought at one time that it might be that the nerves in my shoulder had been burned when I had radiation after I had a recurrence of cancer, and Gilroy, whom I saw before I saw Dr. Poulin, said very earnestly, "We will find out what is the matter this time," because when I was in the hospital last, it was a bad time, last fall, and they never diagnosed. A second opinion was given by a specialist, and they finally decided that it was probably pneumonia, but it was never clear. So let us hope that this time something definite will happen and I can start to live again. I was so tired when I came back; it was two hours at the hospital, I had to undress twice, and the tension and the waiting meant that I got home at eleven and was in a state of shock, but at least I hope I am on my way to getting well at last. Gilroy did say that Prozac would probably have been stopped for a while from doing what it should by this infection that I have now. You cannot win.

Tuesday, July 12, 1994

I HAVE not been able to record for over a week because there was no cassette recorder. Judy finally found one at a reasonable price, I think tried several places, and this seems to be working. I have not been able to record, so a great deal has been lost, but I want to recover a few things other than feeling ill and my despair at the condition I am in.

I remember one evening last week when Susan and I were invited to Margaret and Barbara's wonderful house looking out over Short Sands. As the lights came on, that sight of York Beach, which is ugly in the daytime, at night becomes glamorous. It was a marvelous evening.

But why it was such a spectacular evening for me, such a perfect evening. After dinner Margaret read her poems. An evening that ends with someone reading her poems is special, and Margaret, at sixty, has just begun to discover the excitement of writing poetry and is doing extremely well. This is exciting. She uses a short line. I am trying to get her to try iambic pentameter. At present she uses a two-beat line and sometimes a three-beat line, but not more, so it is a little staccato, what she does, and doesn't flow. And the rhymes are rather trite, so there is a way to go, but the great thing, the exciting thing for me is that she has found this new challenge. She loves to revise; this is one of the signs of a real poet. When I read this true lyric she wrote for me, I had tears in my eyes.

Gentle Deep

for May

Lately when she calls
She says, I'm sick, I'm dying.
Then thinking fails me,
I don't know what to say.
Lost words block my way,
Hobble conversation.
We close the call
When we've said it all.
She lives, she writes, she fights.
Holding with her granite will
A gentle deep—her World of Light.
She'll call again—tomorrow night.
                    Margaret Whalen

Thursday, July 14, 1994, Bastille Day

THIS MORNING Susan helped me begin to clear my desk, which is an unbelievable task. As soon as I put something on this tape, I have one folder of things that have to be answered. One of the things that has been trying this past little while has been that I have had an enormous number of bills, household things that had to be done. Forty dollars just to mend the lights over my bed so that I could see, that seemed so staggering. And then fifty dollars to catch the raccoon; since then another one has come whom Russ has not been able to catch, so God knows what is going to pile up before the end of this month.

But there is still good news. The Japanese are buying many of my books now. The Women's Press is bringing out poems; I am pleased about that. There is lots of good news, but the problem is that I feel ill. It is almost impossible for me to walk. I can get to my car if I have a cane. That is about it. In the house it is a struggle; everything is a struggle for me now. The last test was on Monday, or maybe Tuesday, and it was with a neurologist who came to test the nerve endings of my shoulder where there may be cancer. This is one of the ideas, that my problem is cancer in the left arm and shoulder. We will just have to see. But this was a difficult test; it was complicated for the people doing it, God knows. They put all kinds of little things on my arm and then gave me small electric shocks, and this was fairly nerve-racking, I must say, especially after I had received what the doctor called "a bite," she would say, "We are now going to do ten of these." When you have just had a shock and then are told you are going to have ten more, it is difficult to take. But I am glad to say that the nurse, who was really wonderful, a woman a good deal older than the amazingly young neurologist, about halfway through said, "Miss Sarton, you are doing very well." That was a wonderful relief for me and help because I had occasionally said, "Ow." It really hurt sometimes.

Meanwhile, Susan is doing the impossible. She watered the whole garden today, she said, and she is out doing her walk now. There seems to be a lull in the news. There is nothing but waiting to see what will happen in Haiti. I do not envy our president, for that is a difficult decision.

Wednesday, July 20, 1994

YESTERDAY WAS quite a day because the University of New England, which is chiefly a medical school, sent this professor to do a video of me talking about old age with the idea of helping their medical students to understand the relationship between patient and doctor and also what old age is like. So this left me free to tell how awful it is, and I was happy to do so. I had a letter from the president of the university saying they would like to offer me an honorary doctorate June 3, 1995. I did not think I would ever get another doctorate, old as I am, but it gave me a tremendous sense of pleasure, that there was something ahead, that it is not all finished forever.

It was a good deal easier also than a long interview with Dr. Ijaz in York yesterday. This is the man whom Dr. Gilroy had suggested that I see from the point of view of medicines, to find the right antidepressant since Prozac has simply not worked for me. I decided to have Susan come with me since she is so intimately connected with my life, and I thought it would be good that she know what he is like. Also, she will remember everything that he says if I forget. We had a good impression of this doctor. He is an East Indian, very quiet, very sensitive, and I thought wonderful in that there was no sense of hurry in the interview, which lasted an hour and a half. He asked me a lot of questions about myself, and I gather will now see all the tests that have been made by other doctors, and I am to see him again next week. Also, he has convinced me that it would be helpful for me to have some therapy, not a great deal, but to help me get used to the new drug and to see where I am. I think from what he said about old age that it is also perhaps to help me adjust to old age, a not very easy old age. He was warm about my journals, said they had helped him when he was in medical school. One reason Susan and I liked him so much is that he told us that he went to medical school in New York and after he graduated decided that he must work with AIDS because he felt so little was being done. This was an impressive statement for him to make.

My relief was enormous. I felt as if a ton of bricks had been taken off me. There has been constant anxiety because of not knowing. Now we still do not know, his job is not to diagnose, that will be for Poulin, but he will go over the innumerable tests that have been made. I was afraid, amongst other things, of the bill, but his secretary told me that I would see no bills. Whatever Medicare does not pay, Blue Cross Blue Shield will. So that is wonderful news. I was afraid of high bills.

It was a relief not to think about myself as a patient yesterday, but as speaking to young doctors, young idealistic men and women who perhaps have never really thought about old age and what it is like, the infinite frustrations. Dr. Ijaz was quite definite about the fact that I had a major stroke when I was seventy, but I am now eighty-two, so the two strokes that came last year which were small, unimportant in some ways, took a great toll because there is a twelve-year difference and a lot has disintegrated in me in twelve years. I am that much less able to cope with life.

I realize now that it will be good for me to talk about old age, find out where I should bear down more heavily on myself and where I should let things go.

Monday, August 1, 1994

It is time to put this journal to bed, and I am glad to say that I dreamed that perhaps there would be some better news about my health by the time it ended. The great news is that at last whatever I have has been at least partially diagnosed as inflammation of the bones and muscles, and there are three kinds of this infection or whatever it is which have to be treated in three different ways. Dr. Poulin was impressed by the amount of pain I have been in and really went to work and had a lot of blood tests made which would show which of these three kinds of infection it is and how to treat it. I shall hear from him on Wednesday, when I see him again and he has gotten the results. Also, he wants me to see the neurologist again who did the tests on the nerve ends in my shoulder.

But the best news is that he did not mention cancer. I felt a great burden had been lifted off me because it has been depressing not to know what was wrong, to have as much pain as I have had for months and have no idea what was causing it. The pain-killers prescribed have not done much good. And it is just psychologically difficult not to know what is wrong with you. So I am emerging from this long, difficult spring and summer and believing for the first time in months that by autumn things will look a great deal better than they do now. And I decided to call a number Susan had seen on a truck for Stannah Stairlift. A charming young Englishman came to look things over and give me an estimate, and proved ingenious at finding a way to take care of the two flights and two landings. To make the chair turn the two corners would have cost twenty-two thousand dollars. But by making it take the two straight flights and not turn the corners, I only have to climb two steps at each landing. I had decided I could take ten thousand dollars out of the Trust at Shawmut Bank. Most of that money I have saved myself. This arrangement cost a little over eight thousand dollars.

Amazingly, Stannah installed the lift in one long day with only one man working. The day before, an electrician had organized the question of power.

What a moment when I sat down in the comfortable armchair, pushed a button, and rose gently up the steep stairs. I felt like a child with a toy—what bliss! When I forget my glasses, I can just float down and up again. No problem.

Dr. Poulin approved the idea that Dr. Ijaz had been definite about, that I should have some therapy, and that will begin later in the month and perhaps will help me cope with the miseries of old age a little better than I have been doing.

Ronnie Carpenter-Healy's Christmas present, to do for me some task that needed doing, is surely the best present I have ever been given. I thought of a few things such as cleaning the bird feeder, sweeping the garage, but nothing seemed special enough. Why must it be special? A real challenge. When I came up with cleaning the attic, which I was sure was a fire hazard, I knew that was it, for I shall never do it myself. But I was a little shy of asking. When I did ask Ronnie, she said at once that Jim, her husband, would help and they would bring their truck—why had I imagined such a difficult task as somehow worthy!

So many people offer to help by gardening for me, for instance, offer to serve in some generous way or another, and always I am amazed. How is it that I have acquired so many friends who have never met me yet offer to pull weeds? I feel overwhelmed until I come to see, over and over again, that they want to help me in any way they can as my books and especially the journals have helped them. They are thanking me.

Most who write are women, women of all ages and backgrounds. It is always a thrill to find a letter from North Dakota, for instance, or New Zealand. The people I hear from, from children to the very old, are celebrating their discovery of a writer they consider a friend. They feel free to become themselves because I have done so. What a wonderful reward such letters are!

Yet what have I said? An old woman living alone writes poems, cooks up a supper of asparagus on toast with hardboiled eggs, a woman who is often depressed but has learned how minds change and how to handle the down in weeks or months. Still, I am aware that very few solitary women of eighty-two who live alone are as lucky as I am, surrounded by lovingkindness. How did it ever happen to this old raccoon!

And now, the combination of slightly cooler weather and my being slightly better should be rousing. With that hope I close this eighty-second year.

CREDIT: SUSAN SHERMAN

Acknowledgments